After the Crash
The Emergence of the Rainbow Economy

Guy Dauncey is an author, activist and visionary who works to build a future which will reflect the dreams we carry in our souls, for ourselves and for our planet. He lives in Victoria, western Canada, where he publishes *EcoNews*, and is consultant to the Trust for Sustainable Development. He is a Fellow of the Findhorn Foundation, in Scotland, and of the Royal Society for the Arts.

The author (and details of his Home Page, Earth Future) can be contacted at gdauncey@islandnet.com

After the Crash

The Emergence of the Rainbow Economy

Guy Dauncey

GREEN
PRINT

Green Print
an imprint of The Merlin Press
No 2 Rendlesham Mews
Rendlesham
Nr Woodbridge
Suffolk IP12 2SZ

© 1988 Guy Dauncey
First published in 1988 by Marshall Pickering
Reprinted by The Merlin Press in 1989
New edition 1996

Distributed in Canada by Prologue
1650 Blvd Lionel Bertrand Boisbrand
Quebec Canada J7H 1N7

British Library CIP data

Dauncey, Guy, 1948 –
    After the Crash: the emergence of the rainbow economy.
    1. Great Britain. Economic development. Environmental aspects.
    I. title
    330.941'0858

ISBN 1 85425 082 6

Printed in Finland by WSOY

Contents

This book is dedicated to everyone who is working
to make this world a happier and more peaceful place.

Introduction
by Hazel Henderson

I welcome this new edition of Guy Dauncey's valuable book, which is even more relevant today, as we understand ever more clearly the unsustainability of industrial societies. Dauncey outlines the vision that can help guide us to re-building our communities so that they can be more at peace with Nature and therefore viable for the long-term. In this book you will find a wealth of healthy options available beyond the narrow confines of conventional economics, from left to right, for re-thinking what we mean by 'development' in more human and ecological terms. Further, since Guy Dauncey is a very practical visionary, the book is packed with usable information, names and addresses, organizations to contact, so that you, the reader, can begin to re-orient your own life, take action in your community and fulfill your own visions.

I first met Guy Dauncey in Britain in the 1970s, where he was already busy working out the practicalities of building new communities that empowered members toward seeking satisfying work, productive enterprises and fulfilling relationships within natural resource limits. Only a small band of social innovators then, these social movements in which Guy and I were involved have now burgeoned into the mainstream today – as worldwide concern for the environment has reached a broad, majority consensus. Today, more and more people all over the world are seeking healthy, ecologically-sound lifestyles, voting for Green party candidates, shopping for more environmentally-friendly products, conserving energy, recycling materials, changing their workplaces, investing their money more wisely in community-based enterprises, credit unions, local development projects, socially-responsible mutual funds and ethical investments of all kinds.

Dauncey has tracked all these local initiatives in many countries and is in the forefront of interpreting how all these grass-roots activities add up to a major shift in macro-economic terms. Most conventional economists are hypnotized by the many statistical illusions generated by macro-economic models and fail to look at the new local economies growing right before their eyes.

In today's Era of Global Interdependence, globalization forces unleashed by the Industrial Revolution are driving the daily geo-political realignments, as well as the internal re-structuring of most nation-states. These globalization forces, which I have described elsewhere, particularly those in today's global financial 'casino' are rapidly eroding the autonomy of national leaders and invalidating the theories and tools of macro-economic management. Today's leaders cannot deliver on their election promises. They cannot defend their citizens in time of war, since today's weapons, both nuclear and chemical, are too dangerous to use. Neither can they protect their citizens from global pollution and climate change. They cannot provide full employment in a global 'labor market'. Worse, the siren promise of managing and 'fine-tuning' their domestic economies is now impossible, as over $1 trillion of 'hot money' sloshes around the planet every twenty-four hours.

Today's global casino makes a mockery of monetary policy, reducing central bankers to impotence, while bouncing currencies and interest rates reduce fiscal policy options and create paralyzing uncertainties for investors, managers and politicians. Trade flows are swamped by these huge currency tidal waves, while calls are heard from all sides to 'level the global playing field'. Yet trying to level this global playing field within the conventional economics paradigm leads only to more levelled forests and the homogenizing of more cultures to conform to the economists' appallingly ignorant, narrow, short-term views of what is 'globally efficient'.

Similarly, measuring human progress by indicators such

as the Gross National Product (GNP) is like trying to fly a Boeing 747 with nothing on the instrument panel but an oil pressure gauge! Many more gauges measuring different dimensions of human well-being and development and ecological health are needed. Steps in the right direction include the new Human Development Index of the United Nations Development Program (UNDP) which included life expectancy, infant mortality and literacy measures. My own approach, *Country Futures Indicators*, is broader still, and addresses the problem of over-aggregating apples and oranges into one meaningless number, whether GNP or HDI. The new indicators need to be unbundled, so that they are clear to average citizens, which is why my *Country Futures Indicators* not only correct GNP by adding in poverty gap measures, energy to GNP ratios, military v. civilian budget ratios and including unpaid work, but go beyond to explicit non-money measures of air and water quality, hectares of land lost, resource-depletion, human rights, shelter, as well as literacy and life-expectancy, etc., included in HDI. The whole world game has changed, so we must not only change the rules operating the global economy, but also the 'scorecards' of progress. Only by levelling the global playing field upwards, by raising the 'ethical floor' (the latticework of global treaties and agreements on protecting workers, consumers and citizens' rights as well as the global environment) to a higher level, can we create a new game where the *most ethical* companies and countries can win.

Until this new world order has been achieved – the work of the 1990s for all of us – Guy Dauncey's book provides the kind of road map for sane individual and community action to build home-grown economies that can provide safety-nets, as well as helping shape the sustainable societies of the future.

Hazel Henderson
St Augustine, Florida
October, 1995

Preface to the 1996 Edition

The book you are about to read was first published in 1988. This edition was published in 1996. The main text has been left intact, and two new chapters added, to bring it up to date and add new material. A new Resources Appendix has also been added.

I want to thank the many people who helped me write the book: Liz Shephard, for valuable feedback and commentary on every chapter; Mike Penney, Rosemary Kearney, David Pashby and Gordon Davidson for further chapter-by-chapter feedback; Sandi Somerville, for much personal support; and Nic Albery, Geoff Caplan, Jon Carpenter, Giles Chitty, Michael Clague, Eileen Conn, Kieran O'Donohue, John Elkington, Stephen Fawkes, John Freebairn, Paul Glover, David Grayson, Hal Harvey, Hazel Henderson, Dyfrig Hughes, Vivian Hutchinson, Michael Kinsley, Satish Kumar, Michael and Shirley Linton, David Mansell, Michael Marien, Bill Mather, Ray Mitchell, Mitra, Jan Nation, John Paine, Malcolm Peel, Walter Schwarz, Malcolm Stern, Martin Stott, Nigel Tuersley, Elizabeth Vanefeld and Claude Whitmyer, all of whom helped in different ways. I also want to thank my wife Carolyn Herriot and my mother Mary Dauncey, for their constant encouragement and support; my publisher, Martin Eve, for his commitment to the book; and the many unseen presences which help us fufil our dreams, and create a more loving world.

Since writing the book, I have moved to British Columbia and embarked on a host of new projects. When I revisited the book for the new edition I was greatly encouraged to discover how many of the initiatives described in the book are prospering, justifying the belief I placed in them. It is a good sign, when good initiatives prosper.

Guy Dauncey, Victoria, Canada
November 1995

Chapter One :
The coming storm

Our Earth is in crisis.

If you live in a pleasant home with leafy lanes or parks nearby, this may not seem to be true. Look beneath this surface, however, and the problems are not hard to see. There is not just one crisis, there are four – of the world economy, of global debt, of the global environment and of community collapse. Each crisis threatens a breakdown.

These crises are not really the subject of this book. They are its backdrop; the dark clouds against which the 'rainbow economy', is emerging. A rainbow is caused when the light of the sun shines through the storm, bringing hope, beauty and the promise of better times ahead. The term 'rainbow economy' is used both in this sense, and because the different colours of the rainbow represent the different values which the builders of the rainbow economy are seeking to incorporate into their work.

Most people do not know that this work is going on: it is not often reported in the newspapers or on television. Within the heart of city communities, however, and on housing estates, in busy offices, in country villages and even in the heart of great corporations, people are working to build a new kind of economy, only too aware of the Earth's crises. This book looks at their work and at the rainbow economy which is emerging from it. Behind every dark cloud there lies a silver lining, illuminated by the sun. This book tells of that lining, and of the future it promises. It is a book of hope, telling of ways we can follow to create a better, happier and more harmonious world.

But first, the scene must be set. Without the black clouds of storm there would be no threatened crashes or break-downs, no crises or need for change. It is out of the break-down that new harmony appears. That breakdown must first be addressed.

THE CRISIS IN THE WORLD ECONOMY

The first crisis, the crisis in the world economy, is reflected in the jittery state of the world's financial exchanges.

Amid the constant changes of trade and commerce, the world has always needed some source of stability. For centuries, gold was seen as the one thing that was permanent and stable. When Britain established her empire, the pound sterling became regarded as the world's reserve currency, the bedrock around which other currencies could move and feel secure. After the 1914–1918 War, Britain was economically exhausted, and the world entered a period without economic leadership. It was during this time that the great crash of 1929 and the subsequent depression and war occurred. The USA then took up the mantle of leadership and the 'almighty dollar' became king. Once more, the world knew economic stability and growth.

Being global leader in the late twentieth century is an expensive affair, however. There are army bases all over the world to be maintained, wars to be fought, and an incredible array of nuclear firepower to be tended and updated. Historically, there is evidence that empires topple because they become top-heavy, pouring too much money into maintaining their power and not enough into generating new growth and development.[1] The Vietnam War was a huge drain on America's wealth. Instead of financing it by increased taxation, however, the money was borrowed, chiefly from the Japanese, whose growing industrial success was generating an embarrassing capital surplus. Prohibited from investing in military expansion by the terms of the 1945 surrender treaty, the Japanese had been pouring their capital reserves into industrial development.

In 1981, the USA still had $140 billion in overseas assets. Under President Reagan, however, America went on a spending spree, burying her self-doubts in increased government expenditure and tax cuts, both at the same time. Private consumers picked up the tune, and went on a credit card binge, lowering their level of savings to only 4% of GNP. 'Designer greed' became the hallmark of the decade, accompanied by growing poverty and social inequality. Meanwhile, this show of confidence kept the dollar at an artificially high value, which helped suck in the imports and make life tough for American exporters. By 1987, America had become the world's biggest debtor nation, owing more than $400 billion to the world's lenders. Her economy was sucking in borrowed money to cover $300 billion a year for military expenditure, the budget deficit and the ever-increasing trade deficit. The US fiscal community knew that they were dancing on a volcano.

Meanwhile, vast sums of money were rushing around the world every day seeking a speculative profit on tomorrow's currency and share speculations, which were themselves made more volatile by computerised programs and phone systems. For every dollar that was being placed in solid investment projects, twenty-four were chasing paper gains. (This is still true, so the present tense is appropriate.) Mixed in with this millionaires' confetti is billions of dollars of 'hot money' – money which is deliberately avoiding any stable home where it might be traced because it originates in cocaine dealing, arms smuggling, 'flight capital' from Third World debtor countries, bribery or tax evasion. Instability breeds instability, adding to the risk that the whole charade will tumble. If you think this is an unreliable way to run the world's economy, you are right: many other people, financiers included, think the same.

In October 1987, the markets panicked, triggering the biggest single-day fall in share values in history, and a subsequent tumble in the value of the dollar. Investors were visibly shocked, seeing the crack and fearing the earthquake to come. Apart from generating a healthy – but relatively shallow – debate about the state of the American and world economies, nothing substantial changed. The natural tendency of speculative investment asserted itself, and share values soon started rising again. The cheaper dollar made life easier for American companies to export their goods, but there are still many factors which have to intervene before the deficits fall to any reasonable level – if they fall at all. Everything is so interlinked. If America cuts back too fast on her imports, this will cause producers in other countries to cut back, risking the recession that everyone fears. If America stops importing from countries in the Third World, they will find it even harder to meet their debt payments, putting the banks in jeopardy (see below). If America's borrowing continues, by 1992 Americans will be spending 25% of their annual income on interest payments. This is the kind of figure that gives people sleepless nights.

We have become a globally interdependent economy, but we have not established the instruments of governance needed to guide global economic policy. The system is on autopilot, desperately needing human intervention. It is in this vacuum that chaos threatens.

This is the first of the crises. The second must now be considered.

THE CRISIS OF BANKING AND THIRD WORLD DEBT

The second crisis concerns the black hole that the World Bank and the major British, American and other banks have dug for themselves through their Third World lending policies.

The West's banking institutions were set up to meet the needs of their owners, shareholders and directors, not to meet any consciously ethical, social or global needs. During the 1970s, the banks fell over themselves to make vast sovereign loans to the governments of developing countries, ignoring or forgetting a basic principle of banking, which is that you must have some kind of security on your loan.

Their coffers were filling up with the new wealth of the Arab oil-world, and they were hungry for somewhere to invest it which would bring a good return. By the end of 1988, total outstanding loans to Third World countries stood at $1.2 trillion, a figure which increases monthly with each fresh rescheduling. Many Third World countries are completely unable to pay even the interest on their loans. More loans are now devoted entirely to servicing the interest on the old ones, the money going back to the banks which lent it, making it seem as if the loans are performing.

Officially, the money was meant to finance industrialisation, enabling countries to grow rich and repay the loans, as Japan, Korea and Malaysia had done. In practice, this is not what happened. Loans were given in the knowledge that they were being spent on the most outrageous projects. Susan George gives an excellent and deeply disturbing account of the whole affair in her book, 'A Fate Worse Than Debt'.² She records that in the Philippines, the Marcos government spent $2.1 billion on a nuclear power plant located at the foot of a volcano in the middle of the Pacific 'fire-rim' earthquake zone, which even the International Atomic Energy Authority thought was 'unique in atomic history'. Repayments for the loan for the plant alone are costing the Filipino people $500,000 *a day*. In the wake of Chernobyl, the Aquino government has decided not to start the reactor up, but it still has to be paid for. The Third World is full of examples such as this. The banks never pretended they were involved in 'development'. They saw a chance for profit, and they took it.

Just where all the money has gone may never be known. $1.2 trillion is an awful lot of money to 'lose'. What is not often realised is that most of the money lent has already returned to the countries which lent it in a variety of ways. Some has come back in the form of contracts given to British, American, Canadian, French, German and other companies to build nuclear power plants (four in Brazil, none of them working), steel mills, sugar mills and the like, many of a scale and technology completely inappropriate to the country in question. Some has come back for the purchase of tanks, missiles and military aircraft (which absorbs around 20% of all Third World debt). Much has come back as interest, and more has come back as 'flight capital' – money which secretly disappears into private bank accounts outside the country. Not long after it is lent, the loans are safely back in the economies of the rich nations – but the ordinary people living in poor countries still have to repay the debt.

Some of the flight capital ends up with the banks that lent it in the first place. Karen Lissakers, a former US State Department official who now writes on international banking, reports that one banker told her that his bank regularly 'sends a guy with two empty suitcases' to Mexico City.[3] The banks have designed a range of systems from offshore trusts to fake investment companies to help people get money out of their countries.

As his commission for giving the contract for the nuclear plant mentioned above to Westinghouse, ex-president Marcos personally received $80 million. When President Somoza fled Nicaragua in 1979 he left the country with a $3 billion debt, but only $3 million in the treasury. In March 1986, when Mexico was pleading bankruptcy to the international bankers, a Mexico City newspaper published the names of 575 Mexican nationals, each of whom had at least $1 million in deposits with foreign banks. The ex-president of Mexico, Lopez-Portillo, is himself widely rumoured to have absconded with over $1 billion when he left office and went to live in Rome.[4]

In an attempt to trace the missing billions, New York economist James Henry has done some detective work. On his calculations, from 1974 to 1985 Mexico borrowed $97 billion and sent $50 billion straight back out again. Argentina is reckoned to have 'lost' more than 60% of its foreign borrowing, Brazil 11%, and the Philippines 25%. Doing some arithmetic on the flight capital owned by private Mexicans that is invested in the USA, earning compound interest on a tax-free basis (because the US government charges no taxes on 'portfolio interest' earned by non-residents), his figures suggest that 'by 1984 the value of Mexican flight capital exceeded the face value of all commercial bank loans to Mexico, and that by 1985 it was closing in on the face value of the country's total external debt'. 'The US as a whole is almost certainly a net *debtor* of all these countries, except possibly Brazil.'[5]

The banks appear to have discovered in Third World debt a mythical money-making machine, and a highly effective way of extracting resources from the Earth. Meanwhile, the pressure on the debtor countries and their people is increasing all the time, and the debts remain, growing ever-larger. To enforce repayment, the banks use the International Monetary Fund (IMF) to impose 'adjustments'. The IMF forces debtor countries to cut their public expenditure, push up the price of food, and focus all their resources on the development of cash-crops for export to earn the money needed to repay the debts. The result of this pressure, imposed by the Earth's richest people on the Earth's poorest, is ever-increasing unemployment, poverty, hunger, malnutrition, and for some, death. In Mexico, one study carried out in 1984 showed that half of all the households in greater Mexico City displayed calorie and protein deficiencies. Another study showed that about 70% of lower income Mexicans had virtually stopped eating rice, eggs, fruit, vegetables and milk (fish and meat being long forgotten luxuries).[6] When Mexico signed a new $12 billion loan in 1986, the price of tortillas rose from 45 to 80 pesos a kilo in a single day. In 1985-86, Mexico was paying $27 million a day in interest to its creditors in the rich world. How did they manage to pay this? Among other things, in 1986 Mexico exported over $2 billion worth of fresh fruits, vegetables and beef to the United States, to help pay the debt.

While ordinary Mexicans eat less and less, and while their children grow up undernourished, it is estimated that over 100,000 upper-middle-class, highly skilled Mexican professionals headed north to the USA between 1982 and 1985. One sociologist interviewed members of 28 Mexican families settling in California, each of which had arrived with $4 million or $5 million (thanks to the help of the banks), which they were busy investing in business and luxury housing, adding this wealth to the Californian economy. The Mexican peasants and labourers left behind have to repay this money, plus interest, to the banks. For many, the breakdown is already happening.

For the struggling countries of the Third World, the debt crisis is only half the story. The other half concerns the fall in commodity prices which means that primary producers such as Zambia (copper) and Jamaica (sugar and bauxite) have to sell twice as much today to earn what they did ten years ago. The IMF, in its determination to force countries to produce more primary goods for export, 'forgot' that overproduction would simply force prices down. The situation is not 'as bad as you thought it was'. It is far, far worse.

The banks are trapped. When you examine the details of the loans country by country, it becomes clear that there is no way in which they can ever hope to repay them. In addition to their Third World loans, many American banks have accumulated huge non-realizable farm and energy loans. With each Third World rescheduling, the total debt grows greater. How the crisis will be resolved, nobody seems to know. Third World countries must receive investment capital from somewhere. If they decide simply to stop paying, no-one will lend them anything. Sooner or later, however, this make-believe house of cards has to come down. The threat is that in doing so, it will trigger a full collapse of the world's banking system, bringing chaos and disorder on an unprecedented scale.

From a distance, the crisis is like a mirror in which we see how hopelessly chaotic and unco-ordinated our approaches to banking, finance and development really are. We have become a single global economy, but we lack the global policies to guide our global banking procedures. In the course of this book, a very different approach to development will become clear, and in the final chapter, the debt crisis will be discussed again.

THE CRISIS OF THE GLOBAL ENVIRONMENT

The third crisis concerns the harmony and stability of our whole global environment. We have inherited a birthright which, if there were people from other planets who could see it (which there may be) would probably be judged the envy of the entire Universe. Words fail when trying to describe the incredible beauty of river, lake and stream, of mountain and dale, of forest, field and farm, of oceans, sunrises and deep starry nights. And we ourselves, no less than the bears, the fish and the woodlice, are miracles of creation and life.

For many hundreds of thousands of years, we lived peacefully and harmoniously with the Earth. Nature's overall balance was never at threat from our activities. It was not until about seven thousand years ago that our activities began to make a lasting impact. Around that time, the people of the Sumerian civilizations first started exhausting their soils by practising constant irrigation, which drew the salt up from below the surface and destroyed the fertile topsoil. Mesopotamia was once a garden of paradise. It is now a dusty, sandswept desert. The forest-cover of Armenia and Azerbaijan was probably removed at the same time to fuel the kilns of those pottery-loving people.[7] The Rajputana desert in India – all 250,000 square miles of it – was once heavily populated, and in Roman days, North Africa was the garden of the empire.

Our agricultural practices are still destroying our topsoils today, but at a far faster rate. The various technologies of modern farming produce high yields, but gradually destroy the soil in the process. The United Nations conference on desertification in 1977 estimated that the Earth would lose 30% of its topsoil by 1997 through soil erosion.

The systematic destruction of the rainforests is another cause for sleepless nights. The soil on which the rainforests rest is very thin, unlike the deeper topsoils of temperate northern climates, and when the trees are gone, the land only yields a crop for five years before its goodness is gone, and then it turns to laterite, an infertile hard-baked sand, increasing the Earth's desert areas and upsetting the planetary rainfall cycles.

Once a rainforest is destroyed, it can never be re-established, except in a highly impoverished form. Their astonishing natural beauty and variety make them one of the wonders of the natural world. They contain one quarter of the world's natural species, living in the forest canopy, provide a home for native peoples who know more about them than we ever will, and contain at least 80,000 species of edible plants, few of which have ever been cultivated. Perhaps most important of all, they help to stabilise the planet's atmosphere and climate, anchoring the cycles of rainfall on which billions depend. When the rainforests have gone, the desert areas of the Earth will increase. At the present debt-inspired disappearance rate of 100 acres per minute (or the size of the UK every year), the rainforests will mostly be gone by the year 2000. The main destruction is happening among the world's big debtor countries – Brazil, Indonesia, Zaire, Peru and Colombia. The forests are literally being torn down to furnish the interest-payments for the banks in London and New York.

With loans from private banks and corporations, Brazil is building dozens of pig-iron smelting plants in the Amazon. The plants will be fuelled by charcoal made from the local rainforest, and the pig-iron will be sold to help pay the banks. There are no plans for reafforestation, so when the nearby rainforest is gone, the plants will close down.[8] Similarly, the Grand Carajas project in Brazil will raze an area the size of the UK and France to provide charcoal, oil and steel at cheap rates for the European steel industry. Meanwhile, peasants are being displaced from southern Brazil to make way for huge soya bean plantations, and sent north into Rondonia, where they are burning down the rainforest to clear the land they have been falsely led to believe they can survive on. The soya beans are sold to Europe, where they are fed to cows to make additional milk and butter which added to the European surplus food mountain that nobody wants. This is how we squander our birthright.

The full global environmental crisis is made up of a number of components. Topsoil erosion and the destruction of the rainforests are two; some of the others are the steady heating of the global atmosphere through waste heat emissions from our use of fossil fuels, known as the 'greenhouse effect' which, by melting the ice-caps will raise global sea-levels by four to five feet, flooding many coastal areas and river deltas and submerging many cities; the depletion of the planetary ozone in the upper atmosphere through the use of CFC gases in spray cans, etc.; the continuous emission of pollutants which cause acid rain, which is destroying the trees of Europe and North America; the dramatic genocidal loss of natural species at a rate of at least 10,000 species per year, with the unknown potential that they carry for new foods, medicines, sources of energy, industrial products and biotechnological research;[9] the build-up of toxic and radioactive wastes which are poisonous to natural species (ourselves included); and the evolution of new breeds of bug, pest and organism that are resistant to all known pesticides. On top of this we can add such things as the killing of the whales, seals and dolphins, the cruelty with which we treat our ordinary domestic animals both in factory farms and through scientific research, the steady erosion of wilderness areas throughout the Earth, and much else besides.

Why do we persist with such madness? Partly because we think it is clever to think only with our brains and not also with our souls or our bellies, and so we fail to perceive the deeper wholeness and the fragile network of nature of which we are part; partly because we are still living as we have since eternity, as if the Earth and its resources were infinite; partly because our economic institutions are geared to calculate only the profit, and not the damage, hurt and costs their activities cause, and partly from simple ignorance, confusion and greed.

What can be done about it all? We need to build a new kind of economy, incorporating new values. Before considering how this can be done, however, there is one more crisis to attend to.

THE CRISIS OF COLLAPSING COMMUNITY AND CULTURE

The fourth crisis concerns the collapse of our own sense of community, neighbourhood and culture in the cities and towns where most people live. Before we started the process of industrialization, most people lived in villages or country towns. We shared community, and we shared culture.

With the industrial age came the economic progress that gave us greater freedom. Each new invention seemed to loosen a shackle of social bondage. The human spirit has to break out of social, political and economic enslavement in order to pursue its evolution, and find its freedom. Having come this far, however, many people are beginning to consider what we have lost.

We need both community and culture for our health and wellbeing. During the last 30 years, factors such as poor social planning, poorly thought-out housing developments, the disappearance of corner shops that are driven out by supermarkets and hypermarkets, the break-up of the extended family and people having to commute long distances to work have undermined our ability to meet and know each other in the areas where we live, weakening and then destroying the reality of community, and the support it gives.

As the sense of community disappears, crime rates increase, and the streets become unsafe. Kids have to be kept indoors, and steadily, more marriages fall apart (no necessary connection). As loneliness and inner distress increase, more people take comfort in alcohol, drugs or tranquillizers. In London, half the people now live either alone or with just one other adult.

All this costs money, too. Such things as welfare provision, social services, hospitalization, psychiatric care, the various costs of crime, including prisons, law courts and extra policing, juvenile care and the many other ways of handling community breakdown add up to a growing 'social repair' bill, which absorbs increasing quantities of public money every year.

The rise in unemployment which has accompanied the change from an industrial to a post-industrial economy has brought the problems of collapsing community into sharper focus. There are housing complexes in cities like Glasgow, London, Marseilles, Barcelona, Chicago and Detroit where up to 60% of the adults have no work. The poverty, crime, hopelessness and sense of personal exhaustion which this engenders are tragic. Whole neighbourhoods become defeated. Litter, graffiti and broken sapling trees become the symbols of despair. Occasionally, the frustration breaks out into riot, but what happens mostly, in the privacy of people's homes, is that the distress goes unseen, unheard and uncomforted. Increasingly, it shows up in child abuse, wife-battering, and attempted suicide. When families fall apart, the men and women can sometimes become the homeless people we see wandering on the streets of London, Toronto, New York and Mexico City. Something is very seriously wrong with our societies when this happens. Our sources of comfort, sharing and spiritual renewal are gradually being destroyed.

We need other people to share our lives with, to live, laugh and cry with, and to share the joys and trials of life with. We were never designed to live alone. In many cities, things are definitely getting worse, but at the same time, there is in many neighbourhoods a growth of interest in new community groups, self-help groups, festivals and celebrations. There comes a time when people say 'enough', and start to use their imagination to seek a better way of living. Without this impulse, the emerging 'rainbow economy' would not exist.

A CRISIS IN OUR PLANETARY EVOLUTION

These are four of the crises that are besetting our societies

13

world. Others could be added – the crisis of nuclear competition being the most obvious one. The sources of the crises are connected through the way we perceive and act in the world. Our dominant consciousness is still one in which we see ourselves as separate people, living in separate worlds, surrounded by potential enemies, obstacles and competitors. Whether it is

- another country or superpower,
- another religion,
- nature herself,
- another race of people,
- another class, group or gang,
- another business or company,
- another person in our own family,
- or even our own marriage partner,

we still tend far too often to perceive them as 'them', and to see them as potentially hostile, threatening realities. Not until we learn to trust, to love, and to know that we are all parts in a greater fabric, a greater harmony in which we can say 'we' without exclusion, will we truly overcome these problems.

Behind these instabilities and fears, we face a crisis in our development on the planet as a whole. We are in a no-person's land before the full emergence of a new awareness of who we really are, and a new geo-political pattern which will express our global interdependence. We are at a turning point between a way of life based on materialism and something new, which is just emerging. Many people seem to know this, consciously or semi-consciously. Increasingly, they are seeking to express what they feel in a meaningful way.

In 1968 we saw for the first time that the Earth is a single whole, a beautiful planet floating in beautiful space. We saw that we belonged together in our collective home. From now on, we have to learn to live with each other, not dominate each other.

The realities of global interdependence mean that a nation can no longer act independently of the rest of the world. Japan's export surplus is America's trade deficit. Brazil's import freeze to pay her foreign debt is America's loss of badly needed exports. Britain's industrial pollution is Scandinavia's dying trees. The chemical industry's CFC gases are the world's wounded atmosphere. To attempt to run our economies by the traditional 'win-lose' rules is no longer possible in a globally interdependent world.

For as long as humans have walked, we have walked with fear. Death and danger were never far away, whether from oppressors, enemies or famine. Humans have been conditioned by evolution to protect themselves; to ensure survival.

If we go on acting as if other countries, businesses, people and nature are there to be dominated, we will ensure a collective disaster. The instincts that helped us survive are now an obstacle to our progress. We need to draw on other instincts, which we also possess. Only by coming together and working together, planetarily, nationally, locally, with nature and in our own families, will we find the way through to the sun that awaits us.

Chapter Two :
What is happening?

The crises described in the first chapter form part of a much wider crisis of development and change that is happening on the planet as a whole.

'What on Earth is happening?' is the heart-cry going up from more and more people, as they watch the images of confusion on television and in real life.

The Earth is going through an enormous transition of some kind. We are experiencing greater planetary confusion than ever before, and at the same time a greater sense of what is possible. The chaos we see on our TV screens, the missiles in their silos, the children starving in the desert and the confusion in our own lives is making people sit up and think 'Is this really how it has to be?'. It is sharpening our desire to reach for a different way of living, and fulfil our dreams. But what is happening? Are we heading for chaos, crash and disaster? Or for some incredible breakthrough to a new way of living, beyond the confusion?

At this point I need to state my own personal spiritual and philosophical position, as this shapes and influences the ideas contained in the rest of the book.

Ever since I was 18 years old, I have known that the universe was a unity, both inwardly and outwardly. From somewhere within me, I looked at the world and saw unity, in every way. I knew that disunity could not exist. Even in separation, everything was linked to a greater whole.

It was the 1960s. The Vietnam War was in progress, the nuclear build-up was proceeding, famine was raging in

Biafra and poverty and slums were equally oppressive here in England. On the other hand, I was young, I was filled with an explosive delight in being alive, and my whole being, inwardly, was like a spring morning. I knew that life could be brilliant, for everyone.

I knew I had to work out what was happening, and why there was such cruelty and pain in the world, alongside the love, inspiration and wonder. It just didn't add up.

During two years at university (sociology at Nottingham), a year in India and then a third year graduating at university, I searched and read extensively, seeking the overall comprehension I needed. I found that most major thinkers addressed either social, political and economical realities, or scientific realities, or spiritual realities. None provided the synthesis which would fit these parts into a greater whole, to reflect the unity I knew existed.

Meanwhile, I was meditating, exploring my own worlds within. I didn't come across anything especially dramatic, but I discovered that 'consciousness' was very different from the *content* of consciousness – the thoughts, emotions and images that fill our waking days. When I was able to sit quietly with consciousness itself, separate from its contents, I felt as if I was touching the edge of an entire new universe, something huge in which I was a total beginner, lacking maps, directions or guidance.

At the same time, my fascination with the natural world led me to love and be astonished by our own biological evolution. Here at least was a unity, at least in the physical sphere. The miracle and beauty of the evolutionary process, linking together all living species over unbelievable lengths of time, captivated me. My problem, as someone who was also concerned with the need for social and political change, and for whom the inner spiritual universe was also real, was that Darwin's image of evolution had nothing to say about these realms. As far as Darwin and the neo-Darwinists were concerned, the changes in human culture and society which have taken place over the last 100,000 years have nothing to

17

do with evolution; and the inner worlds of consciousness and spirit were also seen as being completely separate, if they even existed at all. The philosophers seemed to have divided existence into three separate realms – the scientific, the socio-political and the spiritual – which never met – and yet I knew that everything was a unity. I knew that it had to be possible to draw it all together, and understand what was happening.

It was with these questions in mind that I came across the work of Teilhard de Chardin and Sri Aurobindo. Here were two very different people, living at the same time, who never met or knew each other, who had come to similar conclusions. Teilhard (1881–1955) was a Jesuit priest, thinker and palaeontologist, who spent much of his life writing and working in China, exiled by the Catholic church from Europe because of his ideas. Aurobindo (1872–1950) was a western-educated Indian revolutionary, turned yogi and mystic, who on being freed from jail and a death sentence in 1914, spent the rest of his life in exile in the safety of the French Indian enclave of Pondicherry, developing his integrated understanding of yoga. Both these people accepted evolution as a fact; both lived intense inner spiritual lives; and both saw an incredible future lying ahead for humankind. As soon as I understood the synthesis which they had made, I knew that it made sense.[1]

Teilhard and Aurobindo included consciousness in the evolutionary equation. For Teilhard, spirit is present in all life, matter included; consciousness and matter co-evolve, with consciousness becoming steadily richer as matter becomes more complex. When the evolutionary impulse achieved sufficient physical complexity, it continued to work inwardly, drawing humans towards unity, until individual consciousness finally blossoms into a complete realization of its nature, in the wider universal consciousness that Teilhard called 'Omega'. For Aurobindo, evolution is the ultimate yoga, in which consciousness steadily evolves its way through the material level until it achieves union with the spiritual whole. Later, I learnt that the work of Carl

Jung (1875–1961) also fitted into this wider evolutionary pattern. From a lifetime's work as a psychotherapist and healer, he saw that our individual lives are personal journeys towards wholeness. As we make our inner journeys, our separated consciousness gradually discovers the greater wholeness, beyond the merely individual life, and by allowing this greater whole to penetrate our life and personality, healing the separated parts, we come to know the wholeness in our being.[2]

These understandings gave me the threads which served to unite the many things with which I was concerned. Now I knew *why* we carried dreams, and *why* we constantly strove after beauty, love, justice, peace, and a world in which our ideals would be realized. Underneath the surface, we share in a fundamental unity of consciousness and matter. The ideals we carry are the inner voice of that unified consciousness, rising through evolution, reaching towards the whole. The whole of evolution is a process of healing and becoming whole, as each part seeks inwardly to realise its true nature, and find the deeper unity within. Human evolution did not cease when our brains stopped evolving physically, 100,000 years ago. The physical level is only the vehicle to serve the emergence of consciousness, which continues through the development of culture, language, science, technology, and through our social and political struggles and ideals. Our inner potential keeps on striving to realize the fulfilment it knows to be possible. We are on a one-way journey towards wholeness.

During my twenties, I kept on studying, seeking the evidence which might underpin this approach scientifically. Most scientists, I found, were wedded to a materialist and reductionist view of the world. Consciousness and spiritual realities were not measurable or quantifiable, so they were ignored. I found that science's origins in the seventeenth century lay in part with Descartes' division of the world into two realms: 'res mens', the world of mind, and 'res extensa', the measurable world of things extended in space. Descartes considered the world of 'res mens' to be meaningful, but unworkable scientifically, so he placed it up on a shelf and effectively abandoned it, although he himself believed that the two realms were somehow connected through the pineal gland, the biological equivalent of the 'third eye'.[3] Once it was up on the shelf, other scientists were soon denying that it existed at all, claiming that all reality could be described in measurable, material terms. In a world that was discovering the miracles of material existence, and in which men were beginning to believe they could become the masters and creators of their own destiny, this was a more useful belief to hold.

Alongside science's materialism and reductionism, however, I found another tradition, a rich seam of unorthodoxy which embraced such things as systems theory, and the role of fields of energy in the structuring of matter.[4] Through studying and teaching parapsychology, I learnt that many spiritual and holistic traditions emphasized the importance of these energy fields, and that there were close connections between these fields and our inner states of consciousness. I learnt that scientists were exploring such things as the nature of consciousness itself, the unifying nature of the organizational fields, the methods by which healing is transmitted and received, the nature of altered states of consciousness, the role of biological energy, and the connections between our states of consciousness and the strength of our immune systems.[5] By the time I left this work in my late twenties to become involved with work relating to unemployment and to personal and social change, I felt that it would be only a matter of time before a breakthrough would occur which would demonstrate the role that consciousness played in matter, and in evolution. The ultimate unified field theory would be not 'matter = energy', but rather 'matter = energy = consciousness = bliss'. The synthesis I sought would be forthcoming, demonstrating that all life was a single unfolding unity.

Seen within this vision of evolution, the dreams that we persistently carry from age to age serve as the images of the possible future within us. The idealism of the young is not their folly : it is their wisdom, unveiled by the compromises and difficulties of living. We long to walk out of the mud, and into the light. Behind us, far in the past and somewhere perhaps not so far in the future, lies an 'original wholeness'. Seen in this light, our sense of 'original sin' becomes our knowledge that we are separated from the whole, a whole that is known by a thousand different names in cultures all over the world. We are characterized both by the 'sin' or 'error' that comes from separation, and by an innocence that comes from knowing that we belong at some far-conscious level to the greater unity of all existence and life.

I could now see that the many progressive impulses which characterize human life were all fundamental evolutionary movements towards this greater unity, as we grope and strive our way towards the light:

- our steady progress from tribe, to nation, to super-power bloc, and finally to planet, widening the embrace of consciousness with each successive step;

- our constant search to explore the unexplored, and to travel 'where no man (or woman) has gone before';

- our constant search to understand the realms of nature;

- our constant quest for technological development and achievement;

- our steady struggle to overcome material limitation, poverty and hardship;

- the progressive liberation of our potential, the overcoming of blockages and fears, in our quest to know ourselves, and the steady emergence of our inner wholeness;

- the steady dismantling of barriers of sex, race and religion, which hold us apart from our deeper unity;

- our progress towards more participatory forms of government, which overcome oppression and authoritarian rule and allow us the fuller freedom and room for growth we crave;

- and overall, our steady evolution towards human unity, and an incredible future, in spite of our many wars, cruelties and sufferings. 'Hope springs eternal in the human

21

breast', because however dark the night, each new generation always believes in the dawn.

Living with a philosophy as powerful and optimistic as this, I had also to understand why there is such cruelty and pain in the world. Every step in evolution has been accompanied by resistance. New ideas and values have almost always been accompanied by fear, and a determination to resist. A troup of monkeys living on a Japanese island were once fed sweet potatoes by an ethologist who wanted to study their behaviour. The young females were the first to learn that if they washed the potatoes in the sea, it would remove the sand. Their mothers copied them, and the young males were the next to learn. The older, dominant males were the last of all to learn. In evolutionary terms, they are the ones responsible for the survival of the troup as a whole. Innovation is risky. 'Let's see if this new idea works first, before we adopt it' was their attitude. Conservatism slows and stabilises the progress of ideals, forcing us to test our solidity and keep our feet firmly on the ground while moving forwards. Most people have only a faint grasp of the wider, emerging whole, and as separate beings, faced with disappointment, difficulty and death, we want to hang on to what we have, finding security in possessions, position and power. We often hold our ideas, our children and all we call our own too tight, to give ourselves security against the night. When threatened by change, we tend to tighten our grip, not wanting to lose the things we like and believe to be important. All too easily, this leads to conflict, war, and the many cruelties of life.

This interpretation of what is happening here on the Earth integrates the things I know and experience, and provides me with a firm foundation for my perennial idealism, even if it runs against the tide of much current political and scientific thought. Later in my twenties, I went through a sequence of personal experiences which validated my sense that the universe was a miraculous place. I emerged from these experiences knowing that evolution's long and patient search for wholeness can sometimes be focused into a very short period of time in our own lives, and that the process of 'wholing', or healing, is an integral part of all life. Our progress towards our awaiting unity requires personal, social, political, and economic healing. We have to advance towards our emerging wholeness on every front.

My understanding of our present crisis is that we are in the midst of a wider crisis of evolutionary emergence in which we are arriving at planethood, but in which we have so far failed to develop the policies required to express our interdependence, and to function successfully as a whole.

To understand this, it is necessary to backtrack historically, and consider the nature and purpose of the industrial age, and of the agricultural age that went before it.

During the long years of the agricultural age, the western view of the world was relatively fixed. We believed that we inhabited a world laid down by God, in which the patterns of social order were as fixed and unchanging as the heavenly bodies, the seasons, and the turning of the sun and moon. Few people dreamt of trying to change the world itself, and our inner dreams of a different way of life were projected onto 'heaven'. Spiritually, this satisfied the feeling that we were part of something larger than ourselves. Religion bound us into the greater whole.

For centuries, Europe slept. As far back as the thirteenth century, however, people like Roger Bacon were asking in their minds how we could create machines that would enable us to fly, or walk on water. In their minds, they nursed the idea that one day, humanity might master nature, and transform the Earth.

When the Renaissance and the Reformation arrived, rapidly pursued by the birth of science, a spirit was born which sought the fulfilment of its dreams here on Earth. The devotion with which we built cathedral spires, reaching longingly up towards heaven, was transposed into fervent scientific enquiry. The rule of church and inquisition ended, along with the death by fire of those who opposed them, and freedom of the mind was proclaimed.[6]

Science paved the way for technological revolution, as we pursued the goal of mastering nature, and great changes began to sweep the world. New social and political ideals appeared, challenging the existing order. Kings and queens were overthrown. Great journeys of exploration were made to every corner of the Earth. The major nations of Europe grew steadily in strength and power.

In the realm of economics, companies were formed to put the new technologies to work. In sleeping valleys, cotton mills and factories sprang up, blackening the air with their smoke. By a skilful concentration of intelligence, capital, commercial organisation, and the enormous toil of the labouring masses, a miracle was gradually achieved. Over a relatively short period of time, the material nature of our existence in the North of the Earth was transformed. In evolutionary terms, the task we accomplished was incredible. We learnt how to eliminate scarcity, through the processes of creation and synthesis. For those who have known the cruelty of poverty, this achievement can never be underestimated.

In the process of achieving the goal, however, something happened which still haunts our world today. To understand it fully, we must go back to the days before the agricultural age.

For many hundred thousand years, we lived in bands and tribes as wandering hunters and gatherers. Economically, each band was a collective self-reliant unit, running a community economy. Land was never 'owned': it was seen as belonging to nature, or the gods of the natural world, with whom a very close relationship was upheld. Nature was felt to be both a physical and a spiritual power, which humans could learn to embrace by the pursuit of careful spiritual disciplines. If the right inner work was done, aligning self with nature, deer would run into the path of your arrows, and rain could be made to fall in times of drought.

After a time, the women learnt that by collecting and

planting seeds, they could grow their own food, and give the band greater security against times when winters were hard, and when the hunters had no joy. They started to cultivate the land, which over time, tied a band more closely to one spot. It also weakened the close spiritual link with nature, a weakening which the new religions of the agricultural age did their best to encourage. As the supply of food increased, more people lived, and populations grew. In parts of the world where the soil was rich, such as China and Mesopotamia, a settled agricultural existence grew up, displacing the older tribal ways. Ownership of the land was now claimed by individual people, and social divisions arose between those who owned land and those who did not. The latter were forced to work for the former in order to survive. The integrated community economies of tribal days gave way to privately-based economies characterized by dependency and power.

Let us jump now to the end of the agricultural age. The division of the social order into rich and poor has by now been part of life for so long that it is taken for granted as part of the natural order of existence – a belief which the owners of land did little to discourage. As the new agricultural technologies arrived, increasing numbers of peasants found that their labours were no longer needed. The steady procession off the land and into the growing cities of the industrial age began.

In the cities, the division of rich and poor continued. Only those who owned land or who already had capital were considered creditworthy by the bankers, who lent them the money they needed to finance the new factories, mills, railways and mines. A new social division grew up between the owners and their workers, who were often forced to sell their labour for a pittance to keep starvation away. The spirit of economic individualism, which was creating the miracle and powering the transformation of the world, was breeding a shadow, through the cruelty of its ways.

Individually, working people wanted progress and wealth as much as their employers, and shared in the exciting spirit of the age. Both individually and collectively, however, they knew the cost of the transformation. The new philosophy of socialism was born, opposing the greed and selfishness of individualism and proclaiming as its dream the end of social division, the equal division of wealth, and the collective or social ownership of capital. When the Tsarist regime in Russia fell to the organised forces of socialism in 1917, the world was set for the division which has haunted the twentieth century ever since.

In spite of their mutual hatred, the economic philosophies of both capitalism and socialism share many basic assumptions and values, which have underpinned the industrial age. Both are committed to economic progress and the achievement of material goals. Both see nature as a force to be tamed and put to human use. Both place more importance on material than on spiritual goals. Although the socialist movement consciously strove for equality, both took for granted many of the engrained habits of social dominance which we had inherited from our agrarian past, placing men above women, whites above blacks, the powerful above the powerless, 'advanced' industrial societies above Third World societies, adults above children, humans above animals and humans above all nature.

In the late twentieth century, the values which served the industrial age are now proving to be our undoing:

• Our dominant attitude towards nature, born out of our desire to understand the natural world and extend our own abilities, lies behind our destruction of the rainforests, the pollution of the soils and oceans, the extinction of natural species and so much else besides.

• Our commitment to materialism and personal gain, born out of our striving to eliminate poverty and scarcity and to create a heaven here on Earth, lies behind our massive consumption of resources and the ensuing garbage problems, our overheating of the atmosphere (the greenhouse effect) and our loss of wider community values.

• Our commitment to the economic values of

capitalism, born out of the quest for individual freedom, the desire to end poverty and our inability to integrate both individual and social goals, has led to the craziness and irresponsibilities of the West's banking and finance systems.

When you take away the spirit of individual initiative and enterprise, an economy ceases to thrive, deprived of the initiative, motivation and zest it needs to bring prosperity. The Soviet Union, Eastern Europe and China before Deng Xiao Ping give evidence of this. When you take away the wider social values, on the other hand, and encourage businesses, banks and individuals to pursue their own interests without regard for the greater whole, you deprive an economy of the caring and thoughtfulness needed to create a stable, sustainable and happy society, and you get the bad working conditions, insensitivity to community issues, abuse of nature and exploitation of weaker Third World countries that we are so familiar with here in the West.

Capitalism and socialism express two inseparable aspects of human nature, the 'I' and the 'we', both of which are needed for the continuation of the human story. Both creeds seek to realise high human ideals, and both are crippled by the denial of their shadow aspects, which they then project onto each other. Only through the healing of the division and the re-integration of the separate parts will we be able to meet the needs we desire:
- the achievement of prosperity,
- globally sustainable development,
- the strengthening of community and environmental values, *and*
- the development of economic justice in the world.

Today, as part of our global transition, the industrial age is handing over to the post-industrial age, having granted to many the prosperity they sought. Simultaneously, we are experiencing a major shift of values. Growing numbers of people who now experience material prosperity or sufficiency are turning their concerns to other dimensions of wealth and prosperity which they also want, continuing the deeper evolutionary quest in which the elimination of basic poverty is but a stage. Among these higher needs are fulfilment, meaning and love; a richer community life which will provide friendship, fun, and freedom from fear of crime; closer contact with nature; an end to pollution and environmental assault; and an ability to look forward to the future with hope and excitement, instead of fear. Material prosperity and gain are no longer seen as the *only* goal in life: other goals are now important, too.

As these changes in our values are taking place, growing numbers of people are awakening to a new consciousness of the planet as a whole. Inwardly, we are preparing for a planetary existence. For some, the work they do on the inner levels is as important as their outer work.

At the dominant economic and political levels, however, the institutions of government, banking, business and education are still informed by the values and the consciousness of the past. The banks, for instance, rushed to expand their activities to meet the new global realities of the 1970s and 1980s without any questioning of their long-term purposes or values. They have dug themselves a pit, and in the time-honoured tradition of pirates and robbers, are now forcing their victims to dig them out.

Globally, the financial crises which threaten us with crash and collapse express the vacuum of leadership at the global economic level. We are in a difficult and dangerous limbo-land, between American dominance and the emergence of a new global order. We have arrived at the beginning of full planetary interdependence, without knowing what it means. In our emerging consciousness and values, we are experiencing globalization, but in our economic and political actions, we still live in a non-global way. This is the core of our crisis today.

Ecologically, we are still acting as if the Earth were effectively infinite, even while our actions are destroying the very foundations of biological existence. Militarily, we are spending enormous sums of money – $2.5 billion a day – on weapons we know we can never use, consuming the resources so urgently needed for practical development work, because in our minds, we are still fighting the wars of our pre-global yesterdays.

Financially and economically, our activities have become haywire. Enormous sums of money are moving round the world without any overall policy designed to help us achieve our planetary goals. Planetary goals? Such things have not even yet been formulated by the major superpowers except as the expression of the desire to dominate the rest of the planet, or as a result of multi-national corporations planning and managing their assets for the pursuit of profit. No one claims to understand where all the money is, where it is going or even who it belongs to. We allow personal banking secrecy to continue, while countries suffer miseries to repay the billions that have already been stolen and secreted away. We lack any sense of common purpose to guide our common future. The western world's businesses and economies are still guided by values of personal and institutional gain and profit which may have served us during the expansive, constant growth world of the industrial age, but which often have a disintegrative and fragmentary effect in an interdependent, fragile, global, post-industrial world.

Looked at without any vision of what the overall purpose or direction of our evolution might be, it might seem as if the god Chaos has descended and colonized the Earth. Seen in a broader evolutionary light, it is possible to see that we are in the midst of a crisis of global emergence which happens but once in a planet's lifetime. From a thousand directions, the pressures of global integration are urging us to shift to a higher level of operation, and respond in a positive way to what is happening. The longer we remain with the structures and attitudes of the past, the greater will be the discomfort and confusion on the planet as a whole. The consciousness and values which served us yesterday are destroying us today.

We urgently need to evolve new economic practices, values and policies to serve our emerging planetary needs. We

29

have little choice in this: the impact of our pre-planetary behaviour is rapidly undermining the stability of our whole existence, whether through the greenhouse effect, the collapse of our communities or the potential collapse of our whole economy.

As we move out of the industrial age, predictably, our values are on the move. New hopes, new dreams and a new consciousness of the planet as a whole are gaining strength every day. A new impulse is literally besieging the Earth.

In recent years, as the different crises have grown, there has been a steady search for ways in which these new values can be translated into practical economic terms, enabling us to build a new kind of economy to meet our newly emerging needs. For the purposes of this book, I call this the 'rainbow economy', since the colours of the rainbow reflect the values of the new economics which it seeks to serve. These values, and their translation into practical economic forms, are the subject of the next chapter.

The idea that it is *consciousness* which evolves, not only matter, is still quite new, and may seem strange if you have been brought up to view the world in material terms. At one level, it really doesn't matter. If you love life, that is all that matters. We didn't need to understand the nature of our evolution in order to abolish slavery. We needed only our natural sense of outrage and compassion. The same applies today.

At another level, the idea that both consciousness and matter evolve changes everything. It changes the nature of science, for it means that we need to end our Descartian dualism, and integrate our understandings of matter with those of consciousness and spirituality. It changes our understanding of how change happens, for it means that the critical source of change is right here within ourselves in the movement of our own inner consciousness and ideas. It makes us re-appraise the nature of consciousness, and see it not just as the passive background for our thoughts and feelings, but as the active source of energy through which reality itself is formed, and through which the deep unfolding of our evolution occurs.

It makes us realise that as we ourselves are possessed of consciousness, we have it in our power to mould and change reality, not only physically, but inwardly. It makes us realise that the way we handle the consciousness which runs through us determines the kind of life we lead. If we re-create ourselves each day as passive victims, it will be so; if we re-create ourselves each day as beautiful, happy people, it will be so. We are free, with the power to make choices. It means that if we hold within our consciousness a world in which suffering, disaster and hopelessness are seen as inevitable, we help it to be so; and if we hold within our consciousness a world which is growing daily into greater peace, understanding, and love, this too will be so, for we are literally creating this reality within the heart of consciousness, and thereby assisting its emergence on the outer levels, too.

When we perceive our world to be made only of physical matter, in which changes happen because someone makes them happen by physical effort, we set up a situation in which change will always be hard, involving effort and struggle. When we perceive that the world is made primarily of consciousness, on the other hand, a very different view emerges. As we think, so we become, and so the world becomes. The source of the greatest action moves to the innermost level, where it shapes and forms the constantly re-creating and emerging world. A truly different view of life, the world and everything emerges, both in our personal lives, and in our endeavours to change the world.

The world is still practical, however, and dreams still have to be converted into action. With these thoughts, the book continues.

Chapter Three :
The emerging rainbow economy

The world of economics can be a bewildering place, full of long words and mathematical equations. This book is not like that. Its major thesis is very easy to grasp. It proposes that:

- as we think, see, love and do,
    so our economies are;
- and as we change the way we think, see, love and do,
    so our economies change.

Our economies are only reflections of ourselves, expressing the ways we live, and the values we live by.

Over the last few hundred years, the dominant values in the industrial societies of the world have been the economic values of industriousness, endeavour, competition, accumulation profit and material benefit. Businesses have had to struggle to succeed, and the values of struggle and gain have become a deeply woven part of our social and economic fabric.

Today, with the arrival of planetization, we are realizing how interdependent we are. We can no longer assume that the world is an open canvas on which we can happily paint our own designs. We live within a closed system where the repercussions of our activities come back to us.

In response to the emerging dreams of the planetary age, and to the crises which people see growing around them, both globally and locally, a new set of values is emerging and seeking practical expression. These are the seven values of the emerging rainbow economy. The new values are coming from the pressure of our own emerging wholeness. Evolution is not standing still; it is urgently seeking new ways to reach its goals.

The people who are attracted to these new values are expressing them in many different ways and on many different levels, including business, education, personal relationships, health, ecology, inner self-awareness, banking, work, science, community development, politics, conflict resolution, international relations, and much else besides. In this book, it is chiefly the economic expression that concerns me. By finding solid ways to express the new values, growing numbers of people are steadily creating a new kind of economy in scattered places around the world. The rainbow economy is emerging. It is not a planned response to the global crises, but in an organic way, it is *growing*. By sharing some glimpses of what is happening through this book, I hope to encourage others with a new vision of economic hope.

The seven core values of the rainbow economy are as follows:

- Purple, for spiritual values
- Dark blue, for planetary values
- Pale blue, for economic values
- Green, for ecological values
- Yellow, for values of personal creativity and fulfilment
- Orange for local community values
- Red, for social values

Purple, for spiritual values[1]

The word 'spiritual' does not necessarily mean 'religious', although it may include it. It reflects a growing sense that many people feel that we are part of a greater whole, which is a source of wonder and humility. For some, this source of wonder is the Earth itself, floating miraculously in the vastness of space, along with nature, and all creation. For others, the greater whole is invisible – it is God, the silent 'Tao', the breathing Buddha, within them and within everything.

Economically, one way in which this value expresses itself

is through the emphasis on the need for honesty and integrity in the way we live, work, and run our businesses. The Buddhists say that when you steal, it is you yourself from whom you steal, and whom you harm the most.[2] A second way is through a shift away from blaming other people or outer circumstances for difficulties, or for things that go wrong. The awareness is growing that it is we ourselves who create and co-create reality, whether we know it or not, and that by our attitudes, we create the results we want.

Dark blue, for planetary values

Dark blue expresses the beauty of the Earth as a whole. Economically, it asks us to reflect that beauty in the way we live and work. There is no sense in developing a business to provide jobs for local people in one community, if it means ripping off people in another. Companies such as Co-op America, and Traidcraft in Britain only import goods from producer groups working in fair and democratic ways. Scott Bader, a large British workers co-operative which produces chemical resin products, recently faced up to its South African connection, which had been bringing it £100,000 a year in license fees. Instead of simply cutting the connection, they set up a locally controlled Trust Fund to receive the money, from which black South African community economic initiatives such as the Valley Trust, outside Durban, receive support. By our ways of trading, we can help to change the world.

Pale blue, for economic values

Pale blue represents the economic values of efficiency and profitability. When pursued alone, they can be destructive, creating the very problems which are undermining the world. When pursued in their rightful place alongside other values, they play an exciting and essential role in world development. If a business does not succeed, it fails, and is no value to anyone. There is nothing wrong with profit itself – it is simply a measure of financial viability and success. Troubles only arise when the search for profit is allowed to override other values which matter too. It is not profit which is wrong, but the ways in which it is raised and used.

Economic values bring economic vision, as companies seek to realise their goals. If their values speak only of economic growth and profit, inasfar as a company succeeds, the planet's overall environment will lose. The pursuit and realisation of goals are essential evolutionary processes. As with profit, there is nothing inherently wrong with growth – it is the way in which growth is achieved which causes the damage. Company visions must be set within the context of other values, bringing growth which is ecologically sustainable, and the growth of other dimensions of value alongside purely economic growth. (Chapter Eight explores some of the innovations which companies are adopting as they seek to combine the values of efficiency and profitability with other values they see as important. Chapter Nine considers some of the innovations which are happening in the fields of banking and finance, as they too seek to realise goals other than profitability and growth alone.)

Green, for ecological values

The industrial age has created a mode of economic development which is fundamentally non-sustainable : we cannot continue in this way. No one *intends* to undermine our existence on the Earth, but taken all together, the ways in which we function economically are doing just that. The realities of interdependence demand the adoption of a wider economic vision, serving more inclusive values.

As the pressure for environmental policies grows, some companies are beginning to realise the value of adopting an increasingly sustainable approach to business (see Chapter 8). The same is increasingly true of local city governments in Europe and North America. In Canada, every province is drawing up a strategy for sustainable economic development as part of a nation-wide effort to chart a new path into the future. Only by building ecological values into the heart of all our activities, both in our personal lives and in business, and both locally, nationally and globally, can we lay the found-

35

ations for a world in which we enjoy the full fruits of a co-creative partnership with nature. (Chapters Eight and Ten consider these developments in more detail.)

Yellow, for values of personal creativity and fulfilment

Many people are beginning to demand that their work brings them fulfilment, and doesn't waste their lives. Companies are realising that to attract the most creative employees, they must offer the best opportunities for fulfilment. We are learning incredible things about the true potentials we possess. Up until now, we have been like planetary teenagers, only dimly aware of our capabilities.

To develop policies which deliberately pursue the release of our creativity and potential for growth means major changes in the way in which we approach such things as education, welfare, careers advice, business, organizational management, government, and justice. A new world of possibilities awaits us. (See Chapter Five 5.)

Orange, for local community values

Since the early 1980s, a steady renaissance in community economic life has been occurring in Western Europe and North America. Stimulated by the disastrous rise in unemployment caused by economic recession, business failure and corporate mergers, and the underlying weakness of many local economies, new community businesses, initiatives, partnerships and development agencies have been forming, seeking practical answers to the problems of local economic collapse and decline. In our industrial age values, we have treated community in much the same way as we have treated nature, just taking it for granted and assuming it would always be there. As we realise the mounting costs of this blindness, people are seeking ways in which physical communities, and the spirit of community, can be rebuilt. Through the use of community architecture, the development of new community currencies, by running future workshops, by establishing community development associations and neighbourhood organizations and in a host of other ways, a gradual revival and renewal is happening. (Chapters Four, Six, Seven and Eleven explore some of these initiatives.)

Red, for social values

At the top of the rainbow, red represents the values which stand at the core of the social impulse – our concern for justice, for compassion, and for equality of treatment between people. On its own, the colour red becomes oppressive, just as the colour blue becomes selfish, but in harmony and companionship with other values, it expresses an essential need to care about society as a whole, to look after the weaker and poorer members and to ensure that everyone has an equal chance to participate, no matter what their background, age, race or sex.

In the context of the emerging economy, social values are being expressed through the development of such things as cooperatives which are owned jointly by their workers, community businesses which are owned by local residents, other forms of social ownership, credit unions and non-profit community banks which serve the needs of a community, and new approaches to welfare, poverty, education and community need.

Each colour of the new economy has something of value to offer. On its own, however, a single colour creates distortions and imbalances in the way we live, bringing distress, disharmony and disorder. Through their integration and harmonic play, an economy and a way of living can be built which will reflect our interdependent, planetary existence, and satisfy our deepest needs. It is this integration at the economic level which the rest of the book explores.

THE PROCESSES OF DEVELOPMENT

Economies do not suddenly arrive; they take time to grow. The art of development is critical to the success of everything mentioned so far, if we are to get from here to the

37

future we seek.

For the sake of clarity, I will describe seven different models of development, two of which are traditional, and five of which add important new dimensions, addressing the critical issues which concern us today. With each successive model, a new dimension is added to the development process. The models are complementary, not alternatives.

Model 1: Top down, macro-economic management[3]

This is the most traditional model of industrial age economic development, which is pursued in various different forms by most western governments. It places its faith in macro-economic measures designed to help business, industry and the economy expand by controlling inflation, removing impediments to trade, cutting taxes and/or borrowing where necessary to pursue public policies and to pump extra spending power into the economy, investing in the necessary infrastructural supports that an economy needs such as science and technology, research, education, training, health, roads and railways, and creating a stable financial and economic environment. Other policies such as regional development priorities also play an important part in this model.

There is no doubt that economic development requires a favourable climate, and that government policies can do much to encourage or impede development. While it has this value, however, by emphasising purely economic development above all else, and ignoring any planetary, environmental or community issues, this model effectively contributes to the problems already outlined, perhaps not by deliberate action, but by default. It should not be thrown out, but should be thoroughly upgraded and transformed so that it addresses planetary, ecological and community concerns, and is integrated with the models described below.

Model 2: Smokestack (silicon) chasing

Throughout the 1960s and 1970s, this was the main (and often, only) development model pursued locally when economic development was needed. An office would be set up, and attentions focused on enticing footloose companies to come and settle in wonderful Telford, Wichita or Winnipeg. Even in the economically tight 1980s, when 500 towns and cities might be courting the attentions of a handful of companies, this policy still has some merit. Footloose companies clearly do settle somewhere, and even though it is a dog-eat-dog game, if a city doesn't take part at all, it misses out entirely on the prizes to be won.

On a purely economic level, successful smokestack or silicon chasing creates new local jobs, thereby adding to the wealth of the local economy. As a development policy, however, it is sorely lacking. It increases the dependency of a community on outside employers whose prime responsibility is not to the locality, but to their head offices in Tokyo, London or New York; and it fails to address the key planetary, ecological and community issues. By default, it also adds to the problems.

If the policy of smokestack/silicon chasing is upgraded, however, to ensure that an incoming company is willing to integrate with other wider and more all-embracing development policies (regarding, for instance, ecological sustainability), and if it is willing to accept the rights of the local community as a stakeholder in the company (see Chapter Eight), it can form a valuable component in a wider, more comprehensive development strategy.

Model 3: Local economic development

The third development strategy is a child of the 1980s. When the unemployment figures started to rise so dramatically in the early 1980s, cities and towns were compelled to start thinking on their feet. Existing policies were clearly insufficient to meet the challenge of the times, and far more was needed.

Out of this period of crisis has come a whole new local economic impulse. This comes in two versions, the 'lesser' and the 'greater'.

The 'lesser' version focuses its attention on the development of local enterprise, encouraging local people to start new businesses, and giving assistance to existing companies to help them expand or to pull them out of a hole. As an impulse, it has been enormously successful. In Britain, the leading actors have been the local enterprise agencies, which offer hands-on assistance and support to those who want to set up in business, and local enterprise boards, which meet a similar need on a larger regional basis. In France, a similar function is fulfilled by the 'boutiques de gestion', and in the USA by 'business incubators'. (See Chapter Seven.)

As the new agencies have developed confidence, they have expanded their role to include arranging local funding, providing business training, organising group marketing, providing workspace units and running local business clubs. By releasing the spirit of enterprise and resourcefulness, they lay an important foundation stone for the development of a more self-reliant, integrated, balanced and sustainable local economy.

In the 'greater' version, an organised approach is taken to local economic development as a whole, incorporating the lesser version as one part of a wider strategy. The Massachusetts town of Lowell, in the USA, provides an example of this process in action. In the 1970s, Lowell had 13% unemployment, and its mills and industries were in decline. The very name 'Lowell' implied 'economic basketcase'. By 1988, it was being paraded as one of Massachusetts' great success stories, with only 3% unemployment.

In between, three things happened which are essential for the local economic development process. These involve *partnership*, *planning*, and *money*.

Firstly, the leading actors in business, finance and government got together and sat round a table to discuss Lowell's problems, something they had never done before. They then formed a *partnership organization*, the Lowell Development Finance Corporation, which could act decisively on the town's behalf. Next, by working closely together, they drew up an overall *development strategy* known as the Lowell Plan. This included various creative ideas which they actively pursued, among them a National Heritage Park and a Sculpture Trail, which attract a million visitors a year. They did these things by their own will, once they had established an organization through which they could express their will. Before they claimed this power, the people of Lowell were victims of the wider processes of economic change which sometimes lift you, and sometimes drop you in the mud, leaving you little or no control over your own economic destiny.

Once they had a plan, they needed *money*. The local banks had been part of the partnership from the beginning, and were involved in the whole development process. When Wang Computers expressed an interest in basing themselves in Lowell, a $5 million loan at only 4% interest was forthcoming. A new Hilton Hotel and the Wang Training Centre were also enticed into Lowell by the same means.

Two wider regional processes played essential roles in Lowell's recovery. Firstly, the State of Massachusetts, under the governorship of Michael Dukakis, got its own house in order, clearing a $400 million state deficit, and then adopting state-wide policies designed to facilitate the development of local enterprise, and not get in the way (Enterprise Development Strategies). Secondly, *education* and *training* were made absolute top priorities, and given the investment needed to encourage the development of a skilled population. Institutions of higher education like the Massachusetts Institute of Technology have played an important role in underpinning the regeneration process.[4]

In Britain, many cities are busy developing this 'greater' version of the local economic development model, involving partnerships with the business community, development plans, and local investment, though they are hampered by the unwillingness of traditional British banks to play their part, which give their loyalty to London, not to Bradford or

41

Sunderland. Local people's savings, instead of being used to support local development with loans below market rates, are invested on the money markets, if profits there are greater. (See Chapter Nine.)

In parts of Britain, local enterprise agencies and enterprise boards have been broadening their role and taking on the role of local development associations. Throughout the 1980s, towns and cities have made a steady progression from the 'lesser' to the 'greater' version of this model. Lancashire Enterprise Limited, for instance, plays a very active development role as an enterprise board on behalf of Lancashire County Council, engaging in a host of positive 'Model 3' activities – encouraging new business ideas, providing finance under a 'Rosebud Fund' for new small businesses, supporting management buy-outs and mergers, running industrial training programmes, encouraging high technology developments, undertaking urban renewal projects, engaging in property development, providing venture capital for local companies, funding the Lancashire Co-operative Development Agency, and co-ordinating major development schemes like the massive £80 million Leeds-Liverpool Canal Project.[5] *The creation of a local partnership, development company or development association is an essential part of any development process, and is an important expression of the rainbow economy values. The community that does not claim power for itself will always be the victim of someone else's power. Either you create your own reality, or you live in someone else's.*

However, while this model of economic development can create jobs and bring back material prosperity to a hard hit community, it still does not address the critical planetary, ecological or community issues. Lowell is quite happy to entertain defence contract work in its development and Massachusetts still has major problems of homelessness and economic 'apartheid', separating its poorer citizens from its economic miracle. And the question of the ecological sustainability of the new economic developments, as far as I know, has not been discussed.

By starting with a model of development and a partnership which includes only two segments of the community as a whole (local government and business), the problems of economic inequality, poverty and community collapse are left basically untouched.

Model 4: Community economic development

In the fourth development model, a major new dimension is added: the dimension of community.

Community economic development is also a child of the 1980s, and has developed as a response to the problems of unemployment and poverty. Through community economic development (CED), ordinary people who have always depended on someone else to develop their jobs and houses and to undertake economic planning begin to take these responsibilities themselves, taking their reality into their own hands.

CED plays a very important role in the emergence of the overall rainbow economy, and for this reason, a considerable part of the book is devoted to it. For the sake of extreme simplicity, its essential components can be summarized in seven points.

The first, as in Model 3, involves the formation of a *local partnership*, but this time, as well as people from local government and the business community, people are also involved from voluntary groups, community groups, colleges, schools, local organisations, churches, trade unions and other local clubs and societies. Accordingly, the *development plans* which the partnership draws up reflect the hopes, needs and aspirations of the community as a whole. (See Chapter Six.)

The second component is an organised process of *community awakening* which brings local people together in their neighbourhoods, and enables them to pinpoint their biggest headaches, devise strategies to tackle them, and undertake the initiatives needed to build the kind of community they really want. One such process, the 'Future Workshop', is described in Chapter Six.

Once the ideas are rolling, there is need for a third component, a *local development organization* to make things happen. This can take the form of a community development corporation, a community business or a community association, enabling local people to reclaim their power and authority after centuries of living under someone else's. Once local people have their own organizational basis, initiatives such as worker co-operatives, housing co-operatives, self-build housing schemes, childcare facilities, community health plans and new local businesses can be encouraged and established.

All this requires *money*, which is the fourth component. Local banks are not usually too happy about lending to this new breed of community enterprise, so new community financial and banking initiatives are called for, such as credit unions and community loan funds, and new definitions of 'collateral' have to be established. In order that poverty and inequality might be eliminated, it is also necessary to pioneer *new forms of ownership* to allow everyone full participation in the economic progress of society. Without permanent solutions to the problems of poverty, low incomes and non-ownership, the existing conditions of economic apartheid, which are creating an unbridgeable gulf between those who are able to afford their own property, and those who are not, will become ever more entrenched. (See Chapter Nine.)

The fifth component involves policies to encourage a wider process of *personal awakening* among ordinary people. New approaches to education, training and welfare are called for to release people's creative potential, to develop skills, and to encourage people to begin to shape their own realities. (See Chapter Five.)

Large changes to local government are necessary to facilitate and support these developments. The sixth component, therefore, involves the *political and administrative decentralisation of power, and a planned shift away from the normal local government policy of doing things for people, towards supporting people to do things for themselves.* The boroughs of Tower Hamlets and Islington in London, and the City of Oxford, have already begun this process, and demonstrate the possibilities.

The final component is the need for *co-ordination* and *integration* of the many different policies which govern local life. At present, because local people have no effective way of voicing their needs, and no means of meeting them, there is no single vision to serve as a guide for development. Without that vision, people perish. Once the members of a neighbourhood find their voice and begin to build the kind of future they want, the vision begins to appear. Integrated policies and integrated budgeting procedures are then called for to support the vision, and its realisation. (See Chapter Eleven.)

Community economic development is an exciting field in which much innovation and new thinking is taking place. The achievements that are possible when local people start to organize themselves are inspiring, and show what can be done. As an organized development strategy, it is young, but it is growing rapidly, and gaining serious attention. Between them, Models 1, 2, 3 and 4 have the ability to heal *one* of the major planetary crises – the collapse of community. That has to be a good beginning.

Model 5: Sustainable development

Model 1 predominated in the 1960s, with Model 2 being added in the 1970s, and Models 3 and 4 in the 1980s. None of the existing models of development addresses the issue of ecological sustainability on the planet as a whole, however. They predate our awareness of just how critical this matter is. The development of Model 5, which addresses this need, and its integration with the existing models will be one of the most important development tasks of the 1990s.

Many of the necessary components for such a model have already been developed. These include strategies for energy efficiency, source elimination of both pollution and waste, recycling, sustainable agriculture, low car-use transport, community health and 'greening the cities'. Organizationally, these strategies require the formation of local partnerships, and the systematic development of initiatives, plans, incentives, and whatever else is required to achieve the goal: permanent ecological sustainability.

Although it may seem from a distance that this represents a simply massive task, once you get close up to each particular component of the overall problem, and study the emerging strategies that are being evolved to counter that problem, it becomes clear that we are not dealing with one huge, intransigent problem, but with a vast number of small, particular problems, each of which has a practical solution, which is achievable once we put our minds to it. For each of the key components that is needed for a comprehensive strategy for ecological sustainability, most of the necessary research has already been done (see Chapter Ten). The critical task for the 1990s is to integrate this work into the local economy, and into local development policies.

In addition to the nation-wide sustainability strategy being developed across Canada (see Chapter Twelve), several cities and towns around the world are beginning to consider ways in which their policies can incorporate ecological sustainability. The crucial issue in the development of Model 5 will be the willingness of people in every sector of local life, including government, businesses, banks, colleges, schools, community groups and environmental groups to link together in a partnership to develop joint policies and strategies designed to achieve sustainability.

Appropriate initiatives, incentives, agreements and legislative requirements are needed nationally and globally, to back this up.

Model 6: Organisational transformation

The need for organisational transformation arises from the fact that in most businesses and organizations, human potential is denied, participation is not the rule, people are not at the centre of attention, and profits are not shared. In individual companies, major transformations are under way designed to liberate our full human potential, increase the success of the company, and operate in a more holistic way (see Chapter Eight). This process of change needs to become part of a wider and more organized development model, in which the many stakeholders in a business or organization, from the shareholders, governors and directors to the employees, trade unions, local community and customers share in a process of discussion, learning, negotiation, evolution and change. By seeking to serve our deepest human needs, and by serving higher human values, a business or organization becomes not only more successful, but also happier. Once this truth is understood, the willingness to take part in this process of development will appear. In the late 1980s and early 1990s this may seem to be a pipedream, but before long, the pressure of our emergent human needs, combined with the market pressures that force a company to keep evolving, will ensure that it happens.

Model 7: Planetary transformation

The seventh and final development model, planetary transformation, concerns the need for our businesses and organizations to serve planetary goals, and to be part of the solution to our planetary ills, not of the problem. There will come a time when companies which derive income from the production and sale of arms and military technologies, for instance, will be faced with the progress of multi-party peace talks and international agreements, and will need either to diversify their activities or face collapse. This is not fantasy. The steady pressure of our emerging human wholeness, which carried us from separate and warring tribes into nations, is carrying us on into a global family in an ever-accelerating way. This is not an 'ideal': it is a very distinct evolutionary process.

From what we already know from Models 3 and 4, helping a company undergo a systematic diversification and conversion out of arms sales into new lines of activity need not present any insuperable problems. We possess a wide array of techniques for releasing creativity, generating ideas, combining research skills, and spinning off new businesses. By approaching the task of the planetary transformation of business in an organised, collective way, communities can assist their companies to undertake a planned evolution into activities which aid the development of our planet and its people, instead of impeding it. This includes the manufacturers of weaponry, but also the exporters of dangerous (and often illegal) pesticides and herbicides, the importers and exporters of hardwoods from the tropical rainforests, the producers and sellers of tobacco and harmful drugs, the sellers of nuclear plants, and the banks which lend money to finance these and other harmful activities. We managed to abolish slavery, and we outlawed child labour at least in Europe. These are just further steps in the steady human progress towards a higher, more caring, and more loving existence.

This chapter has offered a brief overview of some of the contents of the book as a whole. In the following chapters, the different initiatives and developments which make up the emerging rainbow economy are considered in varying degrees of detail.

The sheer scale of the work involved in these changes may seem to some readers to be overwhelming. There *is* a lot to do: that is undeniable. The single biggest obstacle that stands in the way of our achieving what is needed, however, is the belief that it is not possible. With that idea, we give up, and effectively surrender our evolutionary birthright. Many dedicated activists of the peace movement lost their courage for a while in the 1970s. Whatever you think or feel individually, however, two things don't go away. You can go to sleep for a year or stop reading the newspapers, but when you come back they will still be there. The first is the mounting global crisis, with its accumulating craziness, debt, danger and pain. The second is the constant surge of new life that comes with each rising generation, bringing new dreams, new skills, and a new dedication to heal the Earth and build a better world. Hope is more powerful than despair; life stronger than death; and love more powerful than indifference.

In presenting this material, I am not saying 'Here are all the answers we need'. It is only when I get carried away that it may seem like that! This book only deals briefly, for instance, with the national and international policies that are needed to accompany the evolution of new community economies. Nor does it attempt to spell out the value and relevance of the ideas to development overseas or to the evolution of socialist economies.

What the book *is* saying is 'Maybe this is something worth looking at'. The full rainbow economy has yet to arrive: the evidence shows only that growing numbers of people are being sufficiently moved to seek to live by different values, and to build an economy which serves those values. I honour these people.[6]

In the chapter that follows we begin by exploring one community economic initiative which is capturing the imagination of increasing numbers of people.

Chapter Four :
A harbour in a storm

America may fail to sort out the problems of her twin trade and budget deficits and the markets may decide to bail out . . . a Third World debtor country may have a change of leadership and decide that total default will be their best policy . . . the Japanese or the Arabs may decide that the dollar is likely to fall and suddenly pull their money out of their American banks . . . the Japanese or Taiwanese stock markets, both of which are hugely over-priced, may suddenly collapse . . . an unexpected natural or environmental disaster may have major economic implications . . . if any one of these events happened, the result could be a crash which would be far more serious than the October 1987 hiccup. A future crash could lead to recession, as investors wait to feel if it is safe enough to risk their money again, and as producers cut back on production so as not to lose money through overstocking. If major planetary solutions are not forthcoming, recession could deepen into depression, as lay-offs cut back on people's spending power, causing producers to cut back yet further. In such a situation, people with big credit bills they could not pay would face court orders (how much do you owe on your credit card now?), and people with big mortgages would face foreclosure and eviction (how big is your monthly mortgage payment?). Unemployment would soar, as would homelessness. Families would break up. The emotionally weaker and the lonelier would consider suicide.

It is an appalling outlook: but until there are economic and political policy changes of a very major nature, it remains a risk.

In every crisis there is an opportunity. The very word for 'crisis' in Chinese is *wei-chi*, where *wei* means 'danger' and *chi* means 'opportunity', or 'that from which all change springs'. Is there a 'chi' or opportunity to be found in the immediate experience of such a crash, or in the problems of unemployment and poverty that many communities already know?

Tucked away in a valley on Vancouver Island on Canada's Pacific rim, the small town of Courtenay has been the scene of an experiment which provides this 'chi', and which may benefit the lives of millions all around the world, providing a harbour from the storm. A new kind of local money has been invented which is immune from international recession, debt charges, supply problems, theft, scarcity and currency fluctuations. The world's economy can crash around you, the dollar in your hand can become worthless and unemployment can rise to 100%, but the new money will keep its value and enable you to continue trading with other people in your local community.

The search for an alternative to national currencies as the sole means of exchange has been going on for much of this century. In the Great Depression of the 1930s, communities in Austria, Switzerland and the USA experimented with their own local banknotes as a way to encourage local trade, and the Mormons developed an elaborate moneyless system in the nineteenth century.[1]

When local unemployment rises, for whatever reason, people lose their incomes and have less money in their pockets. They spend less money with local traders, who in turn have less money in their pockets, and then the whole local economy takes a downturn and becomes sluggish. Unemployed people sit at home while shopkeepers watch half-empty shops. The economic creativity which should be the lifespring of an economy begins to dry up.

One response to this wastage is to consider barter: 'If you

51

supply me with a bucketful of leeks from your garden, I'll fix your broken exhaust.' After a few initial attempts, however, you discover that the barters don't often match up, and as a system, it just doesn't work.

A NEW KIND OF MONEY

This was the problem that troubled Michael Linton on Vancouver Island. The recession of the early 1980s had brought an enormous increase in unemployment, and a lot of local people, Michael included, were having problems with their income. Michael tried bartering his own skills in bodywork (being a trained teacher of the Alexander Technique), but found that it was a hopelessly slow method of trading. So he sat down and invented a new kind of money.

The result of his late-night ponderings was the 'Local Employment and Trade System', or 'LETSystem'.[2] The LETSystem puts barter onto a non-profit, multi-centred, community-wide basis. It does this by inventing a new kind of local money called the 'Green Dollar', which facilitates local trade.

Unlike other money, the Green Dollar is invisible. You can't hold it, or stash it in a box under your bed. Nor can you lose it, steal it or accidentally send it to the laundry in the back pocket of your jeans. It only exists as information. The LETSystem has various other special qualities which we will consider later. But first – how does it work?

A number of people who live locally and who want to trade together get together, agree to the LETSystem rules, and give themselves account numbers. Each person then makes out two lists, one of 'wants' and one of 'offers', with prices attached (following normal market prices). A joint list is made up and circulated to everyone. Then the members look down the list, phone whoever has what they want, and start trading. Trading can also happen through newspaper advertisements, or personal contacts. The limits of one-to-one barter are eliminated, as you can now trade with the people in the system as a whole: barter is now a collective proposition.

Green Dollars don't exist as tangible money, and no notes are printed, or coins minted. When people trade, the purchaser calls up the central office and leaves a message on an answering machine saying: 'This is Elspeth Simpson, No 54. Please credit Jock MacIntosh, No 273, with $100 in Green for computer lessons'. At the LETSystem office, someone enters this information into the books, and also into a computer. Jock acquires a $100 credit, and Elspeth a $100 'commitment' or debit, like an overdraft or 'minus account'. Elspeth's debit carries no interest, as the whole system is interest-free, both credits and debits.

And so the trading goes on. Every month, a trades bulletin is sent out to the members. Elspeth didn't have to have $100 Green in her account before she spent it – and Jock, confident that he can earn more Green Dollars from giving computer lessons, can go out and purchase the beat-up old Volkswagen van that he has seen listed for $1000 Green, thus putting himself $900 Green into commitment.

'It's like a freedom – it lets you live like a king, without a penny in your pocket. . .'

'. . . I have a housekeeper, and pay her $6.50 an hour, 50% in Green. I couldn't pay her that much if it was straight cash. And she's really happy, too. . .'

'. . . It sure has given me a whole new perspective on people in terms of trust – like, anyone can be trusted. I suppose I had an idea that this was true, but now I've been able to see it, at first hand. There are a lot of incredible people in the system.'

Gail Pratt, Courtenay member

The LETSystem that Michael invented in Courtenay started trading in 1983. By 1985 it had 500 members who had done over $300,000 worth of trading up to that time, in everything from vegetables and goats milk to dentistry, building work and room rental. By 1987, a dozen LETSystems were operating in Canada, ten more at different points around the world, and new enquiries were coming in almost every day. A Canadian Broadcasting Corporation business programme (ventures) featuring the LETSystem had more enquiries on this than on any other topic in that programme in the whole year, and gave a repeat broadcast. A church organization in Prince Edward Island, on Canada's Atlantic seaboard, hired three people to lay the groundwork for a network of LETSystems throughout the island economy, which has a history of frequent economic depression. The provincial government of Nova Scotia commissioned Michael to make a video about how to start a LETSystem. After three years of being met with a mixture of astonishment and scepticism, interest in the LETSystem in Canada is spreading like a prairie fire – 'an idea whose time has come'.[3] With fears of global recession just around the corner, many Canadian communities are struggling to find ways to regenerate their economies, and the LETSystem seems to provide some useful answers.

'LETS offers Canadians an alternative route. Instead of being stymied by high levels of unemployment, as we have in parts of the country, people have another route to use their talents and potential for economic activity in their everyday lives.'

Abraham Rotstein, Professor of Economics,
Toronto University

'The LETS experiment seems to be overcoming the limits of utopians who have dreamed of decommoditization and the localization of local monies.'

Makoto Marayuma, Keizai Seminar, Nov 86, Tokyo

LETSystems are also operating in the USA, Australia, New Zealand, and in Totnes, South Devon.

Common questions

As soon as people learn about the LETSystem they start asking questions to test it for snags, and to attempt to find its Achilles Heel.

Do you have to pay taxes on Green Dollar earnings?

In Canada, the tax authorities have ruled that Green Dollar earnings in the pursuit of your normal profession are taxable, but that other Green Dollar earnings are not.[4] Thus if you are a carpenter by trade, you will have to pay taxes if you earn $1,000 green for fixing someone's attic; but if your basic trade is anything else, you will not. The tax situation in each country would have to be ascertained.

What about sales tax, or VAT? [5]
If you have to charge 15% VAT on your product, you charge this in ordinary currency on top of your Green Dollar price so that you have the money with which to pay your tax bill.

What happens when I have to buy raw materials in normal currency, and want to sell my product in Green currency?
You can split your charge, e.g. 20% in normal currency and 80% in Green, to cover your costs.

What happens if someone accumulates a large commitment (debit) by spending lots of Green Dollars, and then leaves town, or simply refuses to honour their commitment?
This is a risk, and if it happens, the cost of the default is spread among the whole community, as that much energy is no longer circulating reciprocally. Instead of flowing on, the energy represented by the loss stagnates, and can introduce a sluggishness into the system. There are several possible solutions as follows:

1. Information on a person's accounts can be requested, so if you have doubts about someone's willingness to work off their commitment, you can see a statement of their balance before agreeing to trade. This is the normal LETS arrangement so far.
2. A graph showing all the balances in the system can be circulated each month with the newsletter, allowing people to form their own decisions about how far they should put themselves in credit by earning Green. Other options are

also possible, such as setting general limits, publishing information about extreme accounts, or establishing an elected council to discuss solutions.

'When I was $800 in deficit, I started thinking "I got all this money from the community – how can I pay it back ? Am I good enough for that much ? Could I trust myself to honestly repay it?" I was all alone with my own integrity. Then I discovered that I was good enough, when I repaid it all. The next time, I'll trust myself to go $3000 into debt. I'll start with the understanding "I can trust myself, and my community"'.   Lawrie Milne, Courtenay member

How can unemployed people make use of the scheme, when the law says that people receiving welfare can only earn a very limited amount of money before their earnings are deducted from their welfare?
So far, there are no clear answers to this question. In Canada, Green Dollar earnings are counted in the same way as normal earnings, and deducted from benefit. There is further discussion on this point below.

What about inflation?
The LETSystem is not inflation-proof. Green Dollar prices reflect normal market prices, so if there was annual inflation of 100%, the LETSystem would probably reflect this as people increased their prices to keep up. This penalizes anyone holding on to a large unspent credit, which would depreciate in value by 50% over the year, and provides an incentive to keep the Green Dollars moving.

Why is no interest charged?
The LETSystem is a non-profit community institution, run for the mutual benefit of local people. There is no reason to charge interest as the system is not trying to make a profit for itself. Interest is also used to control and regulate the flow of scarce money. Since new Green Dollars can be created by the simple act of trading, there need never be any

scarcity of them to regulate in the first place. They are as abundant as our own willingness to share our skills.

How is the person who does all the book-keeping paid?
When members join, they pay $15 in normal money to cover start-up costs. A charge of 30 cents Green is also paid on each transaction. Wages are paid in Green Dollars at the local market rate to a LETSystem co-ordinator, out of the system's own account.

Is there any limit to the number of people who can join?
Probably – but it has not been reached yet in any current LETSystem. Ideally, a LETSystem should remain small enough for an individual to understand how it works, and be limited to a geographical area local enough for people to meet each other personally. 5,000 people is probably the natural limit for any one system. If it grew too big, it would lose its human qualities.

Can I sell my services for (say) half Green and half ordinary money?
Yes. The dentist in Courtenay gives many treatments on this basis, and many other people trade in this manner.

What about shops? Can they buy and sell goods in Green Dollars?
Yes – they just need to ensure that they cover their costs in cash. Some shops sell locally produced goods in Green Dollars and imported goods in ordinary dollars, while others offer an overall '10% Green' policy, meaning '90% normal money, 10% Green'. The basic guideline is 'costs in cash, value-added in Green'.

Can other local businesses benefit from Green Dollar trading?
Yes. A business which was seeing its cash-flow stretched to the limit can use the Green Dollar system to increase its liquidity, trading in Green Dollars to members, but ensuring

that any marginal costs, plus money for sales tax and income tax were paid in ordinary money, or by non-members paying in ordinary dollars.

I know a lot of people who haven't got any skills they could sell. Wouldn't they get left out of this just as they get left out of the straight economy?
Everyone possesses skills, but often they get no chance to practise or develop them in the normal economy. When people are not valued, they tend to lose their sense of worth, and assume they have nothing to offer. While the normal economy is increasingly limited to full-time jobs, the LET-System encourages people to think of all sorts of different ways in which they can earn money, ranging from the exotic to the ordinary:
'Kitchen Elf' – overnight kitchen springcleaning, $35
Personal love letters composed, $5 per letter.
Babysitting, $5 per hour
Window-cleaning, $8 per hour
Pair of good muscles, $6 per hour
All your shopping done for you, $5 per hour.

'*People have started to value themselves differently and come alive*'　　　　　　　　(Untraced quote from member)
'*We've encountered some very interesting things about people's self-valuation. People who are used to feeling underpaid, when they get into the Green System, start to feel they are rich.*'　　　　　　　　Courtenay member

Sometimes, people's previous or traditional employment will re-appear because there is Green money available to pay them. In a fully integrated community economy, people's natural skills are encouraged and developed (see Chapter Five), and the idea that people have no skills is given the bash on the head it deserves.

Surely, if a local economy only used Green Dollars, people wouldn't be able to buy things like new cars or video cameras?

The LETSystem is not meant to replace ordinary money – it is meant to be used alongside it. There will always be ordinary money as well. If the circulation of ordinary money in the economy dries up, however, because of unemployment or recession, the LETSystem will keep on flowing. That's why it is so valuable. Green money will be preferred for local trading, and ordinary money saved for the import/export part of the community economy.

Can I be a member of more than one LETSystem, and trade the Green Dollars I earn in System A in System B, twenty miles down the road?
At the moment – no. If it was to happen, it would need careful thought, and agreements to ensure that each LETSystems maintained 100% of its own purchasing power, and kept its self-reliance.

Is the LETSystem computer safe from electronic intrusion?
LETS transactions are recorded on paper first and then transferred onto disc, providing a check against discrepancies. The overall LETSystem account is cross-checked each month to ensure that debits = credits, totalling zero. A hacker who claimed an extra $1000 Green would have to deduct it from someone else's account, and the origin of the theft would show up on the monthly statements.

What kind of opposition has the LETSystem received?
Plenty. In the early days, before it started getting national publicity, left-wingers thought it was right-wing stuff and right-wingers thought it was a communist take-over. Local businessmen thought it must be some kind of scam (contrick) – it really worried them that they couldn't see any way to lose. They see life like a poker game, and can't accept a win-win situation. Where the men were suspicious, the women were generally much more pragmatic – they said 'Let's see if it works, and then get on with it'.

There were other reactions, too:

You're getting <u>angora-wool sweaters</u> with Green Dollars?

How can the LETSystem work in cities? How does a 'community' define its boundaries?
In a big urban sprawl, boundaries are best set by where people feel their natural community lies. Where there are subjective overlaps, people can be members of two or more systems. Alternatively, the 'community' can be defined as being those who choose to join in, wherever they live.

Can I give my Green Dollars away, as I can ordinary money?
Yes. In Courtenay, people have made $100 gifts in Green to the Women's Centre, and to the Food Bank. When you give in Green Dollars, you give in kind, not in cash. For the community as a whole, your gift is 'tied aid', since the energy you give will inevitably return to the community, generating more energy.

Seven qualities of the LETSystem

There have been a number of attempts to create working community currencies – the idea is not new. The Government of the island of Guernsey still issues its own interest-free bank-notes, which are used initially for public works, and in 1932–33, the town of Wurgl, in Austria, created its own interest-free local currency which was distributed in return for local public works. The money circulated rapidly, causing unemployment to fall and local shops to flourish. Its success was so great, in fact, that many other Austrian towns were about to do the same when the Austrian National Bank took fright, took legal action against it, and arranged for its closure. Local 'scrip' currencies were also created in Chicago and Basle, Switzerland, in the 1930s.

The Green Dollar system has seven essential qualities.

The first is its *inherent simplicity*, and ease of operation. It represents the first complete break with the old idea of tangible 'money'. It is effectively self-regulating, because of built-in constraining factors to do with local relationships, trust, and people's desire to have friends. It is compatible with the existing system of money, and above all, it works.

The LETSystem's second quality is that *it enables money to remain exactly what it is – information*. Money is simply pieces of paper which inform you about the values they represent. Once it becomes 'solid' it takes on a life of its own, and all sorts of strange things happen as people begin to deal in money for its own sake. Because Green Dollars have no tangible existence, they cannot be forged, devalued, hoarded, stolen or lost. No one can get a corner on the money supply, bringing trade to a halt and then leasing it out at a high interest, which is how some banks have behaved in the past. Nor can anyone control its flow, and then make a loan dependent on your having material collateral of some kind as security. No one owns the money in the first place, so no one can lend it to you.

Its third quality is its *total decentralization*. New Green money is created in a natural, organic way – by someone creating something of real value, and trading it with someone else. There are no board meetings when the governors sit down and discuss how much money they should create. Its creation is related directly to its source, which is our own creativity as people.

Its fourth quality is that *every transaction is a personal one*, which brings you new friends and relationships. A LETSystem enables a community to discover itself, perhaps for the first time:

'Just about every time I trade through the LETSystem I get to meet someone personally. I've got to know an extra 100–150 people in this way. To me, that wealth of relationships in the community is synonymous with economic wellbeing.'
Lawrie Milne, Courtenay system

'LETS acts as a catalyst by reconnecting individuals with their fellow community members.'
Geoff Slater, Cowichan system

From these new relationships come many important invisible wealths – friendships, childcare arrangements, parties, greater recognition on the local streets, increased security, and a general broadening of the sense of community.

Fifthly, *it encourages initiative and creative energy, and builds self-esteem and self-reliance,* both in individuals and in families. It removes the straitjacket of the full-time job which binds people's self-esteem to the job they have and causes many unemployed people to feel worthless. The monthly listing of wants and offers says to a discouraged worker 'Look at all these different ways in which people are earning Green Dollars. Maybe I am good for some of that, too.' It re-awakens the natural creativity of initiative which we all possess, but which many people lose touch with when they receive a regular salary or welfare-cheque. It begins to address some of the unmet needs that so many people have.

I'm willing to do what I really love doing, and get paid for it. You get the opportunity to put yourself right out there, to put yourself on the line.'
Gail Pratt

'You feel a lot better about yourself when your community asks for things that you like to do.'
Geoff Slater

Its sixth quality is that *the Green Dollar is limited to local circulation within the local economy*, and cannot leave the local economy to buy carpets from Samarkand or Toyotas from Korea, taking the wealth and the purchasing power that it represents with it. Because it *must* circulate locally, every trading transaction necessarily stimulates another, and in this way, the talent and creativity of local people is drawn out.

'The beautiful part of LETS is that Green Dollars are personal dollars. They just keep recirculating within the community.'
Bill Campbell, Charlottetown, Prince Edward Island

'It really gives you a sense of community spirit, because every time you buy something you're not only getting some-

thing you like, but you're improving someone else's cash situation.'

Joy Dryburgh, unemployed mother, Courtenay system.

In the ordinary economy, there is no commitment to the local community built into the patterns of trading. In return, it offers the freedom of the global market, which is also important. The LETSystem does not deny the value of the global economy or of free global trading – it is a complementary, not an alternative system. It simply says that if a local economy becomes too dependent on such trading, it becomes very vulnerable to the vagaries of international trade winds, and that too much global trading undermines community stability and sustainability. Many local economies risk becoming forgotten backwaters far away from the ocean of the global economy, with local people dependent on welfare, if they play all their cards in the global game. In addition to the global marketplace, communities must therefore also set up more limited local marketplaces, through which essential community needs can be met and local self-reliance strengthened.

In fostering community self-reliance, the LETSystem also helps to ground a local economy in its own resources, encouraging local production for local need, and strengthening the resource base and the ecological stability of the area.

Finally, the LETSystem *restores the quality of the gift economy to the modern trading economy.* People in Courtenay who trade in Green Dollars say that they experience an uncommon 'lightness of being' in their trading relationships. Normal trading relationships are often impersonal, reflecting the lack of personal contact between the people concerned. People who use the LETSystem have been surprised at how good it feels to trade in it. The system encourages trust and friendship, not suspicion, and this quality seems to permeate the transactions that occur within it. If you repair Phil's roof, you give him your energy and your craftsmanship, as well as a new roof; if you do the work with love, you are giving him an even bigger gift.

This is not to say that this cannot also happen in the ordinary economy – but when it does, it is the exception, not the rule. In the LETSystem, it seems to become the rule.

In the game of 'Monopoly' there are winners and losers. Our uses of money and our trading patterns follow similar rules. There have been winners, and losers. Millions of people have starved, been robbed, tricked and defeated. People who play Monopoly with world commodity prices still help to inflict pain and suffering on the Zambias and Bolivias of the world.

We have never yet lived or traded as a whole planet – only as parts trying to dominate other parts. The financial plight of the world is reflected back to us in the chaos which this behaviour creates, in a world that has become an interdependent, increasingly integrated whole. We are economically tied together, and we thrive or we collapse together, all losers, or all winners.

The LETSystem is the world's first money-system which is inherently social. It puts the mutuality of 'we' back into our trading. Money which is convivial encourages convivial behaviour. Money which is selfish encourages selfish behaviour. While ordinary money is inherently privatized, and individualistic, Green Dollars are a community money, carrying an inherently social message.

When information about mutual trading commitments was first converted into solid coinage, the 'we' quality that was inherent in the shared information was lost. It became individualistic, and started following 'I' goals. It fostered the competitive game between people and nations in which there are winners and losers, encouraging its holders to follow the rules of personal gain, instead of the rules which hold a people together, such as caring for nature, for your local community, and for each other.

For centuries, local economies remained expressions of their own communities, being protected by sheer distance, and the difficulties of transport. The industrial world has destroyed this skin. Local economies are now invaded by imported goods which sell more cheaply than home-produced goods, a process which will only grow as the cost of communication and transport falls, and as capital becomes a fully globalized commodity. The pay-cheques of Londoners and New Yorkers will soon be processed by low-paid clerks with computers in Calcutta, simply because it will be cheaper. As long as money continues to chase the cheapest bargain, local economies will become increasingly submerged in the sea of global trade, and subject to its storms and vagaries.

Global trade is essential to the wellbeing of humankind, and must be enabled to continue. However, so is community stability. The LETSystem does not attempt to replace global trade: it simply enables a community to maintain its own stability and offers a fully rewarding life to its people, while being part of the growing unity of the world as a whole. Global unity is much needed on our Earth; but the stronger the whole, the stronger must be the parts. This is where the LETSystem, and the many other tools of community economic development outlined in this book, are so important.

Wider applications of the LETSystem

At present, the LETSystems being established are still relatively small, and bear little connection to the wider systems of economy and society. It is interesting to consider what the future may hold.

A LETSystem that spanned a wide range of local economic life might enable people to sign off welfare altogether, earning their living through the LETSystem until they find themselves a stable source of income. A well thought-out integrated approach combining various other elements would be needed to make this possible.

If local government joined the local LETSystem, the monthly trade bulletin might read like this:

Local taxes: payable up to 100% Green;
Street-cleaning: $8 per hour, 100% or 50% Green;

Vacancy, librarian: $22,000 p.a., 20% Green optional;
City Hall Magistrates Court: fines payable in Green;
Parking tickets: payable in Green;
Community daycare/creche: $10 Green per day.

If a local food and energy self-reliance programme were set up, the bulletin might read:
Solar-cells fitted: $1,000, 50% Green;
Retrofit/home insulation: personal estimates, 70% Green;
Guaranteed organic toxic-free manure: $20 Green a bag.
Community food co-operative: home-grown food, 100% Green.

If a community bank or credit union dealing in ordinary money joined the system, you might see:
Loans for local business projects: 5% interest, 50% payable in Green.
Special offer! Take out a no-interest Green loan for your Christmas shopping! Repay by next November.
Need cash for Green? We give a 90% rate of exchange.

By the time the community economy got rolling, with community-owned businesses taking steps to meet local needs, it might read:
Flats, homes, old-folks cluster dwellings for rent, payment in Green negotiable;
Invest in your community bus company: $100 Green per share;
Green Pension fund: monthly savings schemes discussed.

Getting started

There are seven stages involved in starting a LETSystem:

1. A LETSystem can start with as few as 20 people. You can either base it initially among a group of friends, or around a neighbourhood, community or church organisation.

2. Write off for the LETS manual and programs. These are

available on IBM compatible diskettes, from which you can print your own 250-page manual, which the key people in your group should read and digest.

3. Get used to it by playing LETSplay, a simulated version of the system, the rules for which are in the manual.

4. It is recommended that you use an answering machine, and that you get access to a computer to make the record keeping simple. You can also keep the books manually without any difficulty.

5. Getting the LETSystem started requires a willingness to explain how it works many times to interested people. At this stage you should either decide to secure personal commitments from five to six key people who will agree to work at getting it going for at least six months, or seek a grant to fund an enthusiastic part-time worker for six months to get it going. It will not happen on its own without effort – people's astonishment at the newness of the idea is too great.

The use of the Green Dollar system involves a process of personal growth and adjustment. It takes people time to get used to handling a new consciousness about money, about what they can offer, and what their local community can offer. We are conditioned to use money in a very immediate way to satisfy our wants. The LETSystem encourages people to think less about what they want, and more about what is available locally. This doesn't happen overnight.

6. Groups starting a LETSystem are asked to pay a one-off licence fee of $100 Canadian (approx £45) to Landsman Community Services Ltd to cover the costs of pioneering and developing the system. You will also have start-up costs for printing the newsletter, office supplies, etc. which you may be able to pay for in Green if you find a sympathetic supplier. A group of 40 can cover start-up costs of $600 by paying $15 each for lifetime membership.

7. Once you've done your initial planning, you should be able to start trading within two to three weeks. Don't try to start with a lot of publicity: take it slowly so that you can iron out your operating snags while the system is still small. Publicity will look after itself in due course.[6]

The welfare problem and the LETSystem

A group setting up a LETSystem will sooner or later have to confront the welfare earnings rules.

In Britain, the welfare rules state that unemployed people receiving Income Support earning more than £5 a week will have their welfare reduced on a £ for £ basis.[7] In other countries, similar rules may apply, except that in the Whangarei region of New Zealand's North Island, the Director of the Department of Social Welfare has decided that Green Dollar earnings will not be considered part of a beneficiary's total income. As Whangarei has the highest unemployment rate in all New Zealand, he recognises that solutions will only be found by supporting local initiatives, rather than by relying on central government.

If your welfare authority has not passed a ruling on Green Dollar (pound/mark/yen) earnings, you could act ignorant, and wait to see what happens. If welfare is reduced to take account of Green Dollar earnings, you could lodge an appeal and then fight the case to the highest level, making the most of the opportunity for publicity and public support, and running a campaign applying political pressure for a favourable ruling. This strategy is not recommended until your LETSystem is working well, as a negative ruling would be a big setback.

A second approach is to form an alliance with a university department, and try to get a LETSystem accepted as an action research project to examine the effect of the LETSystem on local economic regeneration. Discussions could then be held with the Department of Health and Social Security, with the intention of getting the earnings rules waived for the groups participating in the research. All being well, the results of the research would show the value of the system, and clear the way for policy reform.

Encouraging the growth of LETSystems

Local LETSystems can either be left to seed themselves in a random way, or they can be deliberately fostered.

The logical step forward would be to establish a LETSystem Development Agency (LDA) serving a region whose staff would help local groups set up LETSystems. The running costs for such an agency might be met through local and/or national government funding, such as the Inner City Partnership (UK). Alternatively, grants and sponsorships might be sought. A network of LDAs could work together to encourage further developments.

The LETSystem seems to be an idea whose time has come. Global crash or no global crash, local communities have much to gain from establishing their own systems. It offers a return to the values of community in which we care for each other and support each other. It enables local people to develop their skills, make new social contacts and get on with their lives without necessarily having to depend on a 'proper job'. It provides a boost to the vitality of local economies hard hit by unemployment or recession. And it provides a secure basis for local economic self-reliance and sustainability. In the event of a crash, a thriving local LETSystem would enable a community to keep trading through the storm. The LETSystem is an important component of the economics of love, which can be the only kind of economics suitable for a fragile and much loved-planet.

Chapter Five :
Our emerging potential

It is impossible to separate the need to create new approaches to economy, nature and society from the need to evolve new methods of teaching and learning. The 'rainbow economy' is a learning process, a growth of consciousness as it rises towards more planetary, holistic and unitary levels.

The story of our evolution, and our emerging potential, is quite remarkable. Fifteen thousand million years ago, the universe as we know it began, scattering its many galaxies, stars and planets throughout space.[1] On Earth, life evolved, blossoming into 500 million different species, one of which evolved into us. We were once cosmic light, and then primary elements of matter scattered through space; we were once algae, colonizing the Earth, and once tiny mammals scuttling under the dinosaurs' feet. We once lived in the trees. From this process, we have emerged.

With human life, evolution began to speed up. We left the trees, and began to walk on two feet. We created amazing civilizations, rich with philosophy, culture and art. Just yesterday, in evolutionary time, we discovered the processes of science and began to take astonishing technological leaps. Within the last 50 years, the number of people needed to grow food has fallen to 4% – 8% of the working population, and with automation, the number needed to produce manufactured goods is set to fall to 6% – 10% in the next 30 years. Meanwhile, we are still searching, questioning and exploring. Like a curve that rises gradually from the horizontal to the vertical, the processes of human change are accelerating, moving from higher gear to higher gear. Wherever we are going, we are going there with increasing speed.

As we evolved, each new step – eyes, legs, wings, self-regulating body-temperature, brains – gave us ever greater autonomy and control over our environment. The impulse continued in the human stage with tools, language, art and science. The desire to achieve freedom over the environment appears to be a fundamental attribute of consciousness.

The same impulse underlies our social, political and economic evolution. The political revolutions and awakenings of past 500 years have been the expression of a constant search for more freedom and self-control. There are occasions when a section of the population has yelled 'too fast!', and thrown away its freedom, clinging to an all-powerful leader, but the underlying thrust has always been towards greater freedom, autonomy and self-expression. The whole evolutionary process is a process of steady empowerment.

Consciousness also appears to seek its dreams. What we dream of, we seek to create, whether it is political freedom, ships that can fly us to the moon or schools which can explore our children's potential. All miracles or technology and engineering begin as dreams and ideas. The fundamental unity which underlies consciousness expresses itself through dreams which make us aspire to realise this unity. Ever since its creation, consciousness has seemingly worked to achieve greater freedom, greater self-expression and greater unity. Behind our efforts and endeavours to create a better world lies a dream as old as the universe itself. You will very rarely, if ever, find a human who consciously longs to be unhappy or in pain. At a very deep level, we share in a harmony of hope, whatever our country or creed.

In the industrial age, our fundamental goals were to achieve mastery over the world of matter, bringing an end to poverty, hunger and disease, and to achieve the social, political and economic changes needed to permit the spread of heads of corporations on television, and assume that is where the power must be. Of course, they do have power – but nowhere near as much power as we potentially have within our own hearts and minds, where the real power lies. It only seems as if someone else has the power as long as we fail to claim our own.

To claim this power and build the kind of world we dream of, we need to get together and form local ecological partnerships, drawing together people from all sectors of local life who share the vision, and who have the skills and commitment to work towards the goals of ecological sustainability.

The partnerships will need to establish special action committees to cover each of the areas where sustainability is needed, including planetary issues such as the development of alternatives to pesticides that are sold for export. In developing a strategy, eight main approaches can be used as follows:

1. *Education*, providing individuals, companies, schools and organizations with the information they need to change to ecologically sustainable ways.
2. *Consumer campaigns*, assisting people to become 'conscious consumers', avoiding CFC (chloroflourocarbons)-containing canisters and food-cartons, purchasing organic foods, biodegradable washing liquids, etc.
3. *Research* into technologies and social-economic arrangements which facilitate sustainability.
4. *Campaigns*, using whatever means are appropriate, including boycotts when other means bring no results.
5. *Transformation*, encouraging companies and organizations to develop policies of ecological excellence (see Chapter Eight).
6. *Creating new institutions and initiatives* to develop community participation in ecologically sustainable practices.
7. *Legislation*, creating new local by-laws and regulations,

alienation and wastage.

Consciousness is evolving all the time, pressing on towards wholeness. We cannot deny the planetary reality in which we live and the unitary pressure it is exerting on us. It challenges all our existing institutions which still operate in a pre-planetary mode. To reflect this new reality, we need to plan an integrated evolution of our social, economic and political systems towards a higher level of co-operation and order, which will serve a higher level of fulfilment, empowerment and well-being, both personally and socially. Education needs to become an integral part of all life, serving our need to evolve.

A HIDDEN REVOLUTION

We possess at least seven major dimensions of being, each of which seeks fulfilment:

1. *Physical fulfilment:* establishing a solid basis of physical well-being and health.
2. *Working fulfilment:* enabling us to serve society and the world and to express ourselves through work that is both skilful and rewarding.
3. *Emotional fulfilment:* encouraging the growth of healthy emotional expression and healthy relationships, which generate love, acceptance and belonging.
4. *Creative fulfilment:* encouraging the full expression of the imaginative, intuitive and expressive self.
5. *Mental fulfilment:* developing the mind, and giving it the stimulation, challenges and satisfactions it needs.
6. *Self-empowerment:* encouraging the power within us to create our own realities, both personally and collectively.
7. *Spiritual fulfilment:* encouraging our inner journeys, as we build a relationship with the larger realm of spirit, integrate the different parts of our being and moving towards inner wholeness.

Three key processes assist the emergence of this potential:

- participation/facilitation,
- empowerment, and
- encouragement/support.

The more we participate in the way our businesses, schools, colleges, community groups and local government organizations are run, the more we contribute, giving what we can of ourselves to make them work better. In public opinion polls in the USA, 80% say that they would do a better job if they were more involved in decisions relating to their work.[2] Educationally, participation provides the key to the future. During the industrial age, education has been a distinctly one-way process in which students were discouraged from thinking for themselves. Creativity was banned from the classroom. Many of Britain's teenage schools have more in common with the army than they do with natural human learning processes, in spite of dedicated and hard-working teachers.

Over the last 100 years, children have put up with a system of learning that offends all their natural instincts. Their objections have been met with physical punishment, emotional punishment such as ridicule, and bribery. They were promised that if they sat down and shut up they would get good exam results, and therefore good jobs. When the jobs began to disappear, however, the bribe became worthless, and they began to vote with their feet. Many young people feel immense frustration at being forced to put up with years of mental and spiritual abuse in the name of education.

In Britain, Canada and the USA, rising levels of illiteracy and innumeracy are major factors underlying unemployment. Traditional teaching methods no longer motivate children to learn as they did, and since most teachers no longer wish to force children to learn by physical force, as their Victorian predecessors did, many children often slip through the net, wasting their childhood learning years and starting adult life with an immense handicap. In 1981, 49% of all boys and 44% of all girls in Britain left high school branded as 'failures' without an exam success to their name, because the secondary schooling system has been set up as a 'quality control' process similar to a factory, designed to pick out the best and discard the rest. Convinced that they are 'dim', 40% of all adults over 16 in Britain undertake no further education or training in their lives.[3]

The answer is not increased emphasis on discipline and traditional methods, but a whole-hearted commitment to participative teaching methods, with investments being made in the retraining of teachers. Natural learning happens by a process of trial, error and personal discovery, not by assimilating information from books. Farmers, mothers, small children, hunters, business leaders, engineers, artists and software designers all learn in this way. The books and courses should be seen as an *aid* to learning.

In the midst of a crisis in teacher morale, however, a hidden revolution is occurring at the heart of Britain's educational system. Under such labels as 'education for enterprise' and 'action learning', more co-operative and participative approaches to education are being developed. Young people are choosing and setting up their own projects, planning them and carrying them through on their own. If the project is a business, they raise the necessary capital and repay their shareholders with a dividend if they do well. Youngsters who have been bored and restless suddenly start working through the lunch-hour, because the project is their own, and no one defines in advance what is 'right' or 'wrong'. The process of education suddenly empowers, rather than disempowers them. Following its success, the participative approach is spreading to youth training initiatives.[4]

The same change is occurring in adult education, as tutors learn how to use group skills and facilitative leadership methods. Tutors are becoming the facilitators of people's own learning experiences. In Scotland, where the community education tradition has been pioneering new approaches for many years, instead of sitting in rows and listening, with increasing frequency, students sit in circles and share.[5] Others use outdoor education and wilderness pursuits to encourage people to go beyond their limits, and open up to new possibilities.

At the Taranaki Work Trust, in New Zealand, a community-based approach to local economic healing and renewal, a training programme has been established for unemployed adults called DYO – Design-Your-Own Training Programme. DYO's staff help you develop a clear idea of what you want to do, find someone in the community who will teach you the skills you need, and fix up a training/learning relationship.[6]

As more adults gradually return to learning, education and training are becoming an everyday part of life, not something that stops the day you leave school. In Britain, in response to concern about local economic decline, locally-based community training initiatives are springing up. Partnerships such as the Coventry Consortium are being formed by people who are concerned with adult education and training, to identify local needs, explore possible responses and design flexible training programmes.[7] In Halifax, Yorkshire, for instance, where the old carpet mill at Dean Clough has been turned into a thriving enterprise centre (see Chapter Seven), a training and innovation centre has been introduced which provides tailor-made courses for companies and their staff, using open-learning methods. The centre's staff help the users organize their own self-tuition, locating the resources they need to design their own trainings, and supporting them while they are learning. New developments in extension learning, aided by television, and in self-help learning approaches are in increasing demand.

This impulse towards a participative, facilitative approach to learning is reaching unemployed people, too. In Irvine, on Scotland's west coast, the community education team of ten staff has to meet the needs of 10,000 unemployed people. Rather than provide traditional classes, they set up a Voluntary Action Training Course for groups of unemployed people with potential leadership abilities. They took them to visit co-operatives, community businesses and self-help initiatives to set their imaginations working, and then schooled them in skills such as public speaking, running a committee, raising funds and making local government work for them. They ended with a residential weekend in which each person was invited to plan a community project they would like to run, with the education workers taking the back seat, providing assistance and support. One person took groups of unemployed youngsters on hiking expeditions into the Highlands. Others formed outdoor education groups, set up a community newspaper and launched a campaign to encourage adults to learn in local schools.[8]

Participation can present both a threat and a challenge to people who are used to hierarchic, top-down ways of making decisions, whether in youth clubs, schools or local government. Putting time and money aside for training is important in helping people adjust, and to ensure that new developments are seen as an opportunity, not a threat.

LIFE-PLANNING

Participation is a fundamental principle of natural learning. If you don't know where you are going, however, or what you want from life, it is very hard to get there. The process of self-empowerment, or taking charge of your own life, is a second fundamental principle.

During the industrial age, the physical work of production in factories and offices meant that most people were denied fulfilment and the ability to express who they really were, learning to put up with work that did not satisfy them and brought no fulfilment. In the late twentieth century, in public opinion polls in the USA, only 24% of the people interviewed said they were performing their jobs to their full capacity.[9]

One reason why people stay in unfulfilling jobs or remain unemployed is that they do not know what else to do with their lives. They know they are missing out, but they do not know what to do about it.

In my work as a holistic careers adviser, one of my starting points is people's natural enthusiasms, skills and achievements. Our natural skills are those which cause us to blossom when we use them, and make us feel good inside. Our natural enthusiasms are those which give us energy and inspire us. The word 'enthusiasm' comes from the Greek 'entheos' – 'the god within'. Everyone has such skills and enthusiasms, and when made the foundation of our lives, they can bring us the fulfilment and happiness we seek.

There is a simple exercise called the 'achievements exercise' which can help you locate your natural skills. Think back through your life, and make a list of 20 things you have done which left you with a special feeling of inner satisfaction, and a sense of quiet pride. They can be anything, from the time you laid out a new garden to the time you cared for your gran while she was dying. If they left you feeling rich and good inside, you were almost certainly using your natural skills. Choose your 'top ten', and write a paragraph on each. By examining your achievements, and using a skills list, you can discover your natural skills.[10] As a second exercise, think back again through your life and make a further list of 20 things you have done which generated your enthusiasm, causing you to fill up with positive energy. Take your 'top ten' and write a paragraph on each of these too, spelling out just why you felt that enthusiasm. Within your enthusiasms, you will find your heart.

Once you know where your skills and enthusiasms lie, your next task is explore your practical options, and establish goals. This takes you into the realm of life-planning, which is an essential part of the self-empowerment process. Life-planning helps you to ask very simple, but all-important questions: What do you want? How can you get there? Which path do you prefer? What are the obstacles? Where can you get help and support? What is your first practical step? There is nothing very difficult about these questions, but in practice they challenge many of our inner weaknesses and fears. At its simplest, life-planning says, 'If you want it, go out and get it. Create your own reality. Be who you really are.'[11]

The full success of a rainbow economy development strategy needs the release of all that natural skill and enthusiasm within us. We can never change the world as long as our own lives are still dull and imprisoned. In everyone, there are sleeping hopes, dreams and ambitions waiting to be awakened and re-inspired. What is life when we put 'shoulds' and 'oughts' and 'don't knows' above what we really want? Where is the joy? When we discover the avenues that bring us fulfilment, life becomes a celebration, a bright expression of the joy of living.

The work of releasing dreams is proceeding all over the country, in a scattered way. There are many schools, colleges and centres where the staff are dedicated to serving the release of enthusiasm and the love of life, especially in the young. The realization of the rainbow economy requires that it is done in a far more organized, co-ordinated way. In London, a self-help organization run by unemployed adults called the Job-Change Project runs weekly career-planning and goal-setting groups for its members.[12] We need to see such groups in every community centre, business and college. Making the break from living on autopilot to consciously choosing your own path in life is an essential breakthrough process: ever since time began, consciousness has sought to shape the world around it, chasing its dreams, and seeking its fullest expression in the physical world.

In Sri Lanka, members of the Sarvodaya village development movement, a grass-roots movement led by Buddhist monks, have set up a 'Primary Talents Identification and Development Centre' to help unemployed and dissatisfied young people locate their natural talents. They give them careers guidance, and where appropriate, channel their talents into micro-enterprise development, providing trainings and support.[13]

The release and expression of our natural talents is important for a thousand reasons, not least of which is that within our skills and enthusiasms lie the seeds of new businesses which are vital to the development of a community's economy. When everyone in an economy can truly say

'I love the work I am doing', the full rainbow economy will be finally within reach.

ENCOURAGEMENT AND LOVE

To draw out people's full potential, we also need encouragement to help us take risks, overcome obstacles and pursue our hopes and dreams. Encouragement is a practical form of love. It gives us heart, makes us know we are not alone, and helps us through the bad times. No one ever said the journeys we make through life are easy, but with encouragement, we can survive – and thrive.

The most natural source of encouragement is a happy, fulfilled community in which people know and care about each other. We need situations in which we no longer fear, where we no longer hide our love. Streets where cars have been banned, neighbourhood meetings which bring us together, festivals, pleasant parks and cafés where we can sit and talk – all these things help us build friendships, share our lives, and grow to love each other, learning to let go of our fear.

Encouragement can also be provided in a deliberate, organised way. In Britain, 'London Work-Out' trains adult volunteers in the relevant skills, pairs them up on a one-to-one basis with unemployed youngsters, for whom they provide friendship, support and encouragement to get on with jobhunting, taking up training, joining classes and developing personal interests. Where appropriate, they give help with family, housing and personal issues, acting as friends in a city where unemployment can easily lead to isolation, loneliness and despair.[14]

The chief obstacles which stand in the way of effective life-planning are the negative beliefs and messages which we carry within us. They come from culture, parents, childhood pains and teenage traumas, and make us believe such things as 'I'm not doing well enough', 'I can never really succeed' 'I'm not good enough' 'I'm not worthy', or 'I will never really be loved.' If only we knew what nonsense these beliefs are, that in reality, everything is possible, and miracles can happen every day.

Support groups and self-help groups play a valuable role in providing the encouragement and emotional support we need to see us through the tough times, and in giving us a chance to explore specific issues and talk about our lives. Where people have known trauma or pain, whether emotional, physical, intellectual or spiritual, support groups offer a chance to share the burdens and heal the hidden wounds. The healing of wounds is an essential process for anyone who wishes to know growth and fulfilment, so the value of these groups, and of other healing processes, can never be underestimated. In learning to express our feelings, open ourselves to healing and release our griefs, hurts and angers, we not only clear a path for our own future happiness, but we also rid ourselves of emotional wounds and darknesses which are otherwise passed on to our children. In healing ourselves, we help to heal the future. The more we encourage, love and support each other, the more we grow. In practical terms, there is much that can be done to encourage the development of such groups.

OPENING THE DOOR

When facilitation, empowerment, life-planning and encouragement are put together, the outlines of a new type of integrated service begin to appear, combining personal counselling, self-help groups, life-planning groups, training and career help and other empowerment processes.

In New York City, the youth project called 'The Door' was founded in 1972 to meet the needs of inner-city teenagers. Existing agencies were fragmented and inaccessible, and the team who started it wanted to put an integrative, holistic philosophy into action.

When young people visit The Door, they are assigned to a primary counsellor who keeps in personal touch with them, and encourages them to explore any program which might help them solve their problems or enrich their experience. The centre offers a comprehensive health program, family planning and sex counselling, a prenatal and childcare program, nutrition counselling, a cafeteria (run by the young people themselves), social services, crisis intervention, runaway counselling, mental health counselling, a therapy program, remedial education programs, career counselling, vocational training, job placements, legal help, as well as arts, crafts, music, theatre, dance, martial arts and recreation programs and facilities. The Creative and Physical Arts Program employs practising professionals whose sessions are always overbooked. Members have the opportunity to develop their talents up to professional levels, and to pursue realistic career goals.

The centre's staff meet together for nightly team meetings to share their perspectives on individual young people, and to pursue their belief in an integrated approach. They encourage the growth of the whole person, going beyond the immediate problems to address the deeper issues of personal growth and emerging wholeness.

Many of the 100,000 teenagers who have approached The Door since 1972 have emotional, family, medical, job- or school-related problems. Some are drug and alcohol abusers. Others face crises such as unwanted pregnancy, trouble with the law, or running away from home. The Door's successful emphasis on a holistic person-centred approach has made it one of the most admired youth service agencies in the USA, which is now being replicated elsewhere in the USA and overseas.[15]

To establish such a centre, staff from a variety of departments would need to meet and explore common interests in working in an integrated and holistic way. This would include careers workers, community education staff, youth workers, community health workers, social workers, counsellors and therapists, group leaders, employment advisers, business start-up counsellors and sports, arts and crafts and specialist skills tutors, among others. It may seem like a dream, but there are many who would love the chance to work as a team, offering encouragement, empowerment support in a holistic environment.

WORKSHARING

The vision which this chapter presents is one in which people are busy discovering their own potential, and seeking to express it through meaningful and satisfying work. A further ingredient is needed, to allow the combination of freedom and fulfilment that so many seek.

This involves *worksharing* – not just jobsharing, in which two people share one job, but a whole range of options and choices, giving us the freedom to work in the way we want. Up to 40% of workers, according to some surveys, want to reduce their worktime, with proportional reductions in pay. In a Canadian survey, 31% of all working people and 64% of women professionals stated a preference for worksharing if it were available, permitting a reduction of unemployment from 11% to 6% (1986 figures). A US Department of Labor survey found that 60% of those interviewed favoured worksharing, corresponding to a 4.7% reduction in total worktime. In Britain, a 4.7% reduction in worktime could produce a 2% increase in the number of people in jobs, translating into 420,000 new full-time jobs.[16] Worksharing strategies are clearly important as partial solutions for unemployment, as well as for our personal freedom.

The 40-hour week, 48-week year, 48-year working life is an industrial age straitjacket which traps people into hours they dislike, decreasing productivity and increasing absenteeism and sick leave. When unemployment is so high, it is absurd that people should have to work more than they want to. This is no way to fulfil potential.

The term 'worksharing' includes six recognized workoptions:

1. *Deferred salary leave plans.* In Winnipeg, Canada, the teachers' union has negotiated a deal which allows teachers to take a year off without pay. This is done in an organized way which allows the employers to know that since 20

teachers will be taking time off in any one year, they can afford to employ 20 more full-time staff. A special tax-free salary savings scheme is part of the deal, which permits teachers to save for their year off.

2. *Jobsharing.* There are several thousand jobsharers in Britain. Barclays Bank alone has 2,000. The potential for development is held back, however, by the lack of organized jobsharing registers and agencies.

3. *V-time.* Currently available in 14 state agencies in California, V-time is a time/income trade-off which allows employees to take a negotiated number of days off in the form of shorter working days, shorter weeks or longer holidays.

4. *Compressed and modified workweeks.* Work is compressed into four 10-hour or 3 12-hour days, often alternating with a normal work-week, permitting four or five day weekends.

5. *Flexitime.* A system allowing employees to choose their starting and ending times. This has been shown to reduce absenteeism by 40% and overtime by 50%, as well as reducing staff turnover and raising morale.

6. *Banked overtime.* This system gives employees the option of taking time off at a later date instead of being paid for overtime hours. Full-time relief staff are hired to cover for banked overtime absences.[17]

The ideas are great – so why don't they happen? Simply because nobody has yet organized to make them happen. Worksharing schemes are complex affairs which require careful negotiation between employers, staff and unions. In North America, there is a 'Network for Work Time Options' with 18 member organizations, such as San Francisco's 'New Ways to Work' and Boston's 'Work Options Unlimited'. On Vancouver Island, British Columbia, the Victoria branch of the Canadian Mental Health Association launched a Work Option Resource Centre after realizing that half their clients came in with stress caused by overwork, and the other half with stress caused by unemployment.

A *Community Worksharing Agency*, financed either from the local economic development budget or from the Inner City Partnership Funds for the contribution it can make to creating new jobs, could:

- brief employers, employees and unions about new work options;
- track and promote current examples;
- carry out surveys locally to establish the extent to which people want more flexible working arrangements in the area;
- run educational programmes for the general public;
- establish procedures for negotiations between employers and unions or staff organizations;
- help individuals negotiate new work schedules; and
- set up jobsharing registers.[18]

Once a community has its Community Worksharing Agency, people will wonder how they survived without one for so long.

OUR EMERGING WHOLENESS

Local life is a single unity, where everything interconnects. The style of local architecture, the layout of the streets and gardens, the presence of nature in the local environment, the provision of space where young and old can pursue their interests, the supports that are available to families, the ways we conduct our schooling, our ability through decentralization to enjoy local self-government, the presence of businesses which emphasize shared ownership, participation and teamwork, the existence of welfare systems which encourages self-reliance instead of defeating it – all these things impact on each other, either positively or negatively. If any one area of local life encourages defeat and suppresses someone's potential, our lives as a whole are poorer. We therefore need to pursue a model of development which emphasizes the development of people, their economy, their community and their local biosphere *as a whole*.

Empowerment heals dependency, and releases potential, both personally and socially. A story from Colorado's San Luis Valley illustrates how the empowerment of a community as a whole affects the lives of individual people.

The San Luis Valley stands at 8,000 feet, and members of the impoverished Hispanic community have always kept themselves warm with firewood gathered from common land from old Spanish land grants. In 1980, a corporate land-owner fenced the land and threatened to shoot anyone trying to gather wood, causing an immediate crisis. Some local people knew how to build solar greenhouses using scrap materials, so they taught each other, holding collective work sessions, adding solar collectors and greenhouses to several thousand local homes. This cost $4 million (spent at local businesses), saved $4.5 million annually ($1,000 per family) and generated hundreds of jobs. The devices meet one half of people's heating needs and extend the growing season from three months to year-round, improving both winter nutrition and personal cash-flow. As enthusiasm caught on, wind machines were built, and local farmers created an alcohol fuel plant fed with cull potatoes and barley washings, powered by geothermal process heat. The valley is on its way to energy self-sufficiency, and having gained confidence from this experience, is now tackling its local health problems.

As a spin-off from these activities, there has been a marked reduction in signs of stress such as crime, alcoholism and family abuse. As people realised they had the power to solve their own problems, there was a healing of the dependency that used to characterize the valley.[19] Healing is social, as well as personal. Where a community's problems have social origins, social answers are needed. By privatizing them, we cut ourselves off from the source of healing, which lies with collective empowerment.

Together, we can all be fulfilled and know our potential. We dream of it, so it is possible. Every one of us is part of evolution's journey towards its goal. Each of us carries the precious load of consciousness. Like a diamond hidden within, it persists in saying 'Be more. Be whole. Be who you really are'.

Evolution has laboured long to reach this far: it is hardly going to give up now, within dream-shot of its goal. When we stop to think how far we have come from those early beginnings amid the cosmic dust, every step of our journey has been a miracle, and there are many more steps yet to come. The universe is more incredible, more miraculous and more whole than we imagine – and the adventure is just beginning.

Chapter Six :
Awakening a community's resourcefulness

'Pope John Paul II has suggested that in the Third World people are oppressed economically. In the Second World and the Soviet-dominated zone of Europe, people are oppressed politically, and in our Western society, we're oppressed culturally, because we have a culture that makes us into materialists, that makes us into individualists. We've lost the sense of social solidarity, we've lost the collective political will. We're really quite powerless as a community or as a country to solve our relatively small economic problems.'
Professor Gregory Baum, McGill University, Montreal[1]

The overall process of establishing a full rainbow economy development strategy has many different parts and components to it. They share a common core of five key processes:

- getting together,
- analysing your problems, exploring new ideas and working out what you want to do,
- forming a partnership organisation,
- forming a strategy to achieve your goals,
- and lining up the necessary funding and resources.

Through these processes, the people of a city, town or neighbourhood can create for themselves a new collective political will, and tackle whatever problems or issues they see fit. The process is not a challenge or an alternative to existing democratic structures : it is a complementary process, which allows the members of a community a more direct and participative involvement in creating their own future. In the successful models, local councillors and politicians involve themselves alongside the other members of the community.

This chapter considers some of these processes, and looks at the kind of results that are possible when the will and the commitment are present.

The idea of 'partnership' is on the lips of many people who are concerned with local economic development today. It is usually taken to mean a partnership between local/city government and the private sector (Model 3, Chapter Three). This can mean that local government gives planning permission, provides the infrastructure and generally paves the way for the developers, playing the secondary role, while the private sector finances and undertakes major property developments such as conference centres, malls and shopping arcades and other 'honeypot' schemes. Property values rise, business thrives and the rich get richer, but the poor stay poor, working if they are lucky in the new McDonalds and Sainsburys which blossom in the new arcades. New chain stores drive out smaller local shops, and contribute to continued urban decline in the areas outside the honeypot zone. Apart from unskilled work, local people are often not adequately trained to take the jobs which the developments bring. Community collapse continues. This kind of partnership is based on the continued dominance of economic values (pale-blue), and is one of the causes of the world's crises, not a solution.

The key to a transformative development model is partnership which involves people from *all* sectors of the local community, not just business and government, and which seeks to express the full range of values in the rainbow spectrum, not just one value.

No region, city or town in the world has yet attempted to adopt the full rainbow economy development model as described in Chapter Three, embracing every dimension which is needed to overcome our collective planetary crises. The intention behind this book is to open up just such a possibility, and make sure it gets a place on the agendas of politicians, development economists, business executives, community groups, environmental groups and everyone else who is concerned.

A new community partnership is needed because our existing systems of democracy are not up to the task. We have struggled a long time to achieve real democracy. Our constant quest to control our own lives has brought us steadily closer to that goal, but we are not there yet. The world has become a highly complicated place, changing at a very fast pace, and our structures of democracy have not kept up with the changes. We watch the world changing on our television screens, and feel relatively helpless to do anything. Our non-involvement breeds discontent, and we live in a restless, disempowered way, not knowing why life feels dull and yet not realising how corrosive this deprivation of power really is. We complain, moan and castigate the politicians, saying 'they're just in it for themselves'. Every few years we vote for a politician to voice our concerns, but even the best of councillors, MPs and Congressmen and women find themselves bewildered by the immensity of what they are supposed to do. Our system of democracy is like a model-T Ford that is responsible for taking us on a mission deep into space. No wonder it feels as if things are a little out of control.

Meanwhile, the problems remain. The farmers of Aberdeenshire in northern Scotland turn to suicide because they feel their problems are too immense. Mothers living in drab suburbia take valium to hide their depression. Young people internalize their frustration and powerlessness through drugs, carrying out an internal riot against reality. As Pope John Paul says, we have lost our collective political will; our social solidarity. We are not meeting our need for empowerment and self-determination.

COMMUNITY INITIATIVES

In contrast to this general feeling of helplessness, there are many scattered instances where people have got together in their local communities and achieved remarkable things, without waiting for someone else to come and solve their problems.

In Liverpool, the dockland community of 2,000 families known as the Eldonians faced dispersal through housing redevelopment in 1979. Rather than lose what they valued, they drew up their own plans for a self-build housing co-operative. The Labour-controlled city council (under left-wing 'Militant Tendency' domination) refused to finance the co-operative, and forced them to settle for city-owned council housing. Undefeated, they then conceived a plan for a further co-operative of 145 homes on a nearby derelict factory site, and won financial support from the government's Housing Corporation, along with a £2.1 million derelict land grant. This development is now underway. They are now dealing with the matter of jobs: 40% of their families are unwaged. They have set up a market garden and landscaping business which they own collectively, with directors elected annually from the community and profits going into the Eldonian Community Trust, an arm of the Association. In setting up the business in this way, they achieve an important marriage of economic, social and community values. Their next enterprise is to convert an unused building into an enterprise centre to create space for several other business ventures they are planning, and beyond that, they have their eye on a bigger dream: to become the developers for a whole community-based environment in Liverpool's north docks area.[2]

The path the Eldonians are following is neither 'private'

91

nor 'public': it is a third way, which draws on the resourcefulness of the local community, serves the community's self-defined needs, and returns its profits back to the community for re-investment in further projects.

In the Rocky Mountain ranges of British Columbia, Canada, there is another remarkable story of what a community can achieve by its own resources.

The Sushwap Indians of Alkali Lake have lived in the Rocky Mountains for 8,000 years or more. When the white settlers came to western Canada, the Indians' stable way of life ended. The loss of traditional hunting lands and the rapid seclusion of native peoples onto reserves where their traditional spiritual understandings and paths were discouraged or banned by missionaries brought great sadness, confusion and defeat. Native children were forcibly removed from their bands and brought up in mission schools, creating much emotional loneliness. The white traders brought alcohol, which helped numb the pain of the Indians caused by their cultural, economic and emotional destruction.

The Alkali Lake band were protected from this influence by their relative isolation until 1940, when a white trading post was set up, trading goods for furs, and selling alcohol. By 1960, the entire band was drinking. Between 1960 and 1971 alcohol-related deaths, violence, neglect and family break-ups were a constant part of life. These were their darkest years.

In 1971, one woman, Phyllis Chelsea, decided to give up drink after her daughter refused to come home one evening. Her husband, Andy, followed her decision a short while later, and they formed an Alcoholics Anonymous group in the band, with assistance from an AA counsellor from a nearby town. For a year, they kept the group going on their own, being the only two members. Phyllis set up a grocery shop to provide an alternative to the white trader who had been cheating them, and Andy was elected chief of the band. One couple joined them in 1973, and by their joint efforts, by the end of 1975 40% of the band (total population 300) was sober. There was considerable resistance to be overcome; people feared losing the comradeship of the bottle and of their drinking companions, and bootlegging and alcohol trafficking had to be fought. When people agreed to sober up, they went away to a treatment centre and while they were away, their houses were painted and restored, so that they came back to new beginnings. They began to seek their lost spiritual traditions, rediscovering the meaning and purpose of sweetgrass, the pow wow and the sweat lodge. By 1979, 60% of the band was sober. Through attending a personal development training course, people began to rebuild their inner self-esteem. The power to take command of reality and rebuild their lives was re-instated in their hearts.

By 1985, 95% of the band members were sober, and extensive community development efforts were underway. The band school was being run by native people in a new school building they built themselves, and children were being taught their own traditions, language and culture. Pow wows and feasts were being held regularly. Several businesses were being formed as the band applied its newfound determination to the problems of economic dependency and poverty. Unemployment, which stood at 90% in 1972, was down to 75%.

In the summer of 1986 the band hosted a major gathering of native people from all over Canada to share experiences and discuss ways of tackling alcohol and drug abuse in native communities. In conjunction with the Four Worlds Development Project at the University of Lethbridge, in Alberta, the people of the Alkali Lake band are sharing in the pursuit of a major new goal, which is the elimination of all alcohol and drug dependency from native bands throughout Canada by the year 2000.[3]

Six hundred miles to the south, the people of the Mattole Valley, on the coast of northern California, had their own crisis. The Mattole River used to be so thick with salmon that horses wouldn't dare to jump into it. For countless thousands of years the stunning beauty of the valley had been shared by the Yuki Indians and the abundance of nature's creation. A hundred years after the first white men arrived, the Yuki were all dead. The trees were being taken out, the grass cover was overgrazed, the soils had been washed into the creeks, the hillsides and gulleys were being eroded, the salmon spawning pools had been clogged and the river's depths had filled up with silt. David Simpson, a newcomer to the valley, saw what was happening:

> *'I had read about the decline of the great civilisations of the world, and the process was always the same – over-grazing and poor logging in the uplands and consequent destruction by self-induced flooding of prime agricultural land. I looked out of the window and the same thing was happening here in 1974 as happened in Egypt and Mesopotamia and Sumeria and Greece.'*[4]

With his partner, Jane Lapiner, they got together with local people and started rearing salmon fry in small stream sidehatch-boxes – but they soon realised that the only way to improve salmon habitat was to restore the whole watershed. The residents have now created a web of home-grown institutions to carry out the immense job they have taken on. There are groups involved in salmon-enhancement, reforestation, running their own school where the children take part in the watershed work, even setting up their own dance company to express their feelings about the valley. To the Mattole Valley people, this is real local democracy at work.

This kind of activity is not limited to the industrial north of the world. In Brazil, there is a rural tradition known as 'mutirao' through which village people help each other. In the face of appalling problems of external debt, galloping inflation, IMF austerity pressures and rapidly growing shanty towns, the public authorities have begun to draw on this natural tradition to create an alternative strategy for public assistance. On a single Sunday in 1983, 80,000 people in Goiania working together through community organisations set up 1,000 pre-fabricated homes on land prepared by the city authorities.[5] Similar examples can be found throughout the Third World.

These initiatives are scattered and random, however. They seem to spring up only when there is a combination of a crisis of some kind and the will to work together to make a difference. They arise when conditions become desperate – not as a regular part of life. When they do arise, the results can be remarkable, and they offer a method of development which goes a long way towards meeting the needs of the rainbow economy model. If the wider community is to be involved in an active development partnership, some more systematic way needs to be found in which the huge pool of resourcefulness and skill that lies sleeping in every neighbourhood can be awakened. The answer may lie with 'future workshops'.

FUTURE WORKSHOPS

A future workshop is a social invention which could have as profound an effect on human progress as any other yet invented. It is a participatory process which enables people to get together to explore any issue which concerns them, and to develop creative approaches which please them. It releases people's resourcefulness and invites them to take part in creating the kind of future they want.

The person who has contributed most to the invention is the German writer Robert Jungk, a refugee from Hitler's Germany in the 1930s, who saw how disastrous the results can be when people experience powerlessness:

> *'At present the future is being colonised by a tiny group of people, with citizens moving into a future shaped by this elite. I believe that we should not go blindly into this future.'*
>
> Robert Jungk[6]

95

One of Jungk's early future workshops was run in the coal-mining village of Eisenheim, in Germany. The village was scheduled to be torn down and replaced with modern, high-rise buildings which would bring increased incomes to the developers. The villagers were resisting, but their leaders were being labelled troublemakers and reactionaries who were opposed to change. The villagers felt frustrated and full of bitterness at their powerlessness.

With help from a socially committed planner who lived nearby, they cleaned and painted an old coal wash-house for use as a meeting room, and in the course of one day they then held a future workshop during which they produced dozens of proposals for a modernization programme in keeping with their needs. They voiced their frustrations and pent-up anger, and worked in small groups with large sheets of paper, dreaming up ideas they wanted to see in their village. No one had ever consulted them before – these ideas had lain idle all these years. The coal mine owned their houses, and told them what to do. They wanted to set up a park, a lending library, a youth centre and a local newspaper, and to have a notice board where people could post up their complaints about the estate management's negligence and harassments. They wanted to create a meeting place where Germans and foreign workers could get together, and they considered what could be done for pedestrians, and how the sewers and drains could be restored to working order. Eisenheim, they felt, could become a model for other communities by enhancing its own cultural life, by providing more ways for people to get to know each other, and by continuously involving all its residents.

As long as the villagers remained defensive, they were on the losing side. When they came up with constructive proposals, the authorities had to give way. The village was saved, and a programme of renewal and restoration was put into action following their ideas.

The future workshop comes in five phases:

- Phase 1, the *Preparatory Phase*, occurs before the

workshop begins, when people are invited to a briefing session so that they know what they will be attending. If the workshop is happening over a weekend,

- Phase 2, the *Critique Phase,* happens on the Friday night. People take time to share their frustrations, irritations and difficulties, which are written on sheets of paper and stuck on the walls.

- Phase 3, the *Creative Phase,* takes place on Saturday. Focusing on their main items of worry, people now let their imaginations roll, dreaming up hundreds of ideas which they would like to see take place, using the brainstorming technique.[7]

- Phase 4 is the *Implementation Phase,* which starts on Saturday and continues on Sunday. Time is now spent giving detailed attention to the ideas which receive the most support. Plans need to be drawn up, working groups formed and arrangements made for follow-up. The miracle of birth is over and the long childhood of a community development project begins. The months and years that follow involve labour, trial, experiment and endless learning. The future workshop liberates the spirit that has been sleeping, and the awakened spirit then begins to create a new reality.

- Phase 5 is the *Action Phase* which takes place over the following months and years. Opposition may have to be overcome and internal tensions resolved and lessons learnt from successes and failures.

During the workshop, people grow in confidence, and their horizons stretch:

'In the fantasy phase of a workshop on "Alternative Forms of Work" we were taking a short break. A woman broke the silence by saying "I'm sorry, but I have to say something. I don't know about the rest of you, but I've not felt so well in years as during the last couple of hours. That's all I wanted to say. I just had to

97

get it off my chest".'

'Many workshop participants, even if they have never been politically-minded, become committed in a quite personal way to the search for a more basic restructuring of society. The workshop is not just another problem-solving method – it may have a lasting impact on the participants, turning them into activists for social change.'
Robert Jungk

Through childhood, and in school, college or training, we are rarely invited to contribute our creativity in an open-ended way. We get used to a method of learning which is one-way, in which someone else has the knowledge and expertise. The systems of state examinations allow a few people through the barriers to power and influence, and they then become the experts. The powers-that-be would have us believe that those who do badly at school are simply less intelligent. In this way, people grow used to the idea that someone else will always govern them, be their boss and determine the future of their community. This is why the future workshop is such a critical invention.

'Individuals get an opportunity to spread their wings and discover what they are capable of when serving a larger cause. In the process, their self-confidence grows as they come to realise that they are capable of constructive planning, and thus take their first steps towards adding more meaning to their lives.'

The Aberdeenshire hill-farmers, instead of becoming depressed and committing suicide under the pressure of mounting bills, might decide, through holding a future workshop, to help each other with their emotional strains and worries, to set up a debt-management advisory service, to explore ways in which they could reduce their loss-making operations, to diversify into new operations, to experiment with new crops and organic approaches, to develop the tourist potential of their area, to establish a local development agency to pursue their plans further – and so on.

The running of a successful future workshop requires group leaders who understand the facilitator style of leadership, and who are sensitive to the realities of long-term community development. Workshops could be encouraged by locating people who possess these skills, and asking them to train a group of local people, who would then become a permanent resource. These people could get in touch with community groups and organisations and interest them in holding workshops as part of a wider community awakening strategy.

To return to the overall task of development, the members of the new community partnership have been considering ways in which local resourcefulness can be awakened at the neighbourhood level. They have seen the potential of the future workshop. Something else now concerns them. What happens on Monday morning? A neighbourhood group which has been awakened will need a lot of skills if it is to follow through successfully. It will also need a proper organization to carry it.

Many groups adopt a two-fold structure; a non-profit community association, and a separate profit-making community development company, which returns its profits to the community association. Once a development company has been set up, the community can become an active player in the local economy, and there is very little limit to what can be achieved.

In County Galway, on the west coast of Ireland, the inhabitants of the parish of Ballinakill, covering some 320 square miles, first got together in the early 1970s to discuss what they could do about their problems. Their villages are extremely remote, the farms are tiny and the soil is poor. As in so many other Irish communities, emigration was the normal expectation for many of the 1,700 inhabitants, especially the young. In 1971, they decided to set up a community-owned development company called Connemara West Ltd. One of their first actions was to raise £13,000 from 500 local people and construct nine self-catering thatched holiday cottages, in which the residents became the shareholders. Often, such cottages are owned by outsiders, and the income from rent disappears to Cork, Dublin or London. By keeping the rent themselves, they were able to pay off the debt and start accumulating capital. Their next move was to build a Teach Ceoil, a centre for social and cultural events and for training in traditional Irish music, song and dance.

Learning to work together co-operatively is like building up new muscles – it can be painful at first, but as your muscles grow, you gain increasing confidence and strength. In 1978 they bought a large old Industrial School for £21,000, raising all the money locally, and restored it for community use. This building serves as a base for the development company, and provides space for the Farmers co-op (founded in 1983), the credit union (founded in 1970, membership 420, assets £220,000), the Fish Farming Co-operative (founded 1980), the doctor's surgery, a sports centre, a public library, office space for Connemara West and for local businesses, a shop and a café. Among the businesses using the office facilities are manufacturers of ceramics, pewterware, quilts and patchwork, an iron worker, a potter and a woodturner.

In 1982, they set up a three year craft training programme giving full-time training to 15 unemployed young people. This ended in 1985 with 13 of the trainees qualifying for City and Guilds Certificates. All but one of the 13 are now in work, including five who have grouped together as the 'Letterfrack Woodworkers' and set up production locally. The villagers' next move was to hold a major symposium on wood sculpture in 1986, which attracted national interest. Following this, they have set up a permanent two-year course in fine woodwork and furniture-making and design in partnership with the regional technical college – a collaborative step without precedent in Ireland (or Britain).

A measure of the increased community resourcefulness that these activities have released is in the astonishing increase in the number of local community organizations. Before 1970, there were only six organisations, including the Legion of Mary and the Pioneer Total Abstinence Association. Since 1970, a further 31 community organisations have been formed, including nine organizations furthering economic goals such as the Sheepbreeders Association, the Craft Co-operative and the Farmers Co-operative, four sporting groups (two badminton clubs, an athletics club and a women's tug-o-war club) and the eighty-strong Connemara Environmental Awareness Group. In 1988, with the new woodwork course underway, Connemara West set up a Resource and Education Project with help from the EEC. They are developing community plans for the three villages in the parish, organising night classes and a schools art programme, and considering setting up a community radio station to ensure the free flow of information and debate on community matters. All this from a population of only 1,700 people.

> *'Things don't fail because of money. They fail without commitment. What is needed is fantastic commitment, dedication and a belief in what a community is doing. There is goodwill and potential, but governments can't seem to harness it. For some reason, it seems to be the government in conflict with the people. If the government could channel this tremendous resource in a positive way you could sort out a lot of the country's problems.'*
>
> Michael O'Neill, Teach Ceoil

As well as commitment, there is need for good organizational skills. There is always the danger that the power will end up in the hands of a few professional managers, and stop the process of community-empowerment. Connemara West avoids this by having 12 unpaid directors who

101

are elected every three years:

> '*As enterprises got off the ground and became more complex, we saw that we had two main options in terms of efficient management. One was to employ more and more professional full-time staff and therefore have a larger central office; that's the way most groups respond. We saw that way fraught with danger, in that what tends to happen is that professional managers run away with the whole policy-making function of the enterprise. It can then become more and more divorced from the community and the people who have set it up, and whose support is essential in the future. We wanted to avoid that. We also wanted to avoid a central hierarchical system of management where you have supervisors, and managers supervising supervisors and a general manager supervising managers. It becomes a crazy system in this kind of development, which is really about people. So we felt as an alternative that what we would do was to develop a stronger committee system which demanded more voluntary work by Board members; it does involve a fairly heavy commitment of time for some directors, but they clearly recognise that this is an option we have chosen.*'
>
> Kieran O'Donohue, Connemara West Ltd[8]

One of this book's purposes is to build a coherent vision of a positive future. Community initiatives start off small, and if they are successful, they grow. The work in Connemara started in 1971; in Mondragon, Spain, where 20,000 people now work in a fully co-operative economy, it started in the early 1950s. Community economic development is not like private sector development. It takes time, but over time, developments grow.

In Los Angeles, in the wake of the 1965 rioting, local people set up the Watts Labor Community Action Committee, and as a separate community-owned trading wing, the Greater Watts Development Corporation. They started off doing building and renovation work in Watts after the riot, and moved on to set up a market, a restaurant and a petrol station, using the profits from one activity to finance the next. As their experience grew, they felt confident to take on bigger projects, building a general store, and buying vacant lots, holding onto it for a few years and selling at a gain, bringing the surplus from increased land-value into the local community. They recently took a 25% stake in a $23 million shopping centre project, which will bring them 25% of its profits. By 1987, they had built 600 houses for local people, and had overall command over $50 million worth of community assets. They use the profits both to finance new development projects, and to set up youth training and enterprise programs, childcare and senior citizens programs, and to run a community bus service.[9]

A similar story comes from Cape Breton, a beautiful island in Nova Scotia, on Canada's Atlantic coast, where unemployment is constantly high. In 1973, a local priest, Greg MacLeod, and a group of local people set up the Cape Breton Association for Co-op Development, in Sydney, and helped a local handicraft organisation find new premises by buying a building, using a $20,000 personal bank loan and a $40,000 credit union mortgage. They renovated the building, turned it into commercial space and rented apartments, and extended the mortgage to pay off the bank loan. They went on to buy other properties, and in 1976 they set up a community development corporation called New Dawn, with three divisions covering business, cultural and social activities.

By 1979, New Dawn owned over $1 million in real estate, and had helped to establish a senior citizens guest home, a group home for the mentally ill, two dental centres, a senior citizens resource centre and had sponsored many traditional folk concerts. By the end of 1985, assets had reached $10 million, after two waves of dynamic expansion followed by hasty nervous contraction as they struggled to develop management and financial control methods which were able to handle the volume of work they were doing. Along the way, they have organised or supported a used auto-parts enterprise, a land-clearing project, a computer consultancy group and a ceramics workshop. They view themselves as a very young organisation, with their future still undetermined and open to change.[10]

In Australia, the 500 residents of Tammin, a small wheat-belt town, set up a community company called Farmdale, and collectively raised $30,000 to acquire a disused petrol station and re-open it. They then raised another $19,000 to buy the lease on the local pub/hotel, and re-opened that. There are now volunteer work-ins to tidy up the town around the hotel, and empty houses are being re-inhabited and improved.[11]

In Cleveland, Ohio (USA), nine community-based organizations joined forces to form the Cleveland Housing Network, which is creating affordable housing in partnership with the city and the private sector. The Enterprise Foundation, a non-profit development company, is aiding this and similar community efforts in dozens of cities around the USA.[12]

These new community-based social-economic initiatives *are* the new dawn. They represent a very important aspect of the emerging rainbow economy, showing how a community can claim its own collective will and win control over its own destiny. Wherever they are established, they share similar goals:

- the development of local communities and their economies in ways that
- meet local needs,
- provide meaningful jobs and
- help create long-term prosperity, security and sustainability for the communities.

Many organisers of local community initiatives are immensely frustrated by the question of money, disliking their dependence on the endless process of seeking grants and government money. The people of Mondragon (see

Chapter Seven) and Connemara have been willing to put their savings where their hearts are to finance their own development. In this way, they establish ownership over their own resources, and ensure that the income from activities flows back into the local economy. In moving from spontaneous community initiatives to a more deliberate policy, methods are needed to encourage local people to participate financially.

In Scotland, the Highlands and Islands Development Board observed the success of the Irish community co-operatives, and decided to shape their development policy along those lines. In order to encourage communities to awaken, and start taking initiatives, they offer training, technical and legal assistance, and for every pound raised locally, they provided matching finance. In many remote Hebridean islands, the community co-operatives have now become the principal focus for economic development.

From the Highlands, the community impulse spread to the Scottish heartlands, where it arrived in the late 1970s in the form of the community business movement. A community business is a trading company owned by the members of a local community, which recycles the profits from its activities back into the community to serve local needs. By 1987, there were over 100 community businesses trading in Scotland, doing such activities as providing workspace for small businesses (Govan Workspace, Clydeside), doing stone-cleaning and restoration work (Ferguslie Park, Paisley), providing a security service and a painting and decorating service (Barrowfield, Glasgow), and producing high quality knitwear (Via, Stevenston). The initiatives are still young and vulnerable, as they are being built in some of Scotland's most deprived areas, and many members have to learn skills such as management and financial control from scratch.[13]

A community organization rarely blossoms into existence on its own. The Scottish community business movement is growing because of the support given by the Community Business Development Units, and the funding policy practised by Strathclyde Regional Council, which intentionally encourages a careful step-by-step development process. The council offers start-up grants (maximum £500) to help companies get going, development grants (maximum £500) to pay for feasibility studies, and management grants. As a new business becomes solidly based, capital grants and access to a Revolving Loan Fund become available.

There are numerous other difficulties to be faced, as people who may have never had a personal bank account find themselves becoming company directors, dealing with matters of finance and planning permission. With support, much can be achieved. Without it, people can feel they are being led down the garden path as they move from one government department to another, waiting for committees to meet and falling foul of petty regulations. Most local government officials are not yet geared up to taking a facilitative role, and require training in this area (see Chapter Eleven).

In the USA and Canada, many community development corporations (CDCs) have been established during the last 20 years, fulfilling the same role as Irish community co-operatives and Scottish community businesses, and similar lessons about support have been learnt. In Massachusetts, the Community Enterprise Economic Development Program, which provides small grants, pre-venture start-up costs and administrative expenses to CDCs and other community organizations is credited with helping to increase the number of CDCs in the state to 57 in 1982. A Community Development Finance Corporation with resources of $10 million makes equity investments in economic enterprises sponsored by CDCs in low-income communities, assisted by the Community Economic Development Assistance Corporation, which provides technical, managerial and training support to new initiatives to help secure the loans. Without joint discussions, Massachusetts and Strathclyde have reached the same conclusions about the need for carefully-phased support.

These processes of community awakening enable people to reach towards a vision. We are surrounded by unmet needs, and by problems which often seem to have no solution. We often live for years within situations which oppress us, putting up with poverty, bad housing, hopelessness, environmental decline, unsatisfactory work or just simple misery, assuming there are no solutions. *The only obstacle to change is our belief that there are obstacles to change* : if this one obstacle alone is removed, everything becomes possible. By building the confidence that we can change the world at the local community level, the confidence grows that we can change the world at other levels too.

This is true both spiritually and practically. The changes that will be needed to realise the rainbow economy development strategy, locally, regionally, nationally and globally, will depend on our ability to realise changes locally. By grounding the ideals of change in our local realities, we lay the foundations for a truly planetary world.

In addition to the technical aspects of setting up new community initiatives, there are also the intangible spiritual aspects, reflecting the reasons why people care enough to get involved in the first place. If we forget to nourish these, we can sometimes lose heart.

In New Zealand, a co-operative movement has been growing since the early 1970s and has involved thousands of people, both Maori and Pakeha (whites), in work trusts, co-operatives, credit unions and other co-operative initiatives.[14] Every year or so four or five hundred people meet together for a national or regional 'hui' (a Maori term for a tribal gathering). For several days there is a festival of music, dancing, trainings, learnings, workshops, speeches, debates, planning sessions, networking, and time just spent 'hanging out', enjoying personal friendships. The movement for a new society and a new economy in New

107

Zealand is spiritually very strong, even while its people experience the same difficulties over practicalities that occur in other countries. People remain committed because they care, and because they want to build a new way of living and working that will reflect how they really feel inside, and which will allow them to be who they really are. By holding their 'huis', they renew their dreams, and strengthen their determination to realise the vision.

The Maori people have a tradition called 'mahi', which refers to co-operative work for a purpose other than just pleasing yourself. That tradition exists in all tribal societies, and within the ancestral consciousness of all of us. In countries and communities all over the Earth, it is beginning to re-emerge.

When a community's resourcefulness is awakened, the ideas, skills and energy that are needed to regenerate a community and to create a new economy, serving new needs and expressing new values, are released. We regain our sense of social solidarity and our collective will. We reclaim the future as our own.

Chapter Seven :
The building of a community economy

The rainbow economy development strategy seeks to build a happy, balanced, prosperous, ecologically sustainable local economy which meets people's needs, supports their hopes and dreams, encourages the expression of their highest potential and serves the unfolding needs of the planet as a whole. At higher levels, it seeks to build regional, national and global economies which serve the same goals.

It seeks the realization of 'wealth' in the broadest possible sense of the word, including a deep sense of belonging, rich relationships and a spiritually vibrant environment, as well as material security. The agricultural and industrial ages taught us how to achieve a sufficiency of food and material wealth; our tasks now are to stabilize the ecological foundations of our existence, to ensure that material prosperity spreads to deprived areas, and to achieve prosperity in our emotional, spiritual and natural wealth. The foundations for the next stage of our evolution will then be secure.

The crises which mark the termination of the industrial age have prompted communities to respond in positive ways from New Zealand to northern Canada. In the process, these communities have been building the foundations for a new kind of economy. Based on their experiences, it is possible to draw out some of the steps which lead to the building of a rainbow economy at the local level. This chapter runs through the steps, some briefly and some at length, and considers how they can be incorporated into the development process.

Step One: Forming a partnership

The first step involves the simple act of getting together and beginning to talk. The broader the reaching out, the wider and more solid the eventual development process will be. The rainbow needs all its colours.

Step Two: Establishing a vision

When there is a clear vision of where you want to go, it is easier to get there. How can this be achieved, when in many cities and towns people have been arguing for years over how to approach development?

In some of the most successful initiatives, one person has given a clear and committed lead, saying 'This is the vision: now let's achieve it'. That is one way forward. When a group of people meet together and want to develop a vision without depending on one leader, without knowing what that vision will be, one strategy is to go out and get inspired by visiting and studying other initiatives. Read the literature and set up a series of study groups covering different areas of need; learn about the best practices in the field, and come back to share results. Meetings are also valuable to share more fundamental visions, and to establish basic values. When we step below the level of detail and take time to share what our deepest dreams are, we often find an unexpected degree of agreement. Our values inform our principles, which in turn inform our policies and actions.

Step Three: Researching the local economy

Most people have little idea what goes on inside their own local economy. With care and organisation, it is possible to build up a profile of the community, its economy, its people, and of their basic dreams and needs. Some of the information exists in various public places, and just needs collating. Some has to be sought by questionnaires and surveys. What percentage of local people would like to work fewer weeks a year? How many would like to have more fulfilling work? Answers can be found to these questions only by asking people directly. Some information will need more skilful digging out. How much money is flowing in and flowing out of the local economy each year? How much money is each household spending on imported energy? How much on insurance?

These may seem like difficult questions, but students at local colleges and universities can sometimes build a research project into their studies. People may also volunteer to help gather the information and build up the overall picture. The more who are involved, the greater will be their later participation.

Step Four: Looking for opportunities

At the heart of the rainbow economy development strategy there needs to be a state of mind which sees the whole of life as an opportunity in which something is always waiting for us to make it happen. In the imagination, the dirty, neglected area of wasteland becomes a place of beauty and refreshment. The derelict old mill becomes a thriving centre of new activity. The grey, run-down estate becomes a centre of community revitalisation.

Reality is only what we make it, so when we see something that seems grim or depressing we have to realize that what we are seeing is not a 'thing' that is inherently grim; it is simply a state of mind, arranged in bricks and mortar. It is we who decide whether it is 'grim' or whether it is simply awaiting the attentions of someone who will bring about a miracle. Everywhere there are opportunities. The critical skill in developing the rainbow economy development strategy is to awaken the power in local people so that they begin to see the opportunities all around them, and know that they can take them and turn them into heaven.

111

One of the common features of 'Model 3' in the local economic development strategies outlined in Chapter Three is the choice of a central project to serve as a 'honeypot' for the development – a new museum, landscape park or culture centre, for instance. In the full rainbow model, the emphasis on imagination and opportunity is still there – but it draws the imagination out in ordinary local people, so that it is they who see the opportunities and create the projects.

Step Five: Forming a strategy

By creating a strategy, with targets, goals and timetables, we take a conscious hold over the future, and begin to create the kind of society we want.

Step Six: Awakening local resourcefulness

Most people prefer to leave the future to others, not realizing that this is the very reason why things are not well in the world. Local neighbourhoods can be awakened, so that they release and channel their resourcefulness into positive actions. Chapter Six considered at length how to inspire this local involvement. A strategy for a city, town or region that omits this resourcefulness is like a pie that has been filled with air instead of fresh fruit.

Step Seven: Starting new enterprise

In addition to personal and community awakening, there is need for economic awakening, leading to new business enterprises. A lively initiative on the south-west coast of Australia illustrates the process in action.

Esperance is a small, isolated town of 10,000 people 750 km from Perth.[1] Most of the farms in the area developed in the last 30 years, and until the early 1980s the economy seemed strong. In 1983, however, land prices peaked, there was a bad drought in 1984–85, and the economy began to decline. Without a critical intervention of some kind the town was in danger of fading away. A growing number of such towns in Australia are becoming empty shells, occupied only by the wild animals, the wind and the sand.

The intervention came in the form of one Ernesto Sirolli, a committed enthusiast for one idea – growing people:

> *'Human nature is like a plant: if you give it sun and water the human being will grow. How do you make them grow? You have to give them sun – of love, respect, basic psychological nutrients – and they will spontaneously fulfil their being. I don't give a damn about people making money. What I care for is those people growing. They cried with me. They said "It is the first time someone is caring about me". If I help a person to make money and be unhappy, what is it? It's a different story. You have to have faith, faith in people. I think it is the most beautiful faith to have.'*

Ernesto was asked by the Western Australian Minister for Regional Development if he would go and take a look at Esperance. He turned up in 1985 and asked people one question : 'What would you really like to do?' Then he helped them to do it.

> *'There's nothing I can do in Esperance if no one in Esperance wants to do anything. What I can do in Esperance is according to what the people in Esperance have in their brains. I'm a midwife; they're not my babies. If nobody's pregnant, well, forget it.'*

What Ernesto and the Esperance Local Enterprise Initiative Committee bring is actually a lot more. People need encouragement to remember that everything is possible, given the will to do it. The resources they need to realise their dreams lie within their own intelligence, imagination and resourcefulness. It just needs someone to believe in them and help make them happen.

In Maurie Green, Ernesto found a 53-year-old man who had been manager of the fish cannery, now unemployed.

113

He wanted to smoke fish and needed $4,000 to start, but three government departments had turned him down. Ernesto helped him revamp his application, went to the Department of Employment and Training, and bullied them:

> *'Why have you knocked him back?' 'Oh, because the committee felt he was competing with the fishermen.' I said, 'He is smoking fish, not fishing. He needs $4,000. Come on, give him his $4,000.'*

Working together, they did the feasibility study and looked for a shed. Word got around. The tuna fishermen came next, asking for help. They first had to agree to work together, and then they started exploring ways in which they could get more than the standard 60 cents a kilo from the cannery. All the added-value was being won outside Esperance. They got a $1,000 grant to do a feasibility study and then got a Japanese chef to come and show them what 'sashimi' – smoked tuna – was, and how it was cooked. The chef said their fish looked great – his restaurants would buy it. Maurie smoked the fish they caught, and the restaurant paid them $3 a kilo. Later they would go direct to Japan and get $15 a kilo on average – $60 a kilo on one occasion. Now they have a $2 million annual turnover in sashimi, with extra work on the boats and 15 new part-time jobs on-shore.

Esperance is a small town, where word gets round fast. The farmers came next. One of them had some ideas around conservation and farming, so Ernesto got the farmers and the conservationists together. Some of the farmers put up the money to fund a feasibility study into wild flowers, which they are now selling direct to Japan. Other farmers wanted new ideas about their mutton farming. This led to an operation developing quality sheepskin products such as chamois, boot and handbag linings, and local sausage production.

The government in Canberra heard what was going on

and suggested they apply for a full-time staff member. They set up a committee – the Esperance Local Enterprise Initiative Committee – and hired Brian Willoughby to become a full-time development worker on a very minimal budget:

> Brian had 20 minutes training in the car. 'Look, there is only one thing that you are never to do, that is absolutely forbidden to you', Ernesto said to him. 'I know exactly what this town needs', Brian replied. 'I don't care what this town needs,' Ernesto replied, 'that is not the way we work. We only use our resources – intelligence, creativity, stamina, you name it – on request. We are not here to tell people what to do, we are to help people to do what they want to do'.

Two months later Brian had 45 projects on the go – half of them involving previously unemployed people. A subcommittee which includes six aborigines on it vets the aborigines' own proposals for businesses. This has led to 15 new jobs – panel-beating, graphic arts, a health food shop, a fruit and vegetable market, book-keeping, secretarial services and running a woodyard. They are now setting up their own aboriginal agency.

The abalone divers want to set up their own abalone breeding ground. Someone wants to breed oysters. Someone else is making sheepskin seatcovers. Because Esperance is small, it is easy to see what goods are coming in and what is going out, so they've looked at import substitution in a big way, gathering figures. They found that two and a half tonnes of continental sausage was being consumed every week – all of it imported. So a sausagemaker stepped in and took 10% of the market within three weeks, enabling an extra $1,000 a week to stay in the local economy. They found that 50 tonnes of fresh fruit and vegetables was coming into Esperance each week – so the farmers started talking about ways in which they could diversify out of straight mutton. And so it goes on.

The town is coming alive to the possibilities sitting right under its nose, within its own resourcefulness.

> *'As soon as we have every person in Esperance with someone in his family or circle of friends using this kind of approach, we will see the real thing happening, which is a community, which becomes a community again.'*

Ernesto Sirolli

After ten months' activity, the results are as follows (in Australian dollars):

Operating cost, 1 May 1986 – 31 March 1987 $32,000
New businesses established   35
Full-time jobs created (and many part-time jobs)   58
Cash-flow into Esperance from new enterprises per year
                                               $4,900,000
Cost per job $551
Savings in unemployment benefit $377,000
(Single person's benefit $90 per week; married $160 per week, average $125 per week × 58 full-time jobs created).

These figures are important: a 1000% return on investment is not bad, by anyone's standards. Similar business development agencies around the world are finding that a cost-per-job in the range of £1,000 – £3,000 is more normal, compared to Esperance's figure of £275 ($551).

The new business development agencies play an important role in the overall development of a community economy. They are one of the most important social inventions of the 1980s, and a clear indication of the emerging economy. In Britain, there were 380 Local Enterprise Agencies in 1988, funded by the government and private companies, started by joint initiatives between people from the private sector and from local government. They receive support from 'Business in the Community' (BiC), a national organisation set up in 1981 to encourage greater

116

involvement by industry and commerce in local communities. As in Esperance, the agencies all offer personal counselling and support. Many also offer business training courses, business funding packages, workspace, youth enterprise initiatives and other supportive activities. Studies indicate that they are collectively effecting as many as 90,000 new jobs per year.[2]

In a similar way, Co-operative Development Agencies (CDAs) are helping local people start up new worker co-operatives. In 1988 there were 60 CDAs in the UK, mostly funded by government and by Labour-controlled local authorities, and started by local people who believe in the co-operative idea and want to encourage it. They help new co-ops to start, and provide training, access to finance and other supportive activities. In areas where there is a CDA the annual growth rate of new co-ops is 131%, compared to 28% where there is no CDA.[3] The growth of co-operatives is particularly important to the long-term stability of a community economy, as co-operatives bring a built-in commitment to worker ownership, participation and wider personal, social and community values.

The process of economic awakening needs also to spread to groups of people who do not traditionally think of themselves as potential businesspeople. The growth of Youth Enterprise Centres has been another remarkable invention of the 1980s, catering for young, often unemployed, people with no previous experience of business. In 1988, there were 14 such centres in existence, and a further 46 at the planning stage. By providing carefully organized processes of training and support, very high success rates are being achieved. 'Surrey Business Enterprise' runs self-employment courses for the physically disabled, and for the mildly mentally handicapped.

The same applies for women. In St Paul, Minnesota, USA, the Women's Economic Development Corporation (WEDCO) helped over 550 women to start new businesses between 1983 and 1985 and gave assistance to another 500 already in business. 52% of the women coming in with ideas had incomes below $7,000 before starting in business, and 61% were either single or single parents. 23% had recently been on welfare. WEDCO's success rate is an astonishing 98% – with the 2% representing women who have chosen to move on to something else, and one business failure. They achieve this rate of success because of the thoroughness and sheer professionalism of the trainings they provide, because they give attention to personal detail, and because they share the Esperance principles of never doing anything *for* anyone: help them do it for themselves. They help women write their own 12-step business plans, and start-up finance is available through the regular banks which are willing to lend because they have a healthy respect for the WEDCO approach and track record of success.[4] Stories like these could fill an entire book and still only scratch the surface.

Step Eight: Supporting existing enterprise

The traditional business assumption has always been that 'you're in it on your own', and that business is a private affair both in success and in difficulty. During the 1980s, however, when people in local communities became concerned about business failures and the loss of jobs, they decided that the more that could be done to help new businesses start up and to help existing businesses succeed, the better.

Among the new initiatives that have been set up to support local business are small business workspace units, marketing centres, innovation centres and science parks (linking the needs of business to the research and development skills available in local colleges and universities), trade associations, sectoral initiatives such as Nottingham's Fashion Centre, trade associations such as Islington's Microelectronics in Information Technology in Islington (MITI), training initiatives, business support networks and special loan schemes.[5] The streamlining of local government procedures is also important. The giving of information, issuing of building permits, resolution of land-use problems, sorting out of inter-departmental mud-dles and issuing of decisions all need to be speeded up, simplified and concentrated into a one-door approach, ensuring that government is a source of support not of obstruction. This means retraining administrators in the new approach.

In Britain, some enterprise agencies have begun taking a pro-active approach to business support, not waiting until a business asks for help. The Bathgate Enterprise Agency (BASE) in Scotland challenges local businesses to double their turnover within five years, and helps them draw up development plans. The Aberdeen Enterprise Trust fol-lows up its new business starts, prompting them to con-sider overall strategies and new approaches to marketing, and pairs them up with a business 'foster parent' if they want one, a retired executive or business academic who provides free advice and support.[6]

From these many activities, **a local business support sys-tem** is steadily emerging. This is immensely significant. It spells the end of the traditional separation between busi-ness and the wider community, and the beginning of a new mutuality in which the community cares about business and business cares about the community. In nature, every species is indirectly supported and assisted by every other species, and competition happens against a background of widespread natural co-operation. The same is now begin-ning to happen within local economies, creating an impor-tant feature of the emerging rainbow economy.

This new spirit of co-operation has a subtle spirituality. In the Yorkshire town of Halifax (area population 190,000, unemployment 13%) the massive old carpet fac-tory at Dean Clough closed down in 1982 with the loss of 600 jobs. It had been the centre of the town's life since 1850, employing at one time 5,000 people. For Halifax, it was a complete disaster, until a Lancashire entrepreneur called Ernest Hall bought the place and started to realize a dream.

119

> '*When I came here, I wanted to create an environment which evidenced my belief that the power of human beings is unlimited. The most serious problem which communities like this suffer is a problem of confidence. I wanted to create an environment in which people would gain confidence, enthusiasm and motivation, qualities which I believe are absolutely unstoppable. It was a matter of spiritual regeneration in the community.*'
>
> Ernest Hall[7]

Dean Clough is now the scene of an economic renaissance, drawing on local energy, local entrepreneurship and a strong partnership between business and the local community. By 1988, 180 businesses and organisations had made Dean Clough their base employing over 1,800 people, and giving the town a whole new sense of direction.

As well as the businesses, which include Britain's largest wholefoods distribution co-operative (SUMA), an art gallery, two theatre companies, a restaurant and a pub, there is an Industrial Design Centre, an Innovation Centre, a Small Business Advice Centre, an Enterprise Training Services Centre, the Local Employment Network, the Youth Business Initiative and the Calderdale Partnership, providing the framework of co-operative support in very tangible form.

> '*For those of us who have lived through this period, it has been absolutely tremendous. We have initiated and supported all kinds of activity which add greatly to the total experience of Dean Clough. I am convinced that what is needed is an integrated environment, offering all of the ingredients, not just a place to work but a place to live, a place to learn, and a place to be inspired. What was threatening to become a symbol of permanent failure has become a symbol of new hope. An end can also be a beginning.*'
>
> Ernest Hall

Another expression of the wish for a more co-operative way of business life can be found in the Briarpatch Network in San Francisco. The Network was founded in 1974 as an association of friends in business (or 'Briars') who shared similar values, and as a system of self-reliance and mutual support. It takes its name from the briarpatch in the folk tales of Uncle Remus, where the hero, Brer Rabbit, led a happy life protected from predators by his humble and seemingly inhospitable home of thorns. Members join the Network and consider themselves Briars if they agree with the following statements:

1. You have an insatiable curiousity about how the world works.
2. You seek to do the work you love and to make a living at it.
3. It is more important to you to provide the highest quality product or service than to get rich.
4. You prefer co-operation to isolation.
5. You prefer honesty and openness to deceit and secretiveness.
6. You believe in independence and responsibility.
7. You believe in simple living and environmental preservation.
8. Your financial records are open to the community.
9. You have been in business long enough to have a track record of your performance as a business.
10. It is important to you to have fun in everything you do.

The Network has 150 active members, and in its history over 800 businesses have drawn on its skills and services which come in the form of parties, classes, workshops and seminars, a co-ordinator, and technical assistance on a voluntary basis from fellow members who are experts in their fields. Members believe fervently that business is a way to serve others. They share their skills, care for each other and have fun together. They are mostly under 45 years of age and the majority are women, who seem to respond more naturally to the values of openness and sharing. The Network is a family.

It is also a successful family. When compared to the average 80% failure rate for new companies in the first three years of business in the USA, Briars have experienced a failure rate of less than 5%. The whole network is self-financing by voluntary contributions.

A similarly increased success rate is experienced by businesses helped by the enterprise agencies in Britain. A survey has shown that while nationally one in three new businesses fail by their third year, only one in six of those which receive help from enterprise agencies do so.[8] Co-operation builds up a win-win mentality in which every-one succeeds.

In Britain, a similar network was established in 1986 in the Yorkshire town of Whitby. It is known as the Com-monbox Club, and its membership is open to people run-ning small businesses which are socially friendly (i.e. which do not seek to cheat or exploit), committed to hon-est trading and good quality, and willing to help others where possible and practical by sharing experience and information. In 1987 the Club had 80 members, and as well as their regular monthly gatherings, members were involved in the development of a Commonbox Shop, group marketing initiatives and a partnership with the Whitby Youth Trust to provide ethically-based enterprise training for young people. The Club keeps close connec-tions with the 300-strong Business Network in London, which provides a regular family, meeting place and source of new ideas for business-people who wish to explore ways of combining their business practice with higher social, ethical and spiritual values.[9]

Step Nine: Strengthening self-reliance

For clarity of expression concerning the eighth process in

the building of a community economy, we go to the Rocky Mountain Institute in Colorado, whose staff run an Economic Renewal Program (among many other valuable activities):

> 'To prosper, a community must stem the needless outflow of money. The Economic Renewal Program draws on the achievements of community energy planning to show how communities can more efficiently and sustainably meet their basic needs not only for energy, but also for food, water, health and shelter, the basic needs of the community. Economic Renewal helps people identify where dollars are leaking out, and where an imported product or service can better be supplied locally – keeping both money and jobs at home.
>
> This is not a call for isolationism. No community makes all the products it will want. But cost-effective import replacement and a higher degree of self-reliance can enable a town to develop sustainable commerce and improve its comparative advantage. Resource efficiency and fuller use of indigenous resources increase a community's economic resilience by reducing its vulnerability to external economic fluctuations.'[10]

By looking at the economy as a whole, it is possible to see where expenditure is being wasted and where a sensible policy measure or investment would increase local economic activity, generate more jobs and keep local dollars within the economy. At a cost of only $30,000 US, the 'Oregon Marketplace' program in Eugene created 100 new jobs and $2,500,000 US in new local contracts by helping local firms get some of the business which used to go out-of-state.[11] Farmers can often increase their local sales considerably by organising farmers' markets and joint marketing initiatives, bringing local people fresher food and reducing the amount of pollution caused by packaging and transport.

In the USA, the judicial system permits cities to favour

local commerce. Detroit and Livermore, California, have purchasing provisions which allow contracts to be awarded to local employers even if they bid 5% higher. In Washington DC, the city government is required to purchase 25% of all its goods and services from local, minority-owned firms.[12] In Britain, local government is obliged by law to accept the lowest tender when purchasing goods and supplies. Glasgow, however, runs a preferential policy whereby local producers who can match the price given by the lowest tender are given the contract. Several councils run Meet-the-Buyers exhibitions to ensure that local businesses know how to tender for local contracts, and in Croydon, South London, the local purchasing officer increased the number of local purchases simply by developing an in-depth knowledge of the local economy.[13]

Local purchasing can also be encouraged within the private sector. In Newcastle, staff from Project North-East, one of Britain's most dynamic enterprise agencies, took to lobbying business commuters waiting at the station to catch the train to London, in some cases to meet suppliers. They urged them to consider whether their needs could be more easily met through local purchasing, and distributed copies of their 'Who's Who Directory of Enterprising Businesses'.

Energy expenditure is an area where local policy can increase self-reliance considerably. Out of every pound spent locally on imported energy, 85p leaves the local economy immediately. A high proportion of money invested in energy efficiency measures, however, is spent on labour and materials which can be used locally, and every pound not leaving the economy for Saudi Arabia or the Central Electricity Generating Board is a saving to the local community. After an exhaustive study to ascertain how it could save energy, Portland, Oregon, concluded that it could achieve 5% savings simply by reviving neighbourhood grocery stores. Modesto, in California, switched its city vehicle fleet to locally produced methane from the sewage treatment plant.[14]

Computers allow communities to build up dynamic resource maps which can analyse the movement of money and resources in and out of a community, and show alternative policy paths. By creating integrated accountancy procedures which weigh up the gains and losses from different policy options, local government can increase the effectiveness of its policy decisions in terms of overall community gain.[15]

Step Ten: Generating capital

A community must have access to capital in order to be able to invest in new enterprises and initiatives. It is also important that poorer people with little or no personal collateral are not excluded from borrowing. When loans get too expensive, however, debt charges can become crippling. In low-income areas of Birmingham where loan-sharks operate, some families are paying out 15% or more of their weekly income to service annual interest rates of 1000%. It has also been estimated that if the USA continues its late 1980s level of public and private borrowing, by 1992 it will be spending 25% of its GNP on interest payments. Many Third World countries are only too familiar with the realities of excessive debt-repayment. Through initiatives such as credit unions, community banking practices and community loan development funds, a community can draw on more of its own capital resources and become more financially self-reliant. Chapter Nine considers this area in detail.

Step Eleven: Community economic synergy

When co-operation and mutual support reach a high enough level, the gains begin to increase exponentially. This is when the term 'synergy' becomes justified, referring to the higher level of energy that emerges from within when the different parts of a whole begin to work in harmony.

The Japanese understand this. One reason why they have been so successful economically is that they practice

125

a high degree of co-operation between their businesses, banks, government and research establishments. Among other things, this allows them the luxury of 15-year development loans, which are used for the long-range pro-duct development strategies which have brought them such pre-eminence on the world markets. In the USA, the phrase 'long-term' usually means 2.8 years, because both companies and capital chase after short-term profits at the expense of long-term gains, resulting in a social and economic atmosphere in which individuals and companies think in increasingly separate terms.[16] This achieves the very opposite of synergy, and results in steady social and economic fragmentation and collapse.

The formative energy fields in nature are all integrative. They support the emergence of new growth within the pat-tern of the organised whole, and use synergy to create higher levels of order at which more complex physical structures and higher levels of consciousness can emerge.[17] By creating similar integrative fields in our social and economic institutions, we can achieve quite remarkable results. A visit to Mondragon will illustrate why.

Mondragon is a town in the Basque country of north-east Spain, in the western Pyrenees. From the late 1940s onwards a Jesuit priest, Hose Maria Arizmendiarrietta, worked with local people to develop the economic impli-cations of Jesuit and Catholic theology. He found the answers he was looking for in the writings of the utopian socialists such as Robert Owen, who emphasized the importance of the co-operative tradition. Working from the mid-1950s onwards, local people developed their own metalwork co-operative, a co-operative bank, and then a network of further co-operatives. Today, in 1988, nearly 20,000 people work in more than one hundred separate but linked co-operatives which do everything from man-ufacturing fridges and cookers (stoves) to running the bank, a technical research centre, a college and a social security system. In the 1980s, with Spain's 25% unemployment rate the highest in Europe, and with the surrounding Basque country experiencing similar distress with 30,000 people unemployed, the co-operatives of Mondragon had zero business failures, and only 30 people unemployed and dependent on Mondragon's own social assistance programme.[18]

The co-operatives are achieving these results because they have established a complete strategy of mutual support, setting up an integrative field of co-operative effort which releases the maximum degree of synergy. New businesses are carefully nurtured into existence over a two-year period. Training, product development, finance and marketing support are laid on through secondary co-operatives. Mondragon's early leaders were concerned that each co-operative should have a responsibility to the wellbeing of the community and its economy as a whole, so they founded Ularco in 1965, a secondary co-operative which helps the co-ops support each other. Member co-ops invest 20% of their capital in each other, buy products and equipment from each other, group together for special purchases and offer at least 25% of their workforces for transfer between member co-ops. Ularco also encourages the improvement of working conditions, promotes benefit sharing, arranges technology transfers and acquires new product licenses.

In order to establish local ownership of their enterprises, and to safeguard them from takeovers and pressures from external shareholders with no interest in the philosophy of wider community gain, every worker in a Mondragon co-operative must become a shareholder in the co-op she or he joins. To join a co-operative costs over £2,000, which is arranged as a loan and deducted from pay. When they retire, Mondragon workers must sell their shares, which are by then worth £20,000 to £30,000.

Mondragon's capital needs are met through the local credit union, the Caja Laboral Popular, which has 400,000 members, 133 local branches and £70 million in assets. The bank plays a crucial role in local life, investing people's savings in the development of their own community and its economy, and playing a highly participative role in the co-operatives which it supports.

The Empresarial Division of the bank has seven departments with 120 employees. Once it has invested money in a co-operative, it goes out of its way to make sure the co-op succeeds, helping it make intelligent and informed decisions in the global market.

Every year, each co-operative has to give its year's accounts and cash-flow forecasts to the division's Audit and Information Department, as a condition of the original loan. The department subjects them to rigorous analysis, feeds them into its computers, correlates their future intentions with market analysis for their particular sector of the economy and gives relevant feedback and advice – a bit like the crypton diagnosis (computer check-up) you can get for your car at some garages. The Research Department then provides detailed information concerning the local, national and global conditions in which the co-op is operating. If the read-outs indicate that the co-operative is heading for danger, the Intervention Department will help the co-operative's members diagnose the problems and draw up an appropriate development strategy.

If their analysis shows that a co-operative is in danger because the market for a particular product is drying up, the bank's Industry Promotion Department will offer it one of the new products or foreign licence agreements which its staff have been busy researching and developing. If the co-operative needs assistance with export promotion, marketing, production engineering, personnel matters, administration, financial or legal matters, they will get the help they need from the bank's Advisory Department. If the analysis shows that the co-operative is heading for extinction, the Entrepreneurial Department will help it to find a new product or service, arrange retraining of both management and members and finance its new launch.

Between Ularco and the Empresarial Division of the bank, Mondragon's co-operatives have created for themselves a 'mega-brain' that is able to think ahead, using sophisticated economic analysis, and seek solutions to emergent problems before they become too serious, just as an acupuncturist detects and corrects imbalances in the human subtle energy field before they show up as illnesses or complaints. It is this sophisticated process of mutual support which lies behind the astonishing achievements of the Mondragon co-ops, with their zero business failures and their almost zero unemployment during tempestuous economic times.[20]

Underlying Mondragon's success lies a spiritually based vision. 'Let us make richer communities, rather than richer individuals', is how the Caja advertises itself. Don Hose, the initial encourager of the whole network, wrote that 'Salvation is achieved through community action, and involves the development of the capacity to think, to invent and to serve'. He actively believes that the world can be transformed. 'I plead for the thesis to do the real, within the possible.'

Mondragon's success has prompted the formation of 4,000 further co-operatives in the Basque country, outside the integrated network. Local banks are happy to support them since co-operatives have a good track record in the area, owing to the Mondragon experience.

In Britain, the growth of business support systems (in Step Seven above) could represent an early stage in the development of a similar community economic synergy. If the processes of co-operation and mutual support continue to develop, synergistic qualities will begin to emerge.

Step Twelve: Developing human resources:

Chapter Five focuses on some of the ways in which human potential can be developed.

Step Thirteen: Strengthening the informal economy

The economy of a community or nation has four layers. On the top is the layer of private business activity. Under that comes the layer of public activity. These two layers both rest on the third layer, which consists of the unpaid personal, voluntary and household activity which makes up the 'informal economy', which most economists ignore because it is unmeasurable. This is a highly valuable source of wealth and wellbeing in an economy, and the greater the level of activity within it, the greater is the overall happiness within a community. The fourth layer is nature's own layer, the biosphere, on which all three upper layers depend.[19]

The informal economy can be strengthened by such measures as establishing local currencies (see Chapter Four), by encouraging worksharing strategies among local employers, by ensuring that people have access to physical spaces where they can develop their hobbies, crafts and skills, by increasing local learning opportunities and by strengthening the quantity of community space in a neighbourhood where people can meet, talk, and pass the time of day. The more we interact together, the more we share our lives and our skills with each other.

Step Fourteen: Increasing local ownership

Generally speaking, the greater the degree of local owner-ship in an economy, the greater the stability in that economy, and the greater the commitment of local people. Measures to help people start their own businesses and co-operatives, and to facilitate worker and management buy-outs are valuable here. So too are initiatives which enable people on low incomes to buy their own property, or to share in the increasing land-value which reflects a community's growing economy. Community Loan Funds, Land Trusts and Co-operative Land Banks are able to achieve this goal, and have an important role to play in ensuring equal access to capital and land-value. (See Chapter Nine.)

Step Fifteen: Developing community mutuality

This is perhaps the toughest issue in the building of a community economy. The specific issue that needs addressing

here is the need for a new system of community-based welfare. Existing systems undermine and weaken personal
self-reliance, by levying a close-to-100% claw-back tax on
the personal earnings of people on welfare in order to be
fair to those who are not on welfare, and by asking nothing in return from those who receive welfare. This disrupts
our natural sense of mutuality in which we expect giving
and receiving to exist in balance.

The real problem, however, lies with the fragmentation
of public policy and budgeting procedures. The welfare
payments budgets exist in completely separate boxes from
the budgets for education, housing, training and community economic renewal, destroying the relationships of cause
and effect which ought to connect them, and lead to intelligent policy decisions. The fact that Mondragon was compelled by Spanish law to create its own system of locally-
based social security, the Lagun Aro (Spanish social security systems do not include people employed in worker
co-operatives), and that it has command over its own
polytechnical college where retraining takes place, may
partly account for the almost non-existent unemployment.
Once the relevant budgeting decisions and procedures are
re-integrated at the community level, the natural logic of
cost-effective policy-making re-asserts itself.

Until central government budgeting procedures become
decentralised to the appropriate level, we have to live with
existing systems. Some of the American systems of 'work-
fare', which endeavour to link payment of welfare with
appropriate training and educational provision are quite
popular among recipients when they are implemented in a
person-centred way, and not imposed in a heavy-handed
manner. The resistance to 'work-fare' in Britain stems
from the realistic fear that it might be enforced in an
authoritarian way. A community-based, democratically
governed, participative, person-centred work-fare scheme
which linked a person's retraining to their personal hopes
and aspirations (see Chapter Five) would probably generate support once the fear of having meaningless work or

training imposed died away, since at the end of the day, very few people who are stuck on welfare enjoy being trapped in that situation.[20]

Step Sixteen: Sustaining the natural environment

Chapter Ten is dedicated wholly to this theme.

Step Seventeen: Transforming business holistically

Chapter Eight focuses on this step.

Step Eighteen: Community government

Refer back to Chapter 6, and then to Chapter 11.

Step Nineteen: Planetisation

Many companies and banks have developed to meet the needs of our pre-planetary, industrial age existence. They operate within the military-industrial complex, trade with countries overseas in an ecologically destructive and humanly exploitative manner, and disregard the emerging values of a more interdependent, planetary world.

As we move towards a steadily more interdependent existence, there will be less and less room for such activities. In building up the structures which underpin the community economy, a community develops tools which can be used to assist companies to change their methods of production and trading. With help from the community, they can seek new product-lines and develop new trading relationships with other countries and communities. Organisations such as the St Louis Economic Conversion Project in Missouri, USA, are helping the process along by running workshops to help local communities think through their dependencies, and to recognize the pitfalls of reliance on the military complex for the wellbeing of their citizens. (See also Chapter Eight.)

A similar impulse can inform a community's relationship to incoming companies. The arrival of a new enterprise from outside the community can bring a healthy influx of new people, activities and ideas. If it is just seeking a supply of cheap labour and a new branch factory, however, and if the directors have traditional attitudes to business, labour and the environment, a community should question whether it may not be better off without it.

> *'When recruiting a major new enterprise, a community should ask whether its real goals will be enhanced by the proposed development. Will the new firm hire and train local people who need work? Will it pay its own infrastructure costs? Will the new company compromise community values and squeeze out existing businesses?'*

(Rocky Mountain Institute)

Step Twenty: Celebrating local culture

The final step involves remembering to take time off to celebrate.

> *'The common celebration of great feasts and sacred rites expresses and articulates the social unity of family and of state. Splendour and sacred music serve to arouse strong tides of emotion for all hearts to share in unison.*
>
> *Thus is awakened consciousness of the One Creator: the common origin of all life.*
>
> *Thus is awakened the common will: the co-operation among humans so necessary for great general undertakings that set a high goal for the will of the people.*
>
> *Let barriers dissolve; all hands unite.'*

The I Ching, the Chinese Book of Changes[22]

THE PROCESS OF DEVELOPMENT

To carry through the development processes outlined in this book, there is need both for a high level of experience and competency, and for creative participation by ordinary people, all the way through. Herein lies a dilemma – and an opportunity for creative thought.

One way of handling the process of development is to pay a firm of consultants to make a study of your town or city and tell you what they think should be done. This is usually done in a top-down and non-participative way. 'Public participation' has traditionally meant that the planners work out what they want to happen in advance, and then present their plans at a public meeting, inviting questions, which usually ensures a very passive or unimaginative response.[23]

When the staff from the Rocky Mountain Institute in Colorado, USA, work with a town using the Economic Renewal process, they combine a highly participative process with a tightly organised approach in which learning *and* becoming skilled as you go along are part of the process. They help a community to organize itself around four pre-decided principles:

- plugging the leaks;
- investing in yourself;
- encouraging new local enterprise; and
- recruiting appropriate new business.

After an initial town meeting to introduce the whole idea and generate enthusiasm, a 'preferred future' exercise is held which enables local people to step back for a moment and focus on the values, goals and visions which they hold in common. People normally find that they agree on 95% of local issues: they all want the place to be safe for their children, for instance, for the air to be clean and for unemployment to be ended. This enables personal agendas to be set aside so that work towards community-wide solutions of mutual benefit can proceed.

Over a series of further meetings, groups use workbooks and casebooks which the Institute has prepared to analyse their local economy and to learn what other communities have done in similar circumstances. In this way, they explore local business opportunities, and the economics of energy, food, health, housing, waste management, water and finance, educating themselves as they go along. On the basis of their research, they form an overall Economic

Renewal Plan, and choose appropriate projects on which to embark.

The virtue of this approach is that it emphasizes wide public participation, while ensuring that the quality of debate on development alternatives remains high by use of the workbooks and casebooks. To ensure that this balance of participation, expertise and learning is maintained after the RMI organiser leaves, local people are trained in group facilitation skills.

In Chapter Three, seven models of economic development were presented, embracing progressively wider dimensions of change and transformation. In Britain, most local economic development work (Model 3) is conducted by local authority-initiated economic development partnerships, companies and enterprise boards. While many of these are doing valuable work (e.g. Lancashire Enterprises Ltd), they are not generally attempting to carry out community economic development work (Model 4) or to work in a participative way.

To carry through a full rainbow economy development strategy (models 1 – 7 inclusive) four main areas of expertise are called for:

- group facilitation skills,
- understanding of the full range of policy options,
- organizational, financial and project management skills, and
- the political skills of persuasion, negotiation and selective compromise.

Alongside any strategy, therefore, these skills should be taught in an organized manner through adult and community education classes.

In the smokestack/microchip-chasing model (Model 2), the community itself is hardly involved at all. No personal growth or evolution is required. As we move beyond the traditional models, progressively greater levels of personal growth are called for. We are asked to see more, and to relate to each other in new ways, learning to listen and to share. We are asked to give up old habits and addictions of

135

dominance and submissiveness. The models are not just social-economic systems which can be taken off a shelf – they are also expressions of consciousness, and of our own inner growth. They invite us to evolve along with them. Without our own growth, they are empty shells, transforming nothing.

We are not simply changing our social and economic systems, or our world. We are changing ourselves.

> *'When one has fully entered the realm of love,*
> *the world, no matter how imperfect,*
> *becomes rich and beautiful,*
> *for it consists solely of opportunities for love.'*
> Søren Kierkegaard

Chapter Eight :
The transformation of business

As we evolve, moving steadily closer towards that unity to which we are drawn, our societies evolve with us, reflecting our changing consciousness. Business, which is an expression of consciousness applied to the economic world, evolves too.

This chapter considers the transformation of business that is underway, as it evolves towards holistic values and practices. Much that is written can be taken to refer also to non-business organizations such as social services departments, hospitals and schools, where a similar, less publicized evolution is under way.

THE EVOLUTION OF BUSINESS

When business first became a major part of modern life several hundred years ago, there were no laws controlling or regulating business, and no unions or environmental regulations. You stood alone at the centre of life's maelstrom, and tried to make what you could of it. Picture Charles Dickens' London, those streets full of teeming activity, tiny workshops and endless toil. There were businesses whose owners thought nothing of deceiving and exploiting to augment their profits; there were businesses whose owners struggled hard to pay a decent wage and trade in a fair and honest way; and there were others, the great majority, which fell in between. This can be called the 'First Era' of business.

The 'Second Era' evolved out of the hardships of the first. Technology advanced rapidly, opening up the world and bringing many changes in its wake. Workers organized to protect themselves and their children against exploitation, campaigned for laws about health and safety, worked to make employers pay a living wage and to place limits around employers' belief that they possessed a divine right to rule in whatever way they thought fit. Governments eventually brought in rules and regulations to protect the urban environment and to achieve a variety of other goals. The 'we' of the wider world was demanding that some of its needs be met.

Some employers fought, and still fight, every move to take away their powers, like kings, queens, emperors and barons of old. There are still Dickensian sweatshops in *our* societies, and companies whose directors view life as a constant struggle against laws and regulations, even regulations which attempt to control such things as the dumping of toxic, carcinogenic wastes. Other companies have moved their operations overseas to countries where there are fewer unions, far lower wages, no health and safety regulations, and no troublesome environmental laws.

Many employers go along with second era realities, fostering good worker-management relations and striving to meet safety and environmental standards. Some even set it as their goal to pursue excellence in everything they do.[1] In their fundamental structures, however, they remain second era businesses, owned by their shareholders and directors, pursuing private goals of profit and gain, and perceiving a clear line of boundary between business and the outside world. In the alignment of left and right, of 'we' and 'I', business has sat firmly on the right, defending itself against what it sees as attempts by the left and by workers and environmentalists, to take away its initiative and control. We have established in our minds a destructive duality between the need for efficiency, productivity and profit, and for personal, social, ecological and planetary values.

Today, a huge evolution is occurring. Step-by-step, business is moving into its 'Third Era'.[2] The leaders of an evolutionary process are always few, their steps rarely seen by the mass who remain behind, but where they tread the others surely follow, five, ten or fifty years later.

3M, in Minnesota, USA, makers of magnetic tapes, computer discs and a thousand other things, is a good example of a company that is leading this evolution. 3M is the Minnesota Mining and Manufacturing Company, and with 87,000 employees it is one of Minnesota's most important companies. The company has a strong commitment to decentralization, and seeks to preserve human-scale qualities of smallness and flexibility. Its average plant size is only 115 people, and these are often located in small-town America.[3] 3M makes a big effort to nurture the creativity of its workforce, aiming to make at least 25% of its annual sales from products introduced within the last five years. It has been listed by *Fortune* magazine as one of the USA's three most admired companies, and it takes its community and environmental responsibilities very seriously. Through its 3P Program – Pollution Prevention Pays – it 'gives individuals or groups of individuals who contribute innovative pollution prevention ideas and accomplishments an opportunity to gain recognition for their efforts'.[4]

> *'Instead of simply adding on pollution control equipment at the end of a manufacturing process, 3M has stressed the prevention of pollution at source. The 3P Program has focused on the elimination of pollution through product reformulation, process modifications, the redesign of equipment and the recovery of waste materials for re-use. It also lays a good deal of responsibility on the individual employee to identify actual or potential pollution problems, and rewards creative solutions.'*
>
> John Elkington, The Green Capitalists

Nurturing creativity, worker self-management, participation and teamwork, setting up profit-sharing and employee-shareholding schemes, promoting the role of women and meeting childcare needs, encouraging work-sharing and flexi-work patterns, supporting employees' own personal journeys of growth and self-empowerment, breaking down hierarchical organizational structures and authoritarian modes of management, setting high standards of health and safety and of general business ethics, paying well and rewarding individual endeavour, building good management-union relations, pursuing environmental excellence, encouraging community involvement – these are some of the signs which mark a company's evolution into the Third Era.[5]

One of the fundamental processes which underlies this evolution of business into the Third Era is the re-integration of the separated 'I' and 'we'. As businesses begin to move beyond the dualistic view of the world which sets the pursuit of productivity and profit (the 'I' goals) against the pursuit of social, planetary and environmental goals (the 'we' goals), their managers and owners are discovering that by emphasizing higher values alongside those of economic profitability and gain, the values become not only compatible, but symphonic – the different goals assist each other and add up to a greater whole. *Serving personal, social and ecological values as well as economic values actually brings greater prosperity, for all concerned, raising the whole business operation to a higher level of synergy and consciousness.* In evolutionary terms, each cell becomes awake, and contributes the fullness of its consciousness to the whole.

As businesses develop more holistic ways of working, they begin to tap into the benefits of the natural harmony which comes when the laws of business are in accord with the inherent laws of nature, honouring the need for evolution in both the parts and the whole – the individual, the company and the world as a whole. In the language of Chinese philosophy, they are discovering the 'Tao of Business'.

Is this a left-wing process? or Is it a right-wing process?. It cannot be described in these terms at all. The trans-mation is based on the integration of values which come from traditionally polarised worlds:

- traditionally right-wing values of initiative, individuality and enterprise;
- traditionally left-wing values of caring for the workforce and the community as a whole;
- green movement values of environmental concern and human-scale organization;
- values from the human potential movement of caring about personal growth and fulfilment;
- values from the spiritual tradition of honesty and integrity; and
- values from the movement for global development of international justice, co-operation and interdependence.

A synergistic wholeness emerges from this meeting of different traditions, and their values, in which the different stakeholders in a business contribute to the success of a business, and are in turn nourished by it. This degree of integration rises above dualism and draws out new qualities and potentials. The business changes gear and discovers a range of freedom and ability not previously explored.

There are some very tangible reasons why this evolution is happening, in addition to these changing values. It is by no means just a question of idealism:

- The post-industrial age is a knowledge-based age. People have overtaken land, capital and material resources as the single most important resource. As people develop, the business develops.
- Global competition means that companies cannot afford to lag behind in anything which will increase their levels of innovation and productivity. To drop behind is to risk dropping out. Company investment policy has to anticipate the future. Governments have relatively short-term considerations in their sights, but companies like Shell or General Motors must plan for 20 years ahead in research and development (as governments should, too).
- Employees are bringing in better rates of productivity

when they are treated in a non-authoritarian manner, allowed to organize themselves in small self-managing groups such as Volvo's group-based production teams, and involved in the company through participative methods, profit-sharing, productivity bonuses and company share-ownership.

• High-quality employees want to work for high-quality companies which use participative management methods, and which respect their employees as people, not just as employees. Companies which do not meet these requirements are losing their best workers.

• Computers are rapidly eliminating line-management functions, speeding up the introduction of self-management.

• Consumers are voting with their credit cards to buy high quality goods. If Japanese companies can offer high quality goods because their team-work and company management methods produce better quality results, consumers buy Japanese.

• Business is increasingly vulnerable to environmental and consumer group pressure; company image has never been more important. In Britain, 80% of the general public is either concerned or highly concerned about such things as toxic waste dumps. Companies which continue to abuse the environment will suffer increasing sales losses, and as consumers turn elsewhere for their shopping, profit margins will dwindle rapidly.

Businesses are being forced to evolve to keep up with competition, and with changes in employee and customer demands. Commercial pressures, technological developments and changing human values are prompting the evolution of a more holistic approach in which economic values are integrated with personal, social, ecological and planetary values.

Figure 8.1 presents a model of a holistic business. When you examine the diagram you will see that the stakeholders are also the beneficiaries, completing a circle of

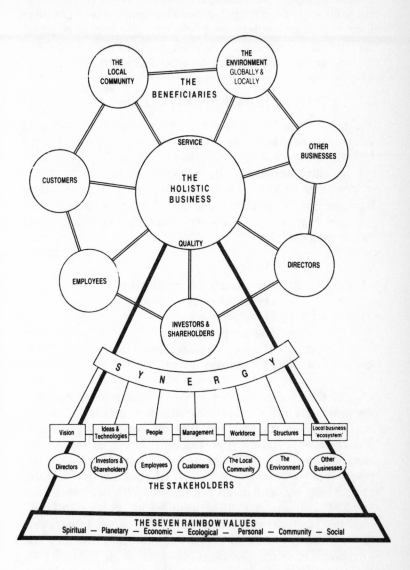

Figure 8.1   Holistic Business

mutual benefit. The business becomes a wider partnership, through which everyone gains. This chapter will consider first the stakeholders and owners, then the essential dimensions of production and service, and then the beneficiaries, giving examples of holistic developments.

THE STAKEHOLDERS AND OWNERS

Traditionally, the directors and shareholders own and control a company. The shareholders are represented (at least in a nominal way) by the Board of Directors, who govern the company in the way they think fit.

The 'stakeholders' are a far wider group of people who have an interest in the company, without necessarily having any ownership or control over it. There are seven major stakeholders:

1. The directors
2. The shareholders/investors
3. The employees
4. The customers
5. The suppliers
6. The local community
7. The environment

One of the evolutionary processes that is moving businesses into the Third Era is *the extension of ownership to this wider group of stakeholders.* The mushrooming growth of worker co-operatives expresses one aspect of this evolution. From 1971–1975, there were just 10 worker co-operatives registered with ICOM (the Industrial Common Ownership Movement) in Britain. In 1980 there were 300, in 1984, 900 and in 1986 around 1,500, with a £200 million per annum combined turnover. This remarkable growth-rate of around 58% per annum illustrates the growing desire that workers have to be in control over their own livelihoods, and to be able to create a harmony between their values and their working lives.[6]

The growth of employee-share-ownership is another reflection of the process. Publix Super Markets, Florida's largest retail food chain, is completely owned by its employees – and turns in a profit per dollar of sales twice that of Safeway, America's largest retailer. In 1976 there were just 843 ESOPs (Employee stock-option plans) in the USA, covering about half a million people. In 1984 there were more than 5,700, covering some 9.6 million workers, about 7% of the US workforce, a growth rate of 27% per annum.[7] In Britain, (a trade union bank), the Unity Trust and the National Co-operative Development Agency have been pioneering ESOPs. Profit-sharing plans are another expression of this evolutionary process which show a similar degree of growth. The message is coming over very clearly: employees are already stakeholders in any company they work in. Now they want to extend their stake to include actual ownership, giving them a share in the profits, and hopefully, in the power and decision-making, too. If the USA continues to keep to its present annual growth-rate of ESOPs, the whole American workforce will be working under an ESOP plan by the year 2004.

'Employee-ownership is good for business': that's the news from the San Francisco-based National Center for Employee Ownership, which conducted some studies in 1987. Among its findings were the following:

● A sample of 43 'majority employee owned' firms grew at about 3.9% per year compared to a weighted rate of about 1.1%.

● A sample of 13 'publicly traded firms that were at least 10% employee owned' outperformed their rivals 62% – 75% on such measures as sales growth and return on equity.

● A sample of 13 failing firms that were then bought out by their employees had an employment growth rate twice that of comparable conventional firms.[8]

Source: New Options, Washington, May 30, 1988

Under present rules, as long as company shares are owned by people who care most about the personal gain they make on their shares, stakeholders who have no legal way of making their voices heard have to shout from the sidelines. When the corporate raiders come to town, offering increased dividends to shareholders, companies can find themselves being taken over by people who have no interest in the needs of the other stakeholders. This is one way in which the 'octopus economy' gets a hold, with larger companies sucking money out of local communities, or closing down the whole company or plant. 'In business schools our future executives are taught that the corporation exists *solely* to maximise the net worth of stockholder equity.' (Lester Thurow, 'The Zero-Sum Solution'.)

In 1987, to the alarm of Minnesotans, Minnesota's 3M was threatened by a hostile take-over bid. 3M was not just 'any old company'. It was *their* company, and they were damned if anyone was going to seize control of it! On 25 July, the Minnesota State Legislature passed, by an overwhelming majority, legislation to limit the takeover activities of corporations in Minnesota. The legislation includes strict guidelines about shareholder voting procedures, and the financing of takeovers. Part of the legislation states the following:

> '*A director may, in considering the best interests of the corporation, consider the interests of the corporation's employees, customers, suppliers and creditors, the economy of the state and nation, community and societal considerations, and the long-term as well as short-term interests of the corporation and its shareholders, including the possibility that these interests may be best served by the continued independence of the corporation.*' [8]

The take-over bid did not go through, and Minnesota's example may signal the beginning of an upturn in favour of local ownership and social values. In the same year, the glass firm, Pilkington, successfully fought off a takeover bid from BTR, mainly because the local community in St Helens, Lancashire, rallied to their defence. Over the years Pilkington have put considerable effort into developing a new kind of relationship with the local community, and strengthening the local economy.[9]

THE PRODUCTION OF GOODS AND SERVICES

A holistically-oriented business seeks to achieve three goals:
- a quality of service which will please both customers and employees;
- increased productivity, so that more is done with less in a cleaner and more efficient way; and
- the achievement of synergy in which the different factors of production combine in a mutually enriching way.

> '*A high quality well-motivated work force interested in working together as a team to raise productivity is ultimately the major source of productivity growth.*'
>
> Lester Thurow[10]

There are seven components of production, which, when they work in harmony together, they will create this synergy (syn-ergos = joint work). These are
- vision,
- ideas and technology,
- people as individuals,
- management,
- the workforce,
- organizational structures, and
- the local business support networks (see Figure 8.1).

Vision

> '*We believe the first ingredient in re-inventing the corporation is a powerful vision – a whole new sense of where a company is going and how to get there. The company's vision is a catalytic force, an organizing principle for*

everything that the people in a corporation do.'
  Naisbitt & Aburdene, 'Re-inventing the Corporation'.

The traditional goal of many companies has been simply to increase the annual profits. A developing holistic vision must contain more. It has to have the power to inspire people so that they will feel enthused to fulfil it.

Jan Carlzon's vision for SAS (the Swedish airline) was a market where 'the customer is always happy, costs are trimmed to the bone at head office while more money is spent on service, businessmen are pampered without paying any extra on the standard fare, tourists fly for the price of second class rail travel, and 'profits will flow in like clear water from a mountain stream.'[11] A year after Carlzon turned SAS upside down to make it customer driven, an annual loss of $17 million per year had been turned into a profit of $54 million.

A renaissance of entrepreneurial vision is occurring. Robert Schwartz, who set up a school for new entrepreneurs at Tarrytown, outside New York, says of them:

> 'Entrepreneurs are the mutants and abherrants of our society. They feel out of step, and they have a nagging sense of mission that keeps them more interested in challenges than rewards. They feel suffocated by too much security. They're the poets and the packagers of the new ideas. They're visualizers and actualizers – that's their disease.'[12]

A new spirit of vocation is alive among them : 'They are motivated almost entirely by a high achievement need. They believe it is time to *move* – not passively, but actively – to the stage where new ideas embody the new vision. Their vocation is fully holistic 'Right Livelihood':

> 'Right Livelihood is work that engages the heart as well as the mind and the body, work that develops selfhood, fosters companionship, and nourishes the earth.'
> Robert Schwarz

A clear vision establishes an inner reality. Before the cathedral comes the vision of the cathedral. Business leaders are learning from the methods that artists, musicians, mountaineers and gold medal winners use to achieve success. When a clear vision is combined with a wider and deeper vision, a business enters the Third Era.

Ideas and technologies

A computer, a car, a shovel – these are ideas, cast in matter. All technology consists of ideas, painstakingly developed over time. In a highly competitive world, it is only by nurturing a steady flow of new ideas that a company continues to grow.

In the early 1970s, the British company Lucas Aerospace was planning widespread redundancies (permanent lay-offs). Many skilled engineers were facing unemployment, a fate which they rebelled against, knowing that their skills could be usefully deployed making socially useful products rather than filling military contracts. A Shop Stewards' Combined Committee was formed from the 17 trade unions operating in the company, which circulated the workforce with a questionnaire, asking *'Are there any socially useful products which your plant could design and manufacture? How could the plant be run by the workforce itself?'* (now called self-management, and practised by Honeywell, Volvo, General Electric, Hewlett Packard and a host of other companies, and in workers' co-operatives all over the world).

The Committee took great care to explain what they were seeking, and to involve their fellow workers in the process. The result was 'The Plan', which contained both a critique of traditional top-down line management, foreshadowing the cross-disciplinary teams of Apple Computers, 3M and Campbell Soup, and proposals for over 150 practical products of a socially useful nature, including heat pumps, kidney machines, vehicles that can travel on both road and rail, new braking systems and a host of other ideas. Their proposals included an employee development programme which called for the creation of working organizations 'in which the skill and ability of our manual and staff workers is continually used in closely integrated production teams, where all the experience and common sense of the shop floor workers would be linked directly to the scientific knowledge of the technical staff'. The Plan also contained constructive proposals for new training methods, re-education processes, worksharing, breaking down working divisions, employee development and the humanization of the workplace – themes which are critical to the evolution of a holistic company.

Lucas turned down the Plan, saying 'your job is to work, not to have ideas', and later sacked Mike Cooley, one of the pioneers of the strategy.[13]

This story ended in failure, but it illustrates the wealth of managerial, organizational and technological ideas which lie within the employees of a company. In the Second Era, this creativity, resourcefulness and potential wealth is not tapped, because directors and managers maintain an oppositional attitude towards their workers, seeing them as 'labour', and as a cost to be reduced, not as a source of new ideas and creative potential which could bring increased profit and productivity to the company as a whole.

Japanese quality circles achieve the active involvement in the processes of working which the Lucas trade unionists sought. At IBM, technical managers are permitted to spend up to 15% of their budgets on 'off-the-record' projects. In Sweden, a 'School for Intrapreneurs' teaches the skills of turning vague ideas into business plans. 'Intrapreneurship' – the deliberate fostering of creativity and new ideas within the company – is the in-term for what the Lucas shop stewards were trying to do in the mid-1970s. It is a key component in the synergy that is needed for company success.

One of the failings that lies behind our current economic chaos is the fetish for immediate results – the 'get rich

now, worry later' syndrome. In many western corporations, 'long-term' means two to three years. Company pay
structures and promotion ladders are geared to please the
stock markets and to produce the best quarterly results,
not to plan for long-term research and development.
Lawyers and accountants who have no understanding of
the technologies their companies depend on dominate the
company boardrooms, arguing for enrichment by merger
and take-over, not for technological innovation. This is
bad news for the development of new technologies which
need five or ten year development schedules. The need for
companies to nurture a long-term vision of a sustainable
future goes hand-in-hand with the need to nurture new
ideas and technologies.

People

The third ingredient is the people who work in the company, whether as executives or as office cleaners. Each person is an individual, and needs to know that he or she is
appreciated as an individual, not just as a 'manager', 'production assistant' or 'filing clerk'. With each passing year,
more people are saying that they want their work-lives to
offer them room for personal growth, as well as security,
income and job-satisfaction.[14] They are looking for non-
authoritarian leadership styles, equality, participation,
flexible working patterns, health and fitness policies,
opportunities to attend training and growth workshops,
and above all a creative atmosphere in which they will feel
stimulated and excited.

At W. L. Gore & Associates (often listed as one of
America's best companies), the founder, W. L. Gore,
believes that 'people given freedom within the necessary
creative restraints become unbelievably enthusiastic,
energetic and creative, achieving things that seem virtually
impossible'. As a new employee at the company you are
not assigned a specific task. You are told to 'look around
and find something you'd like to do' for your first three
months, and when you find your chosen task, you commit

yourself to it. You will be supported by your 'sponsor' – another, more experienced employee who is responsible for guiding you technically, and acting as your advocate if you want to develop a new project. The management structure at the company has no titles or organised hierarchies – it consists of a 'latticework' of sponsors, building on natural person-to-person methods of communication. Pay is calculated on an individual basis, dependent on your contribution to the company.

> *'The simplicity and order of an authoritarian organisation make it an almost irresistible temptation. Yet it is counter to the principles of individual freedom and smothers the creative growth of man. . . It is commitment, not authority, that produces results.'*
>
> Bill Gore

The company employs 4,000 people making the light-weight rainproof Gore-tex fabric that is used in outdoor wear, pollution control filters and as an anti-corrosive coating for steel products. Sales and earnings at the company are growing at a rate in excess of 40% a year.[15]

The idea that people want to seek personal growth through their work is relatively new. In most worker co-operatives, the idea is taken for granted. A rich network of personal friendships and support systems develop naturally because no one tells you not to. Personal happiness is an essential ingredient in the overall synergy which is needed to produce overall company success.

Rainbow Builders is a solar construction co-op in Shutesbury, Massachusetts, one of over 800 co-ops in New England:

> *'A real shift in the way I experienced the business happened when I no longer just saw it as a way to make money and support myself, but rather I realised that the business itself is a service to others.'*
>
> Bruce Davidson, Rainbow Builders

The Body Shop, Britain's fastest growing holistic business, was set up in 1976 by Anita Roddick and her husband Gordon in a small shop in Brighton, and was valued by the market in 1988 at some £5 million. With 3,000 employees and franchise holders around the world, care for the personal growth of the staff sits side-by-side with selling natural body products and environmental excellence as company goals:

> *'The individual is forcing the change. People are shopping around, not only for the right job but for the right atmosphere. They now regard the old rules of the business world as dishonest, boring and outdated. This new generation in the workplace is saying "I want a society and a job that values me more than the gross national product. I want work that engages the heart as well as the mind and the body, that fosters friendship and that nourishes the earth. I want to work for a company that contributes to the community".'*

Anita Roddick[16]

Management

Traditional management styles disappear in holistic Third Era businesses. Linda Ackerman, a much sought-after management consultant in the USA, identifies three types of management style: Fear State, Solid State and Flow State. An organization reflects the level of consciousness of its dominant managers, who set the tone and create the energy dynamic which underlies the action in a company. Fear State consciousness embodies authoritarian attitudes. It keeps people working out of a fear that they will lose customers, miss deadlines, fall short on production standards or simply do something wrong. Solid State managerial consciousness is concerned with organizational security and stability. 'Don't rock the boat', 'We've always done it this way' and 'You'll have to go through the correct channels' are three of its favourite sayings. Flow State consciousness, by contrast, seeks a confluence of employee and managerial commitment and enthusiasm. It encourages a relaxed, yet dedicated, state of mind in which a flow of positive energy is released, enabling work to be achieved with an unusual ease and harmony. The manager's task becomes one of carrying out an energy-scan of her department, generating, releasing and unblocking human energy, organizing and directing the energy towards the desired goals, managing and maintaining the flow of energy, and knowing how to transform energy from one state to another. To achieve this, she or he has to become a sensitive personal and organizational counsellor as well as a leader, creating an environment in which personal and group creativity is released, and in which its flow is constantly nourished.[17]

At the front on the new managerial wave in America, consultants such as Roger Harrison and Celeste Powell are daring to talk about tapping the power of love, by building a supportive culture within the organization. Love is always available as an energy if we allow it to emerge, and although managers rarely acknowledge it, it plays an important part in keeping organizations on the road through the care which many employees put into their work and the support they give to each other. As such, it already provides the underpinning for much everyday continuity and achievement. To foster it in a conscious way means aligning the company with natural processes which emerge when people feel trusted, free, unexploited, and able to commit themselves to what they are doing. It means taking conscious steps to appreciate and give credit, teaching, encouraging and nurturing talent and effort, rewarding and honouring, listening, responding and giving, producing high quality work, caring about little details which no one sees, caring for the immediate physical environment and for the whole environmental impact of the company, caring for the community in which the organization is rooted, and caring for the organization as a whole.[18]

In many workers' co-operatives, these things happen without management consultants to explain how they should be done. Love is a natural process, and once we feel free to contribute to life with our higher qualities, surrendering defensiveness, self-importance and organizational possessiveness, it appears on its own. This is just the way life is organised.

The workforce

This is a useful place to pause and take stock. In a business' Second Era, the workforce is seen primarily as a cost, to be minimized where possible by restricting wages, holidays and benefits, and by keeping the workers at their workplace by a host of managerial devices such as clocking-in systems, statutory toilet breaks, piece-work pay systems and time-and-motion studies. Without trade unions, most businesses would never have advanced out of the First Era – and in the Second Era, trade unions are needed to protect workers' rights and ensure that they get proper recompense for their labours.

Businesses' evolution into the Third Era, with the attendant benefits of higher productivity, increased profits and salaries, greater employee creativity and commitment, reduced absenteeism and higher quality achievements, requires the full evolution of the whole organism. If the commitments to increased worker-ownership, democratic involvement, shareholding and profit-sharing (for instance) are excluded, attempts to raise productivity levels by such things as 'flow-state management' will be perceived quite rightly as another gimmick out of the managers' Second Era bag of tricks. At the end of the day, the directors and shareholders will be the beneficiaries, not the people providing the sweat and toil (however creative it might be). Progressive managerial techniques can easily be used to foster selfish, Second Era goals. The progression into Third Era business methods must be seen as a whole. *It is the commitment to the core values of economic,*

After the crash

human, social, ecological and planetary wholeness which
creates the foundation for a holistic business.

In Britain and America, trade unions have tied themselves closely to the Second Era struggle between managers
and workers, and are in danger of failing to perceive what
is happening. In the USA, union membership is down to
17% of the workforce, and in Britain membership is falling year by year, for a variety of reasons. If the main
preoccupation of members and their leaders continues to
be wages and conditions, the decline will continue. Unions
need to adopt a new agenda to reflect the changing values
and concerns of their workforces, and to bring pressure on
their companies to move in an evolutionary direction.

This agenda needs to include matters such as worker-
ownership, shareholding and profit-sharing, productivity
bonuses, participative self-management processes, board-
level representation, flexible work patterns and worksharing options (see Chapter Five). It needs to cover holistic
policies towards redundancy and lay-offs, non-dis-
criminatory hiring practices, positive measures to ensure
the promotion of women and minority group employees,
personal health and stress programmes, the ending of
separate management canteens, parking places and toilets,
the ending of restrictive quotas, practices and demarca-
tions, the formation of one-company unions, commitments to ecologically sound practice, and so on.

Women may provide the breakthrough energy that is
needed to achieve these goals. The entry of women into the
mainstream job market has been one of the significant
social developments of the 1980s, but their needs and
potentials have been ignored as much by their unions as by
their employers. The Consumers United Group, a
Washington DC worker-owned insurance company (1985
sales, $45 million, 165 employees), has developed a com-
prehensive program for women's personal growth, covering finances, health, social supports, careers and legal
issues. Wang Laboratories, the USA's second largest makers of office automation systems, provides free day-care at

its main office, and is an aggressive equal opportunities employer. The provincial government of Ontario, Canada, has introduced equal pay legislation, with appropriate adjustments to be phased in over several years. Maternity leave, flexibility in working schedules, job-sharing, work-sharing and day-care all need to be pushed on to company and trade union agendas. A study at Texas Women's University showed that a $50,000 investment in a day-care program can save some $3 million in employee turnover, training and lost work time.[19] Ragged Robin, a women's clothing co-operative in central Wales, was set up with day-care facilities included in an integrated way from the start.

Women will play a key role in holistic businesses because for cultural and historical reasons they are on the whole less dogmatic, less ego-bound, less committed to macho-management styles and more concerned with the quality of relationships between people.

Organizational structures

The themes which matter here include decentralization, small autonomous teams, a strong organizational core that protects and spreads the company's vision and values, organic networking structures in place of hierarchical top-down ones, the maximization of communication and sharing across departments and the establishment of cross-disciplinary teams. 'Jan Carlzon of SAS erased the corporate pyramid and redrew his concept of the new organizational structure as a wagon wheel, with the Chief Executive Officer (CEO) at the hub and operating departments revolving around him'.[20] At the Kollmorgen Corporation in Connecticut, USA (makers of electronic and optical equipment with 5,400 employees), Bob Swiggett persuaded his top managers to throw out all their structures, regulations, time-clocks and policy manuals and to replace them with a new system based on trust and autonomous profit centres. Each centre has fewer than 500 employees, with its own president and peer-elected board of directors.

Bonuses are paid to each centre according to its return on net investment. Kollmorgen's sales have increased by nearly 500% since the old rules were thrown out in 1973. They call their new system a 'biological' form of organization.

In Britain, in the Staffordshire Potteries, the Coloroll Group is pioneering an employee participation programme framed around monthly small group team briefings for every member of staff, a formal report-back system, an ideas programme, save-as-you-earn share options schemes and profit-related bonuses. John Bailey, representative of the Ceramics and Allied Trades Union at Staff Potts, one of the group's companies, has seen management evolve over 16 years through three distinct phases, from 'iron rod' management, to the company's first experiments in participation, and to the arrival of the full Coloroll scheme. He finds that the new system allows people on the shop floor to get to know their managers as individuals, so that smaller problems are solved simply by talking about them, rather than through a mire of procedures. Team spirit and partnership are encouraged throughout the company.[21]

By sharing the ownership fully, worker co-operatives eliminate the inequalities of power and position which plague so many companies, making authentic participation difficult. When organizational problems arose at Neal's Yard Bakery Co-operative in London (30 full-time workers, £0.5 million turnover) due to their increasing size and success, the members were able to discuss things fully among themselves at their weekly meetings, before deciding to introduce new trainings in management and commercial skills. As part of their training, five workers went to visit other co-ops in France and Italy to learn and compare notes.[22]

Local business support networks

Chapter Seven described how local business support networks or 'ecosystems' are gradually emerging, as businesses find new ways to support each other (e.g. Briarpatch, Common Box), and as communities develop new ways to assist companies. This achieves its fullest expression at Mondragon, in Spain, with correspondingly remarkable results. As businesses move out of the relative isolation of the First and Second Eras, they become more integral parts of the whole community economy, both giving and receiving in new ways.

The product

All this is fine – but what if the product itself is not very holistic? There is no such thing as a holistic nuclear missile or a holistic uranium mine. In the south-eastern area of Britain (including London), 600,000 people draw their incomes from defence and defence-related industries.

Once the willingness is present, the answers can come from within, with help from the wider community. The Lucas Aerospace initiative showed that there is no shortage of new product ideas among a company's employees, once they are invited to put their ideas on paper. Once it is given priority, a systematic strategy of conversion and diversification can be undertaken. Japanese steel companies managed to move out of steel with no loss of workers, when Korean steelmills started undercutting their minimum cost-levels. The emerging business support network has a large role to play in assisting companies with this process of conversion (see Chapter 7).

THE BENEFICIARIES OF PRODUCTION

As business develops in a holistic direction, the stakeholders become the beneficiaries. The first beneficiaries are the *customers*, who gain from a higher quality product, and a higher quality of personal service :

> *'Quality is a statement of who I am. It is part of a value system that you try to carry throughout every aspect of your life. Whatever I put out there I have to feel really*

> *good about. Every time I make something I try to make it a little bit differently, as a challenge. Quality is something I learn about also from other people's feedback. Quality is a mirror. You can't presume that you have achieved quality unless you can hear other people's reactions. All marketing situations are sort of a showdown, in that respect.'*
>
> Teri Joe Wheeler, custom fibre designer[23]

Person-to-person customer relations are one thing. When it comes to country-to-country customer relations, however, many Third World countries come off very badly indeed. Multinational corporations have a controlling influence in many sectors of Third World economies. '80% to 90% of the trade in tea, coffee, cocoa, cotton, forest products, tobacco, jute, copper, iron ore and bauxite is controlled in the case of each commodity by the three to six largest transnational corporations (in that industrial area).'[24] A transnational corporation becomes a dominant concern wherever it chooses to operate. Planetary values are crucial to our future, and businesses which conduct international trade must develop and abide by codes of conduct which honour the needs and values of the people and the environment in the countries they trade with. This brief comment serves only to open the door on a huge area where the most profound change is desperately needed.

The second beneficiaries are the *directors,* who gain from the knowledge that the business is prospering and achieving a new holistic vision in their hands, serving values which address crucial planetary concerns. One of the functions of the Business Network, in London, (see Chapter 7) is to open up a dialogue with people at senior levels of industry and commerce, giving encouragement to those who are cautiously seeking ways to express more spiritual and holistic values in their work.

The third beneficiaries are the *providers of capital*: the shareholders and investors. The evolution of banking, finance and investment institutions (see Chapter Nine) will hopefully mean that major shareholders will no longer be able to get rich so easily by playing Monopoly with other people's livelihoods. With the spread of share ownership to company employees, and with the legal widening of the definition of 'stakeholders', financial institutions may in future be less able to encourage impersonal investment in companies purely on the basis of likely profits. In the Third Era, the stakeholders are partners in a business, and the providers of capital are just one stakeholder among seven, all of whom require satisfaction.

Next come the *employees* themselves, who in addition to the incomes that their labours earn them, gain financially through profit-sharing schemes, productivity bonuses or the growth of personal capital stakes. They also gain the personal satisfaction, challenge and growth offered by working in a holistic context. They no longer need to separate 'work' from their search for fulfilment and wholeness. When pay differentials reach 1 : 100, the workforce is hardly encouraged to feel part of a team of equals. In Mondragon, differentials of only 1 : 3 are permitted without any loss of trading success. Many other co-operatives either adopt similarly low differentials, or have pay equality for all.

The fifth beneficiaries are *businesses* which have close trading relationships with the company, either as customers or as suppliers. Their security is tied up with the security of the host company, and they gain both from the increased stability of a holistic business and from the increased quality of its products. In order that this becomes true in developing countries where businesses trade, holistic codes of conduct need to be drawn up, setting down desired standards of trading conduct internationally, so that company conduct can be monitored both by management and by outside groups.

ENVIRONMENTAL EXCELLENCE

The sixth beneficiary is the *environment*, both locally and globally. This requires some examination, as it is partly through changes in company practice that the global environmental crisis will be overcome.

When environmental policies are seen by companies as just another costly 'add-on', the policies are vulnerable to attack from company accountants and pressure to show good quarterly returns. The 'add-on' approach to environmental policy (better waste disposal, purchasing smokestack filters, etc.) is a Second Era response to an unwanted reality. For the Third Era, company structures and policies need to evolve so that negative environmental impact is eliminated or minimized at source.

This involves companies in a radical rethink of their environmental policies. There are seven very sound business reasons why companies should pursue environmental excellence (in addition to the obvious environmental reasons):

1. As public sensitivity to environmental issues grows, consumers are increasingly demanding to know that the products they purchase are environmentally clean, and will steer away from companies with a dirty image.
2. The market for environmentally sensitive technologies will continue to grow, and companies which pioneer environmentally clean processes and technologies will gain good business worldwide and gain a good reputation.
3. The pressure for change worldwide guarantees that future legislation both at home and in Third World countries will be much tighter than it is today, setting new standards that companies will be contractually obliged to meet. Products which take 10 years to research and develop will have to meet legislative standards which have not yet been enacted.
4. Reducing our use of fossil-fuels on the planet is a critical environmental need. By introducing demand management and energy-efficiency strategies, companies can save money and lower their operating costs.
5. Local environmental regulations are increasingly

demanding that the cost of site clean-up be incorporated into the sale-price of redundant sites, demanding that toxic waste be cleaned up before the capital assets tied up in the site can be realised.

6. The cost of lawsuits for damages from environmental disasters and mishaps will continue to grow (witness Bhopal) – as will the cost of insurance.

7. As the social investment movement gathers steam, the proportion of capital on the market which is screened for social and environmental considerations is increasing, and it will gradually become necessary for companies to meet the screening conditions before the capital they require is released.

The public first sat up and took note of environmental issues in 1962, when Rachel Carson's book 'Silent Spring' was published. Industry is now beginning to get the message, if not for idealistic reasons, then for commercial ones:

> *'The needs of future generations must rank equally with those now on Earth. Yet the unborn do not vote, invest or demonstrate. Someone must speak for them.'*
> Bruce Smart, Chairman, Continental Group

> *'The exponential growth argument has gone out of the window. All the trends point towards smaller, more efficient plants. Our most important task is to get more and more out of less and less. That is the industrialist's mission. And we are getting pretty good at it. That's not because we are boy scouts. It's for bloody good business reasons.'*
> Sir John Harvey-Jones, ex-Chairman ICI[25]

The development of technologies such as the superchip, the biochip, solar photo-voltaic cells, 'smart' energy-control devices, extremely high-efficiency refrigerators, stoves, engines and motors, superconductivity, ceramics, new materials, fibre optics, and biotechnologies and microbial pesticides move us towards greater possibilities for sustainable development. Most of the new 'technologies for sustainability' exist; what we lack is a strategy to guarantee that we start using them. Under pressure from Swiss environmentalists and legislators to produce an outboard motor oil which would not pollute lakes and waterways, Castrol's researchers came up with an oil formulation called Biolube 100. This cuts oil emissions by 65%, has enhanced biodegradability, and now outsells other comparable oils.

Rolls-Royce have spent large sums of money on research that seeks to improve the pollution performance of its engines ahead of existing legislation. Their new 535 series engines are up to 40% more fuel-efficient than the previous generation of engines, and emit between 10% and 20% of the carbon monoxide, smoke and unburned hydrocarbons emitted by jet engines of the 1960s. Weight reduction stemming from the use of new materials plays a large part, as do intelligent electronic control systems. In a world where commercial pressure for cheaper flights and consumer pressure for quieter flights and less pollution is increasing all the time, the investment in research is paying off handsomely: Rolls-Royce looks set to capture a good share of what could be a £15 billion market by the year 2000.[26]

The Body Shop (mentioned above) exemplifies the possibility of building a business on environmental principles from the very beginning. The world of cosmetics is a huge producer and consumer of chemicals, animal experimentation and packaging. The Body Shop built its success from the beginning on simplicity, natural products, minimal packaging, and breaking all the rules of the cosmetics industry. Anita Roddick goes out of her way to seek out natural products that have been used for millennia by traditional peoples in countries such as Lapland, China and India, to ensure that the ingredients for new products can be grown in the Third World, and to avoid any animal-testing. They always use recycled paper, and in conjunction with ICI, Britain's largest chemical company, they are developing a biodegradable sugar-based plastic for their bottles and containers.[27]

Good environmental practice meets consumers' needs – and this has always been the best formula for business success. The rhetoric and the realities are both encouraging, but as an industrial culture we have hardly dipped a toe into the water of sustainable development. Unless companies adopt rigorously holistic energy policies, for example, every additional percentage point of economic growth will heat up the global atmosphere by an equivalent microdegree of temperature, bringing mega-disaster on our heads in less than thirty years (see Chapter Ten). The U.N. World Commission on Environment and Development (the Brundtland Report) has emphasized the problem:

To bring developing countries' energy use up to industrialized country levels by the year 2025 would require increasing present global energy use by a factor of five. . . Threats of global warming and acidification of the environment most probably rule out even a doubling of energy use based on present mixes of primary sources.[28]

In his excellent book 'The Green Capitalists', John Elkington describes some of the ways in which companies are seeking to evolve to meet the Earth's environmental needs. He draws up 'Ten Steps to Environmental Excellence' which will enable a company to develop top-rate environmental policies.[29] These are:

1. Develop and publish an environmental policy.
2. Prepare an action programme.
3. Build environmental responsibility into organizational and staffing procedures.
4. Allocate adequate resources.
5. Invest in environmental science and technology.

6. Educate and train your staff.
7. Monitor, audit and report.
8. Monitor the evolution of the green agenda.
9. Contribute to environmental programmes.
10. Help build bridges between the various interests.

COMMUNITY PARTICIPATION

The final stakeholder and beneficiary is the local community.

Communities have often welcomed local businesses and branches of multi-nationals, thanking them for the jobs they provide, but hating them for the frustration and powerlessness they sometimes engender. Workers being suddenly fired after many years' loyal service, legitimate demands for pay increases being refused, company branches being closed down without the possibility of a worker buy-out being raised, toxic wastes being dumped in areas where children play and where the wastes filter through to the underground water-table, companies that milk a community of its resources while putting next to nothing back in – the history of business is full of incidents that distress and frustrate local people.

The final step in the evolution of business into a holistic form is the cultivation of a positive, participative relationship with the community which is its host. Over the last ten years, some British companies have been experimenting with community participation. Mass unemployment, inner city rioting and the burning of banks and teenage despair and suicide made many company directors ask whether they could do something positive to help.

Out of this questioning has come BiC (Business in the Community), an organisation which encourages companies to focus their potential for goodwill in practical, results-oriented ways (see also Chapter Seven). Simply giving donations to help the local art gallery or ballet is not enough. Growing numbers of companies want to be involved in the regeneration of inner city communities, the creation of new jobs and the uplifting of the local economy. Companies like Pilkington, BP, Levi Strauss and a host of others have been realising that 'What's good for the community is good for business'. They have been getting involved in local economic recovery partnerships, seconding or assigning fully-paid staff to run enterprise agencies, helping set up Youth Enterprise Centres, supporting local environmental and 'Greening the City' projects, helping ethnic business development initiatives, and generally using the skills they possess to contribute to community life.[30]

A similar process is occurring in the USA. In Boston, USA, in 1982, 200 local businesses got together and struck a deal with the Boston Public School System known as the Boston Compact. The deal stated that if the schools would cut drop-out rates and guarantee minimum competency in reading and maths, the companies would guarantee employment to every graduate school-leaver by 1986. With only a third of high school students being able to a read to a standard comparable for their age, more youngsters dropping out of school than actually graduating and school-leaver unemployment running at 25%, Boston had a problem. The employers backing the Compact set up working groups to pursue reforms in 11 areas, including counselling, athletics and remedial teaching, and staff from businesses became involved as volunteer tutors and careers advisors. By 1986 the Compact had met its target, and had gone on to conclude agreements with the local universities and construction unions.[31] A similar compact has been concluded in London, promising jobs to school-leavers in the Docklands area, and other compacts are being planned.

High-minded talk and actual practice can often be two different things. Sir Peter Parker, Chairman of Mitsubishi UK and of the Rockware Group, has this to say on the development of social policy:

'*Managers are beginning to look at their organisations*

> *and ask questions: 'Have we got an established social policy, flexible, unembarrassed and inequivocal? Has the Board succeeded in getting this philosophy down the line, so that the individual manager knows that if he acts like a human being he will not only not lose marks, but actually gain them? Has it got an employment, educational and training aspect that is adapting to the new, imaginative patterns that are about to burst through? And in particular, have we got a community programme?'*[32]

The community-business interface is still a new one, which will yield many surprises yet.

MAKING THE TRANSITION

This chapter has shown how a growing number of businesses are evolving in a holistic direction. How can this evolution be encouraged? In the following five ways:

Educating and campaigning brings issues to public attention, and encourages companies to develop in innovative and socially responsible ways. Local groups can publish annual surveys of local companies, choosing the 'Ten Best' and 'Ten Worst' and awarding appropriate prizes.

A strong *'conscious consumer' movement* creates market pressures in favour of holistically-produced products and opposed to environmentally harmful and socially unsound products. To help them develop holistic shopping habits, consumers need to have regular reports giving environmental impact and holistic production ratings in Britain, the new 'Green Pages' books have started to meet this need, and it is hoped that Britain's 'Which?' magazine for consumers will follow suit.[33]

The third way is that of *company development*. Companies can consciously choose to develop holistic transition strategies, using future scenarios, future workshops (see Chapter Six), working groups, and surveys and questionnaires, creating the participative impulse which will release the creativity needed to achieve the transition.

Regulatory and legislative pressures can also be brought to bear upon companies. There is ample scope for the use of the creative imagination – local companies might be required to publish an annual social and environmental audit, for instance, in return for being given planning permission.

The transformation of business is an integral part of the overall rainbow economy development strategy, and the fifth path is the development of an *integrated transformation strategy*, drawing concerned people together into a partnership, and working out a strategy to encourage development. *We cannot afford to wait and hope that businesses will evolve in their own time.* Concerned people within business must meet together locally, and start discussing how they could assist each other. The Briarpatch/ Commonbox/Business Network models provide a good beginning, spreading awareness of holistic practices, permitting new initiatives, and drawing people together in an evolutionary context, building new friendships and alliances. In Sweden, 55 people have been trained in the Briarpatch approach to business, each of whom is now training other business people in the same approach.[34] Once the will to evolve is there, the rest is a practical problem-solving exercise.

In a holistic, sustainable context, productivity and profit-making are compatible with a sane, humane and ecologically sustainable future, as are technological development and economic growth.

In a *non*-holistic context, when these activities are allowed to overrule our deeper personal, local and planetary needs, the result is personal, local and planetary crisis. When pursued alongside human, social, ecological and planetary values, in a holistic context, the doors of a very different future open before us.

Chapter Nine :
New finance for a new world

Many people find the world of finance, money and capital bewildering and confusing. International takeovers, mega-deals and commodity speculation seem far from the sanity Earth needs to ensure a sustainable existence. This chapter considers some of the new initiatives in banking and finance which may show the way to a more enduring future, and then asks what steps are needed in order to incorporate them into a rainbow economy development strategy.

Historically, the division between rich and poor has occurred because ever since the tradition of private land ownership began, the ownership of land, property and capital has been restricted to a minority of the people in a society. In spite of recent moves in the direction of greater personal share-ownership, most people are still excluded from capital ownership of the businesses they work in, and many also from ownership of their homes. Throughout the world, poverty is closely related to non-ownership.

When people have a personal capital stake in the homes they live in, the businesses they work in and the communities they inhabit, they experience a much greater sense of personal involvement, commitment and responsibility in these areas. They also directly share in the increase of capital value which follows from the community's collective economic progress.

Conversely, when people are forced to rent their labour and their homes, they often experience a low sense of commitment and involvement. The collective increase in capital value passes them by and they often find themselves trapped in poverty. Whole communities can be excluded in this way from the general increase in prosperity which economic progress creates.

For a community economy to reflect the true hopes, values and skills of its people, there must be a high degree of personal and community ownership within that community. Only when people know that 'this is ours' do they devote their full energy to the care and development of their habitat, its economy and its future.[1]

Our present systems of banking and finance follow traditional economic values, in keeping with the value-preference of the industrial age as a whole. The decisive questions normally asked of an investment are 'Is it a sound investment?' and 'Will it bring in enough profit?'. Questions relating to other values are not considered relevant. They fall outside the instructions the company takes from its shareholders, which are simply to make money.

Many problems stem from this predominance of economic over other values. These include:

- the lending of money to financially profitable but environmentally harmful projects;
- the pre-occupation of money managers and company directors with short-term gains and quarterly returns, at the expense of longer-term considerations;
- the separation of company shareholders from the activities of their companies;
- the unwillingness of banks and lending institutions to advance loans that are not backed by tangible collateral in the form of the borrower's house or other property, making it very hard for non-owners to break out of the cycle of poverty;
- the ensuing dependency of people living on low incomes on money-lenders who charge exorbitant rates of interest;
- the net flow of capital resources out of poor areas

171

through the banks and savings institutions, which collect the savings of local people, but do not re-invest them in local development;

• the subsequent poverty and dependency of many people who live in public housing estates, and the growth of ghettos of poverty in inner city areas, outer city fringe estates and many rural areas;

• the reluctance of banks and lending institutions to lend to business propositions that are unusual or unorthodox, such as community-owned businesses or worker co-operatives, compounding the difficulty people have in trying to escape from poverty;

• the dominance of town and city developments by development companies whose idea of development is often only that which will make them money, and who receive backing from the banks precisely for this reason;

• the lending out of multi-billion pound and dollar pension and insurance funds on the same 'money-first' principles, while the very cities and towns where the depositors live often decline for lack of investment;

• the creation of the insoluble world debt crisis, and the poverty, famine and hardship which result from it;

• the global ecological crisis, as strictly 'economic' investments contribute to soil erosion, rainforest devastation, acid rain and many other bad ecological practices, through the desire by bankers and investors to realise quick financial return without regard to the wider social and environmental costs;

• the feeling which many people share that they are estranged from their economies, both locally and globally, and that the world economy is completely 'out of control';

• the vulnerability of the global economy when so much of the world's monetary resources are tied up in the pursuit of paper gains, commodity and currency speculation, take-over bids and in military-industrial and environmentally destructive investments, when the need for investment capital to finance long-term projects of a sustainable economic and ecological nature is so pressing.

172

Foreign exchange markets turn over about $150 billion
daily,[2] not one penny of which finances anything real.
While the banks and lending houses turn from one disaster
area to another (Third World lending, US farm loans,
energy-related loans), the poverty of millions in industrial
countries increases, the decline of large urban areas continues, and globally the gulf between rich and poor
becomes ever wider. To cover their risks, the banks simply
raise their interest rates, increasing the very risk they are
trying to protect themselves from by adding to the burden
of repayment.[3]

The British writer, James Robertson, has spoken
eloquently of the comparison between the role of the religion at the end of the Middle Ages and the role of money at
the end of the industrial age:

> '*The local church was the most prominent building in
> almost every village; today the prime sites in almost
> every high street are occupied by branches of banks,
> building societies and other financial concerns. The
> centres of medieval cities were dominated by cathedrals;
> centres of today's cities are dominated by the tower
> blocks of international banks. Today's army of accoun-
> tants, bankers, tax-people, insurance brokers, stock job-
> bers, foreign exchange dealers and countless other
> specialists in money procedures and practices is the
> modern counter-part of the medieval army of priests,
> friars, monks, pardoners, summoners and other
> specialists in religious procedures and practices. The
> theologians of the late Middle Ages have their counter-
> part in the economists of the late industrial age. It is
> funny, but true. Financial mysteries hold us in thrall
> today as religious mysteries held our medieval ances-
> tors.*'[4]

The vast power of the medieval church met its match in
Martin Luther and the protestant reformers who followed,

who exposed its contradictions and trod a new – still religious – path. The monasteries were dissolved. Scientists, engineers and rational thinkers brought a new impulse and a new set of values into society, clearing the way for the complete transformation of the material, individual and social world.

Since the mid 1960s, new understandings, perceptions and values, and new Copernicuses, have once again been arising in the Western world, as the shortcomings of the industrial age have in turn become apparent. By the mid-1970s some of the new global thinkers were turning their attention (among other things) to the pioneering of new forms of banking and investment, asking themselves 'Can the power of money be used to build a more humane world, embracing more loving and more ecological values?'.

Some of the questions they have been asking are:

• Can new banking and finance institutions be set up which will live by new values, by-passing dependency on the banks? ('Creating new banking and financial institutions.')

• Can the vast resources of people's personal savings, of pension, insurance and investment funds and of banking deposits be channelled in a new direction, away from activities that increasing numbers of depositors no longer identify with, and towards constructive activities that contribute to the building of a better world? ('Socially responsible investment.')

• Can local banks become responsive to the needs of people in the communities they serve, and not just monetary vacuum cleaners which suck money out of local communities and invest it elsewhere for the benefit of the banks' shareholders? ('Local community banking')

• Can the traditional definitions of 'collateral' be changed so that people who are otherwise permanently excluded from capital ownership can acquire loans? ('Social collateral.')

Although there is still a long to go, the answer to these questions, remarkably, is a clear 'yes'. The fundamental rethinking has been done. The task now is to spread the new practices as far and as fast as possible.

CREATING NEW BANKING AND FINANCIAL INSTITUTIONS

Credit unions

Wherever unemployment and poverty lurk, moneylenders are never far away, like vultures over a corpse. Credit card companies asking 30% interest have nothing on this breed. One company trading on housing estates in Birmingham (England) charges 1163% p.a. to local housewives, many of whom survive on welfare. In Calcutta, some rickshaw owners will agree to defer the daily rent the rickshaw wallahs owe them, if they fall sick, at a mere 25% per day – or 9125% p.a.[5]

One solution to economic vulturage of this kind is to form a credit union (CU). In Britain and the USA, a credit union is an association of people who share a common social bond which creates a degree of trust sufficient to serve as a guarantee for a loan. They may be members of a church, a local community, a place of employment or a set of values. Members save in a collective account, and lend their accumulated capital out to each other for consumer (not business) purchases. In Canada the laws are much looser, almost anyone can become a member of a CU, and loans are given for business as well as consumer loans.

The union is a non-profit institution owned by its members, serving its members' needs, so interest rates are low. In Britain, CUs charge 12% interest, or 1% per month – one of the best kept secrets in the financial world.

In Ireland, 460 credit unions serve 800,000 people, fully 20% of the population. In New Zealand, credit unions are growing very fast: in 1987, 180,000 people had savings of

$125 million, a total that is increasing at 15.5% p.a., or doubling every five years. Worldwide, there are 200,000 credit unions. Britain has only 83 CUs, with 25,000 members and £5.8 million in assets. London's taxi drivers have a CU with £1.5 million in assets, but so far, credit unions in Britain are still an undeveloped force.

The town of Greenock on Clydeside (Scotland) was hit very hard by the closure of the Clyde shipyards. The last local bank closed down 20 years ago. In the Strone/Maukinhill area the local church has been active in building the Greenock East Credit Union. Starting with 11 founder members in July 1984, by February 1988 they had 1,000 members out of a total population of 50,000, and had lent out £140,000. It is run by a board of 15 local people, mostly female and unemployed, who collect savings and distribute loans from collection points in halls around the town.[6] Credit unions are being seen as increasingly important. In Birmingham, the council has set up Britain's first Credit Union Development Agency to encourage the formation of new CUs, which led to the formation of 14 new CUs in low-income areas of Birmingham within the agency's first 18 months of operation.[7] The laws in Britain are very restrictive. Membership is limited to 5,000 people, savings to £2,000 per member and loans to £2000 above a member's savings – these laws are in urgent need of revision (see below).

No such restrictions apply in Canada, where CUs are often as big as the banks, occupying buildings just as large. With a few exceptions, they are also as conservative as the banks, and while they are democratically controlled by their members, for the most part members have not yet used the opportunity to pioneer innovative policies. VanCity Credit Union in Vancouver, one of Canada's largest CUs, with 165,000 members and $1.6 billion assets in 1987, has been among the first to end the tradition of conservatism. In 1983, David Levy and some other members noticed that VanCity was getting into real estate speculation and investments outside British Columbia, and over the next three years they swept the vacant board seats at elections and began to steer VanCity in a new direction.[7] They put the emphasis back onto small business loans (lending \$23 million in 1985), and launched a half million dollar seed capital fund for young entrepreneurs and community economic initiatives. VanCity is redefining what is meant by 'collateral':

> *'We are saying that experience and education count as equity, so they don't have to come in and have \$50,000. They have to have a good idea, a good plan, and show us how they intend to draw on the strength of the community to move an enterprise forward.'*
> Joy Leach, Director, VanCity Credit Union[8]

At the same time, VanCity launched a \$3 million Ethical Growth Fund, to be invested in Canadian companies which
(a) practice progressive industrial relations;
(b) avoid business with countries that promote racial hatred or bias;
(c) are not engaged in military business; and
(d) companies whose major sources of revenue are from non-nuclear forms of energy.

> *'It's a matter of putting your money where your mouth is. Many people frequently have high principles on these matters, but will invest or allow their money to be invested in the most outrageous ways. I think it's because they are disconnected from their wealth and don't recognize that everything they care about can be subverted if they do not pay attention to what they do with their money. It's as silly as watching your local community go down on its knees economically, but running into Vancouver to spend.'*
> Joy Leach

British Columbia has \$6 billion dollars on deposit with credit unions – a figure large enough to allow the province to become a real pioneer in the field of sustainable community economic banking, if local CU members woke up to the possibilities and started using their democratic rights to bring in new community-based lending policies.[9]

Community Development Loan Funds

A second approach to the problem of getting capital resources into poor communities is to set up a Community Development Loan Fund (CDLF), a nonprofit organization which can receive loans from individuals, religious organizations and other investors. The CDLF then lends these funds to community organizations that develop housing, employment opportunities and other resources and services for low-income, unemployed and other economically-disenfranchised people.

In New Zealand, the Co-operative Enterprise Loan Trust (CELT) was set up in 1980 to provide finance for new workers' co-operatives and community enterprises. Its members are organised into regional committees and play a large part in decision-making about loans, which allows them to be responsive to local needs. Deposits are secured by guarantee, interest paid slightly under the market rate, and depositors can participate personally in deciding which ventures will get loans from their deposits. CELT also gives business start-up advice and assistance with business planning, management and marketing, organises trainings, keeps co-operative groups in touch with each other and promotes the development of the co-operative idea in New Zealand.[10]

In England, the Industrial Co-operative Ownership Finance (ICOF), launched in 1973, lent one million pounds to 110 co-ops in the following 14 years. In 1987 it increased its loan capital by £500,000 by issuing Co-operative Shares earning 6% interest, repayable after 10 years. In Germany, the Oekobank' (Eco-bank) was launched in 1987, with starting capital of 6.8 million Deutschmarks (£2.3 million) raised from 13,000 trustees among the environmental, peace and women's movements. Low-interest loans will be given to finance small owner-operated companies and co-operatives.

Community Development Loan Funds have come furthest in the USA, with nine new funds being set up in 1986 alone. In January 1987 28 CDLFs were jointly managing $31.4 million, consisting of $25.8 million in loans from 1,400 members and $5.5 million in permanent loan capital. Among the 1,100 loans given out by the CDLFs are (for instance):

- a $43,000 loan to a newly formed co-operative of 13 low-income families who were about to be evicted from their mobile home park in New Hampshire, to enable them to buy the park;
- a $50,000 loan to Co-operative Home Care Associates, a home health care co-operative in the Bronx area of New York.

The Institute for Community Economics has been leading the CDLF movement since the 1970s. In 1985 they organized a major conference which led to the formation of the National Association of Community Development Loan Funds:

'The NACDLF and its members are committed to dispelling the myths of poverty that contribute to the credit starvation of low-income people. In many instances, the problems of the poor are a result, not so much of a lack of resources or capabilities, but of patterns of ownership – of land, housing, employment and financial institutions – that drain resources out of lower-income communities. They are denied the credit needed to purchase homes, find security, build equity, and leave a legacy for their children ...

... CDLFs have already changed the minds of many early sceptics – those who said that while the social needs were indeed great, community investment was not financially possible. The funds are setting an exam-

ple of creative capital management and providing a veh-
icle through which growing numbers of investors can
strike at the roots of poverty and express an affirmative
vision of economic democracy.'

Greg Ramm, Co-ordinator, NACDLF[11]

SOCIALLY RESPONSIBLE INVESTMENT

One of the most encouraging signs of the spread of
holistic and planetary values is the extraordinary
growth of the social investment movement in the 1980s.

In the USA, a host of new investment funds have been
meeting the needs of the steadily increasing number of
Americans who want to put their money where their
ideals are. The idealism of the 1960s is being translated
into the hard-headed social change of the 1980s. Dis-
contented with companies which pollute the environment, trade with South Africa, grow rich on the arms
race or exploit their workers, they have set in motion a
new social movement that is concerned with 'socially
responsible investment' (SRI).

The Calvert Social Investment Fund, launched in
1982, is one of these fast-growing money funds. It seeks
out companies which:

• deliver safe products and services in ways that sustain the natural environment;

• are managed with participation throughout the
organization in defining and achieving objectives;

• negotiate fairly with workers, create an environment supportive of their wellbeing, and provide options
for women, disadvantaged minorities, and others to
whom equal opportunities have been denied;

• foster awareness of a commitment to human goals
such as creativity, productivity, self-respect and responsibility;

and avoids companies which:

• engage in business with repressive regimes such as
South Africa;

- manufacture weapons systems, or
- are involved in the production of nuclear energy.

During 1985, their funds grew from $16 million to $36 million, and yielded a return of 26.97%.[12]

Working Assets, another fund, was launched in September 1983 with one million dollars' capital, and by June 1985 had over 10,000 shareholders with assets over $84 million. There are plans to launch a $20 – $30 million venture capital fund, to permit equity investments in socially oriented enterprises.

The total amount of funds that are being screened for social considerations of one kind or another is growing at an impressive rate:

> 1984 : $40 billion
> 1985 : $100 billion
> 1986 : $300 billion
> 1987 : $400 billion[13]

In 1985, while assets for equity funds grew by 40.06%, assets of the typical ethical fund increased by 87.6%. Furthermore, there is no trade-off with ordinary investments when it comes to financial returns. In 1985, nine ethical mutual funds tracked by Lipper Analytical provided yields ranging from 18.6% to 31.41%, averaging 25.24%, against an average mutual fund yield of 24.95%. The four funds with a 10-year track record all outperformed the Dow Jones Industrial Average.[14] The US magazine, 'Good Money', has designed a stock average for 30 socially responsible companies, which is compared to the Dow Jones Industrials. From 1976 – 1986, Good Money's 30-stock average was up 396% in capital gains alone, while the Dow Jones average was up only 89% for the same decade.[15]

'The fact that we can keep our investors' returns on par with those of more conventional managers has helped validate the field of socially responsible investment

> *much more quickly than I could ever have imagined.'*
> Joan Bavaria, President,
> Franklin Research and Development Corporation[16]

> *'I discovered after a while, to my delight and surprise, that <u>clean</u> investment in conventional securities and <u>alternative</u> investing in socially positive activities could be conducted with very superior financial results.'*
> Robert B. Zevin, Economist and Vice-President,
> United States Trust Company[17]

That socially responsible investments show a greater rate of financial return than non-screened investments will not be a surprise to anyone who is familiar with the kind of business development outlined in Chapter Eight. When businesses move towards greater environmental responsibility and greater employee ownership and participation, they bring increased productivity and increased profits. The success of the co-operatives at Mondragon is further evidence of this trend.

The movement has been slower to take off in Britain, but gathered steam in 1987 with the launch of six new funds. Friends Provident's Stewardship Unit Trust leads the field with assets of £75.4 million, showing a return of 23% against a market sector average of 11%. The Ethical Investment Fund and the Merlin Ecology Fund provide further opportunities for investors to back well-researched socially responsible opportunities. Fund-managers for the new ethical funds are able to obtain advice from the Ethical Investment Research and Information Centre (EIRIS). The Ecology Building Society channels money into ecologically sustainable initiatives. It is now possible for individuals in Britain to invest ethically for all their major needs such as pensions, endowment mortgages, life assurance and savings plans. The Financial Initiative offers a personal advisory service covering all of these areas.[18]

PENSION and INSURANCE FUNDS

The collective wealth which ordinary citizens and working people own through their various pension and insurance funds is truly massive. In 1987, UK pension funds totalled £192 billion. In California, many counties or cities have over $100 million in public pension funds. This money is invested by money managers who follow what is known as 'fiduciary responsibility', which obliges them by law to obtain the maximum financial return on investments, *regardless of other considerations.*

Clearly, these resources would make a tremendous difference if they were invested in ways which contributed to the growth of sound and sustainable economies based on human, social and ecological values.

The critical question here concerns the predominance of economic values over other values, which has characterized the industrial age. Pension fund and charity trustees have followed this rule, investing wherever they could obtain the highest financial return, irrelevant of social or environmental costs. This insistence on the pursuit of monetary gain regardless of costs represents the supreme item of faith of the materialist set of values.

It has always been accepted by the courts that the interests of fund beneficiaries can go beyond investment returns, however; the trustees of a temperance charity are not expected to invest in breweries, however profitable they may be. As many socially responsible funds bring in consistently better financial returns than unscreened funds (see above), fund managers can no longer claim that pursuing socially responsible policies will put them in breach of fiduciary trust. This opens the door for a major transformation of the whole pension fund scene.[19]

As the rainbow economy of the post-industrial age emerges, social and environmental responsibility will sit alongside financial responsibility as the principles which guide investment, and the old habit of 'either-or' thinking which is so immensely destructive of our social and environmental stability will be seen as a temporary industrial-age departure from natural values.

In the USA, city and state pension funds are coming under increasing public pressure to re-invest in a socially responsible way, and fund managers are no longer able to hold up the 'breach of trust' defence. Jeff Friedman, portfolio manager of the Dreyfus Third Century Fund, an SRI fund with assets of $182 million in 1986, reported a heavy increase in enquiries from state and municipal pension funds in 1985, resulting from employee pressure.[20] In addition to pension systems, some 30 state and 24 city governments in the US have ethical investment guidelines that apply to all public sector funds (1986 figures).

In Britain, there has as yet been no noticeable pressure on pension fund managers from employees. The interesting developments relate to the use of pension funds for local investment, in response to the crisis of unemployment. Strathclyde Regional Council, with an employees pension fund of some £3 billion, has invested £5 million (0.16%) in a special venture fund to encourage local businesses. Rank Xerox Pension Fund has set up an arrangement with the London Enterprise Agency and the Tyne and Wear Enterprise Trust to channel resources into new businesses. In Wigan, fighting 20% unemployment, a £26 million redevelopment of the town centre has been backed with funding from British Coal's pension fund. Berkshire County Council has allocated £0.5 million from its pension fund to invest in small local firms which receive advice and support from the Berkshire Enterprise Agency. The Northumbria Unit Trust and the West Midlands Regional Unit Trust (among others) channel pension funds into local businesses in those areas. These initiatives are still few and far between, however. Pension and insurance funds cannot be rechannelled in a socially responsible manner until new financial institutions have been set up, both locally and nationally, to receive them. The next ten years will probably see a major expansion in this field.

In 1986, Maxine Waters, black member of the California State Assembly and head of the Assembly Democratic Caucus, forced approval of legislative amendments which required divestment of California's state pension funds holdings of over $50 billion from companies with activities in South Africa. The counsel for the Board of Regents, who administer the fund, said that 'investments carefully carried out should not breach any fiduciary responsibility'. In return, Maxine said that fiduciary trust should be legally redefined, and that rather than having to prove that social criteria do not violate fiduciary responsibility, *trustees should be legally obliged to show that investments satisfy socially and environmentally responsible, as well as financially responsible standards.*[21] By enshrining the new values in law, much can be done to stabilise the chaos of the present world, and provide secure foundations for the emerging rainbow economy of the post-industrial world. California has always been seen as one of the 'bellweather states' which point the way that other states will later follow. Within legal moves of this nature lie changes of tremendous potential impact.

LOCAL COMMUNITY BANKING

A third area where innovation is badly needed is local investment.

In the late 1970s, exhaustive and difficult research showed that residents in an older ethnic neighbourhood in Chicago had deposited $33 million in a local savings and loan association, but received back only $120,000 in loans. In the whole of the USA, only one out of 14,500 commercial banks (the South Shore Bank of Chicago) puts more money back into low-income neighbourhoods than it takes out. Local banks and saving institutions (which proliferate in the USA) have no problem in taking local people's savings, but they are not so keen on lending them back to assist in local development. Some older districts are 'red-lined' and considered no-go areas for loans, their residents considered 'bad risk', and denied the chance of capital accumulation. Some banks hate lending at all – they prefer to store their deposits in Treasury Bills or long-term certificates of deposit. One bank in West Virginia (USA) lends out only 7% of its deposits. Other banks will lend huge sums of money for buy-outs and take-overs, while ignoring actual business development projects. In 1983 mergers and acquisitions, excluding leveraged buy-outs, absorbed 69 times as much capital as net venture start-ups.[22]

When a community's savings are controlled by a banking, saving or investment institution whose commitment is to its own profit-line and not to the wellbeing of that community, the community finds it very hard to gather together its own resources to finance its own development goals. In Lowell, Massachusetts (see Chapter Three), the local banks joined in the development partnership and made a solid commitment to the town's regeneration, lending money at considerably below base rate to the Lowell Development and Finance Corporation to finance the refurbishment of vital downtown areas where the need was greatest. In Bradford, a comparable city in Britain, which is still experiencing the problems of industrial decline which Lowell has now addressed, the major banks and building societies refuse to make similar funds available, as they are answerable to their head offices in London and are told to follow the rule of maximum return, no matter what Bradford's own needs might be, or what the actual investors of the money might want. A community economy requires community banking.

Elsewhere in Britain, the crisis of unemployment and the urgent need for local economic regeneration has begun to make certain banks and financial institutions think in terms of backing local development goals. In the London boroughs of Hackney and Tower Hamlets, the insurance company Lloyd's of London (a member of Business in the Community, see Chapter Seven) gave £50,000 to the Tower Hamlets Centre for Small Businesses to finance start-up loans for local businesses, the first £1,000 being interest-free, and the rest at 5%, up to a maximum of £3,000. The National Westminster Bank has appointed Business Development Managers in five inner city areas, with explicit instructions to build up links with inner city communities, and to channel loans into those areas. In 1987, their lending in these areas was over five times greater than the deposits received.[23]

In Britain, some enterprise agencies are beginning to set up linked investment funds for local development, such as Highland Opportunity Ltd in Scotland. Eleven agencies have formed the Local Investment Networking Company (LINC), which acts as a marriage bureau between investors (through the LINC Investors Club) and firms requiring venture capital up to £100,000. LINC helps to channel investment away from wealthy areas like the South East to regions where there is a shortage of investment funds. The merchant bankers Lazards have helped to set up several regional unit trusts, including the Northumbria Unit Trust, which receives money from pension funds and charities[24] (see above), as have the enterprise boards in Lancashire, Merseyside, the West Midlands and London.[25]

In Minneapolis St Paul, USA, ten insurance companies grouped together to establish the Community Initiatives Consortium, which provides investments to businesses which have traditionally had difficulty raising capital from institutional sources. 58% of their borrowers are ethnic minority business-owners, and 44% are women's businesses.

In Quebec, Canada, more than 30 communities and regions have established an alternative form of credit union called the Caisse Economique d'Entraide (CE). These are established and managed by community members who invest a portion of their personal funds in the CE, explicitly to support the development and retention of small local businesses within the community or region.

In Le Mené, a small rural area in central Brittany, France, which suffers from rural depopulation and overcentralist French government policies, 26 local parishes grouped together in 1965 under the leadership of Abbé Paul Houée, a local catholic priest, and formed the Comité d'Expansion, which helped several new business enterprises and cultural initiatives to get going. In the early 1980s they decided that without their own source of loan credit they would never get far, so they set up the Institut de Développement Economique du Mené (IDEM), a small non-profit banking institution which they jointly control. Local people put their savings into the bank, receiving interest 2% above the market rate, and potential entrepreneurs borrow the money at 3 – 5% below the market rate – the differences coming from the non-profit nature of the bank, the sole aim of which is to serve the needs of the community. The 26 communes have set up a collective loan guarantee fund, using public money (invested by the Crédit Mutuel de Bretagne) to back the community's lending.[26]

A different example of community banking comes from North Dakota, USA. At Christmas 1987, banks in 16 small towns offered interest-free loans of up to $1,000, not in cash but in scrip, which can only be spent in local stores. The stores collect the scrip and are reimbursed in cash by the banks. This helps to keep local money in town, and helps to offset the usual haemorrhage of money away from the local economy into the huge shopping malls of cities as many as 250 miles away.[27] (North Dakota is a pretty big place with large distances between cities.)

In the small town of Berkshire, Massachusetts, a local bank agreed to establish a separate program called a SHARE account. Deposits to this account made by town residents receive a competitive interest rate, and loans are then made by a separate non-profit board of directors, and are made only to locally-owned enterprises which contribute to local self-reliance. Depositors to the account know that their money will help finance local development.[28]

South Shore Miracles

One of the outstanding examples of local community

banking is the South Shore Bank in Chicago, which is pioneering a wholly new approach to local banking on the South Shore lakefront nine miles south of the city centre. The district is home to 80,000 low- and moderate-income residents, 95% of whom are black, who live in 265 large blocks. During the 1970s the district was caught in a spiral of decline, its abandoned apartment blocks becoming targets for arson and drug deals.

Ronald Grzywinski owned a local bank, and during the 1960s, with help from two black activists, he ran a successful program lending to black entrepreneurs. In 1973, with 11 other investors, he bought the South Shore Bank, intending to pursue his policy of making enterprise loans to local businesses. Between 1974 and 1980 the bank loaned out $6.7 million, but with dismal results. The real problem was the collapsing physical condition of the district, which made it seem a hopeless case for businesses and residents alike.

In the 1980s, Grzywinski and his colleagues changed their approach, brought in developers to do some subsidized rehabilitation projects, and started lending to people who wanted to renovate the buildings themselves, something no other bank had been willing to do. This turned out to be the critical step. By 1987 the bank had given out 'development loans' for mortgages and rehabilitation work totalling over $75 million, and had facilitated work on more than 200 buildings – nearly one fourth of all the apartment buildings in South Shore. Their lending policy nurtured a group of entrepreneurs who found a means to get involved in rehabilitation work, and set off a self-generating development process.

Humans possess a natural tendency to take positive action on their own behalf. The instinct for self-empowerment gets blocked only when something concrete impedes it, such as the denial of opportunity to develop personal talents, or the denial of ownership. If a blockage continues for long enough the habits of self-empowerment become rusty, and are no longer passed down from generation to generation. New generations have to relearn them, but only once the blockages have been removed.

Under US law, banks are prohibited from initiating development projects or investing equity capital. By teaming up with a non-banking development corporation, the South Shore Bank was able to involve itself in the kind of activities needed to help people re-learn this instinct for self-empowerment. In 1978 the bank started three non-bank affiliates to enlarge on its neighbourhood renewal program: the City Lands Corporation, a real-estate development company which targets particular areas of the neighbourhood, the Neighbourhood Fund, which gives equity finance to minority-owned businesses, and the Neighbourhood Institute, a non-profit economic and social development corporation which helps tenants organize themselves into 'sweat equity' co-ops, organizes trainings, and helps people organise themselves for neighbourhood planning and crime prevention. A further initiative called 'ACCESS' – the Action Centre for Entrepreneurial South Shore Women – makes micro-loans to individual low-income women to encourage self-employment and small business development. These development activities have helped to establish the critical mass of social and financial investment that is needed for the process of community self-renewal to get started.

The South Shore Bank goes out of its way to lend to people who have been disempowered by generations of poverty, unemployment and tenanthood. It also seeks to succeed as a business. In 1986 its return on average assets was 1.1%, while the industry norm is 1.0%, and it made an overall profit of $1 million. Nearly half the bank's loans are invested locally, which is three times the average for other Chicago banks, and it has a 98% repayment rate on its loans. By re-investing local people's money in the area, and bringing in new money, the bank has reversed the flow of capital out of the South Shore district. It runs a program known as 'Development Deposits' attracting $52 million (39% of the bank's assets) from outside investors, and lends them out as 'Development Loans' within the South Shore and other low-income areas. In this way, they are reversing the flow of capital which always runs out of poor communities and into wealthier ones because of traditional bank lending policies. By deliberately seeking to foster social and community values as well as economic values, the bank has been able to achieve both social and economic profits. This is a win-win situation, in which everyone gains.[29]

> *'It's not easy. You need a long-term commitment. Bankers see much quicker and easier short-term profit opportunities. If your shareholders demand profit maximization and no deviation from standard commercial lending policies, this isn't going to happen . . . Can you imagine what would happen if the big money center banks put half of their deposits back into their communities?'*
>
> Joan Shapiro,
> Vice-President, South Shore Bank[30]

Under the 1977 US Community Reinvestment Act, federal regulatory agencies are required to encourage financial institutions to help meet the credit needs of their local communities and assess how well they meet those needs, and banks are required to make a public CRA statement outlining their local community and the types of loans available. Although compliance has been patchy, the CRA has stimulated local investment in a number of cases. Local effort is needed to persuade banks to comply.

The value of local banking is demonstrated at its best in Mondragon (see Chapter Seven). In 1959, the workers formed a credit co-operative, the Caja Laboral Popular. They could not rely on outside help, and so had to provide their own capital. The Caja is now the central mainstay of the whole network. It serves as the bank for the employees in the co-operatives and plays an extremely active part in the generation, support and regeneration of the co-ops.

People can see that their savings are helping to support their own jobs, as well as the jobs of friends and neighbours. It is a good example of a bank that truly serves the needs of local people and their communities. People often say 'you can't replicate what they've done at Mondragon', but this neglects the fact that work to build a community economy began in 1943 when Don Jose Maria opened a technical school, and that his students borrowed the £2,500 they needed to buy the stove-making company which became their first co-operative in 1955. Mondragon have a 30–40 year lead on community initiatives starting in the 1980s.

SOCIAL COLLATERAL

The fourth area of innovation which is important to the growth of a community economy concerns the nature of collateral. Collateral is the security which you are expected to provide when you are being considered for a loan – usually a capital sum of your own, or the title deeds of your house. This is the bank's way of insuring its risk. If you are poor and do not own a house, the bank will not usually lend to you.

Most bank managers are conservative, and don't like lending to things that are new, such as co-operatives or community-owned businesses. This reticence can also extend to business proposals coming from women, young people, and members of minority ethnic groups. Three ways have been found to by-pass this obstacle to community economic progress, which can collectively be called 'social collateral'.

The first involves the establishment of a *community loan guarantee fund*. Students at Malaspina College in Nanaimo, British Columbia (Canada), who wanted to build their own businesses in the summer vacations put their own funds into a special bank account, and used this as a loan guarantee fund to lever business loans out of local banks. In Modena and elsewhere in Italy, small businesses have linked themselves together to form a Loan Guarantee Consortium to guarantee each other's loans. This credit co-operative negotiates a rate of interest 1.5% below market rates, and pays the bank in the case of default. Since its foundation in 1976, it has guaranteed loans for £4.6 million, and lost only 0.7%.[31]

Women's World Banking (WWB), a not-for-profit financial institution founded in 1979 with over 50 affiliates worldwide, encourages local banks to work with small-scale enterprises and women entrepreneurs, particularly in low-income communities and Third World countries. WWB enables local banks to make loans which they would not normally consider, by virtue of having established a Capital Fund of some $5 million (1987 figure). This serves two purposes. It is used as a Guarantee Fund, which by joining with local guarantee funds set up by the affiliated groups is able to induce local credit sources to lend to local women by guaranteeing repayment of 75% of each loan they make, and it provides a regular source of income to sustain WWB's activities. By 1988, the number of loans guaranteed had reached 25,000. The Capital Fund is fed by grants and by the sale of debentures which pay 8% interest, leaving a surplus which enables WWB to build the movement worldwide.

> '*I want to see women have a role in making investments in the world economy. That's the only way it'll be a strong and safe economy.*'
> Michaela Walsh, President, Women's World Banking[32]

In Britain, Mercury Provident Plc, a licensed deposit-taking institution with loans of £1.5 million (1988), makes use of the method in a slightly different way. Mercury Provident takes some of its philosophy from the German philosopher Rudolf Steiner, who taught that the spiritual and social energy represented by money needs to be used in a conscious way. As well as enabling members to make loans to projects and initiatives of their choice, and to choose the rate of interest which they ask, Mercury sometimes asks borrowers to create a 'guarantee community' of friends and supporters who agree to underwrite the loan. A loan of £40,000 might require a guarantee community of 100 supporters. At first this might seem a daunting request, but the process of building the guarantee community is an excellent way of raising awareness, involvement and support, which benefits the business enormously. This process of guaranteeing a business creates a very direct link between the guarantor and the business.[33] In this respect Mercury's method is partially similar to that practised by Muslim banks which follow the principles of 'Sharia' law, and do not charge interest. Usury is prohibited under Muslim religious law, as it is in Christian ethics (though with little effect). Instead of charging interest, Islamic banks (with assets of US $15 billion) pass the risk on to the investor, who shares in the gains or losses accordingly.[34]

The second method involves a change from
  – seeking security in case of failure,
  – to seeking to avoid failure by the development of an *active business support strategy*, as outlined in Chapter Seven.

The person who attends a good business training course, works closely with an enterprise agency to develop a sound business plan and then joins a business self-help club stands a much better chance of surviving the critical first three years than a person who jumps in at the deep end and goes it alone in the traditional way. A survey of enterprise agency clients has shown that the failure rates in businesses assisted by agencies are cut by 50% to one in six instead of the usual failure rate of one in three (see Chapter Seven). 56% of enterprise agencies in Britain have linked loan arrangements of some kind, which reflects this increased lending security.

The model is practised at its best at Mondragon, where the integrated business support system gives the co-operatives advance warning of looming difficulties and creates appropriate strategies to enable them to adapt and steer on to a new course, resulting in a 0% failure rate. At WEDCO in Minneapolis (see Chapter Seven) the failure rate is only 2%. The morals are very clear: *community support paves the way for economic sustainability,* and creating social collateral through a local business support system (in place of personal collateral) provides greater financial security to lending institutions.

The third alternative to orthodox lending policies lies with a system of *peer-group social guarantees.*

To grasp how this system works we have to go to Bangladesh, one of the poorest and most crowded countries on Earth. Conventional banking policies here – as everywhere – lend only to people who have tangible assets as collateral. The landless and the poor are seen as bad credit risks, and forced to go to the village money-lenders, who fleece the poor so much that in the end they are driven off the land and into the city slums. Even with this lending policy, agricultural banks still only recover 50% of their loans, and industrial banks less than 10%.

The Grameen Bank was set up in 1977 by Muhammad Yunus. Instead of insisting on personal collateral, the Grameen Bank asks landless villagers to form into groups of 50 people of the same sex (Bangladesh is a Muslim country), and then to form into smaller groups of five. The ten groups of five each meet regularly with a bank worker for training, and with each other to discuss their business ideas. Each loan has to be approved by the smaller group of five, by the larger group, and finally by the bank's officer in the field; Grameen does not believe in having huge city banks. Two people in a small group can then apply for a loan. The average loan size is £35, equivalent to about £5,000 in Britain, given the annual incomes of landless peasants. Women borrowers use their loans for such things as buying a milch cow, paddy husking and cattle fattening, while men tend to invest in paddy and rice trading, cattle fattening and setting up grocery shops. After six weeks, if the first two have been regular in their payments, the next two members get their loan, and after another six weeks, the final member. The loans are not analysed by the bank – they leave it up to the villagers to do the analysis. As they depend on each other's success in repaying them, the system works.

The bank was launched with finance from the Bangladesh Bank, and later from major donor agencies – they were turned down by the World Bank. By September 1987 the bank had 347 branches servicing 5,600 villages, and had made loans totalling $54 million to over 290,000 borrowers, 75% of them women. The default rate is only 2.7% – a 97.3% on-time repayment record, and in the last three years the bank has made a profit on its activities.[35]

To gain such repayment figures while breaking the conventional laws of banking says something important about the emergence of community banking practices. It is the banks' loans to Third World governments that have set up the trillion dollar debt which now threatens to bring the global banking system crashing down. The majority of those loans were not targeted at particular business activities – they were simply thrown at governments in a head-in-the-sand belief that 'countries can't go bankrupt'.[36] If Grameen banking operations had evolved fifteen years earlier, and the lending spree of the late 1970s had been channelled through village groups instead of through dictators and governments, we would not now be facing an imminent crash, we would not be witnessing increasing poverty and starvation all over the poorer world, and the global economy would be in a far happier position.

Grameen banking operations are being developed in India, and in South America, where people in 60 cities and towns in 12 countries are benefiting from loans organised by Accion International. The South Shore Bank in Chicago is beginning an experiment in rural Arkansas based on

Grameen principles, linked to other community economic development strategies. The annalists of the twenty-third century may be able to write that for the poorer people on the Earth the invention of social collateral and peer-group lending was the single most significant economic break-through of the twentieth century.

CREATING A LOCAL BANKING STRATEGY

In conclusion, we need to return to the towns and cities of the industrial world, and ask how a local strategy could be developed which would serve the capital needs of the rain-bow economy development strategy, bringing the benefit of these innovations to people living in deprived communities, and to the many who are trapped on the downside of economic progress by virtue of non-ownership.

The first step involves the formation of a working group of interested people, who will meet together and explore ideas and possibilities, educating itself about initiatives by studying, corresponding with and visiting those that seem the most relevant. Possibilities for local action then include following:

• holding discussions with local banks to discuss the possibility of their developing more locally and socially oriented lending policies, and setting up socially responsible deposit accounts;

• publishing information and raising awareness on local banking, lending, and community economic approaches, including an annual survey of the social and environmental policies and practices of local banks and lending institutions;

• holding discussions with managers of local pension funds and city or council capital funds with a view to achieving re-investment on a socially responsible basis;

• forming a network of local financial consultants, encouraging them to offer socially responsible investment possibilities to their clients, or establishing a consultancy to provide the needed service;

- forming a local shareholders network, bringing a holistic perspective into local businesses and encouraging their evolution in transformative and socially responsible directions;
- establishing a credit union, or (in Canada) taking one over by democratic process and moving it in a socially responsible direction;
- launching a local investment fund or a community finance corporation, to channel local savings and pension fund money into local businesses which operate with holistic values;
- establishing a community loan guarantee fund, to lever loans out of the banks for people who cannot provide their own collateral, and for community-based enterprises which have difficulty in getting loans;
- strengthening the local business support system, and negotiating with the banks to revise their lending policies to permit a more liberal approach to businesses drawing on this support;
- in the USA, and in other countries where banking laws permit, buying or setting up a community bank.

Nationally, in Britain, legislation is needed to raise the limits which surround credit unions, to permit individual savings up to £50,000, loans up to an equivalent level, and the ability to issue business loans to members. It would also be useful if banks and other companies were required by law to include information on their social and environmental policies in their annual reports. The establishment of community banks and loan funds would be easier if the effective monopoly of the 'Big Five' banks were ended and current restrictions reformed.

COMMUNITY OWNERSHIP

The area of community ownership is very new territory for

social change. The socially responsible investment movement is less than ten years old (with the exception of a few older non-alcoholic and non-gambling funds), and awareness about the need to develop community banking operations to serve the newly emerging community economies is very new indeed. It needs time to develop, and it needs support.

In a sustainable community economy, all but a small minority of passers-through should be able to participate in the general increase in the capital value of land, housing and enterprise which is created by the collective endeavours of the community as a whole. A society which excludes some of its people from this value is practising economic apartheid. Post-industrial technologies are creating a very major social rift between those who benefit financially from the increases in productivity and those who are exiled into unemployment and poverty. The advanced industrial societies of the world are passing through a crucial time. Fuelled by the productive capacity of the new technologies, the capital value of land and property are moving far beyond the reach of first-time house buyers who lack capital. In most areas of southern Britain it is impossible for non-property owners on low incomes to afford a mortgage on a house or flat, however small. Property owners pass their homes on to their children, along with the accumulated value, but the children of non-owners inherit nothing, and unless something is done they will remain a permanent minority, excluded from the growing prosperity of the many for generations to come.

This problem needs the most urgent attention. The answers may lie with new forms of shared and community ownership, in addition to private ownership and self-build operations financed by new community banking arrangements. In the USA, the community land trust movement is pioneering new approaches to the community ownership of land and housing. A Community Land Trust (CLT) is a democratically run non-profit corporation which buys and holds land for the benefit of a local community, and provides permanent access to land and housing at affordable rates for low-income people. The land trust keeps ownership of the land itself, and leases it to people who are assisted to buy property on the land. Even though the increase in land-value remains with the CLT, not with the purchaser, the approach is proving popular enough for there now to be 25 CLTs in the USA, such as the South Atlanta Land Trust and the Ozark Regional Land Trust, and the movement is growing fast.

In Massachusetts, a special $30 million fund has been set up by the legislature to support new ideas and approaches that might help solve the housing and homelessness problem.[37] A linked idea is the Co-operative Land Bank, through which a company or trust is formed to hold possession of the land of a street, neighbourhood or town, and individual property owners become shareholders in the company, participating in the increasing (or falling) land value through their shares. Houses are sold as normal, minus their added land value. This structure allows the process of land ownership to become a social, and not just an individual procedure, and makes it possible for policy measures to be introduced ensuring the inclusion of all inhabitants as land bank shareholders, eliminating the socially disastrous exclusionism of existing land-owning policies.[38]

In Britain, where many of the economically excluded live in public housing schemes, some of which are in need of demolition, there is need for a highly sophisticated strategy, combining the following:

● local participation and planning (with appropriate training and technical support);

● the formation of community companies to hold the ownership of land, and/or new housing developments based on community architectural methods; and

● large-scale capital grants and loan finance to fund the development costs of rehabilitation and rebuilding.

In the event of a major economic crash, many people would find themselves unable to meet their mortgage repayments and under threat of eviction. The lending institutions (banks and building societies) would find themselves in possession of houses which in many instances might be worth less than the amount lent. By grouping together, local people can form community companies and borrow the money to buy the houses from the banks and reinstate their original owners, who would then become participants in a community or shared ownership scheme, instead of being strictly private owners.

Community ownership is a concept which is new to people in the capitalist world. In the Soviet Union, seventy years of state ownership of property has proved its ineffectiveness as a policy, and government-owned apartments are now being sold to tenants, assisted by the provision of very low-interest mortgage finance. Community ownership offers a form of security which allows full participation in the growth of value that a society achieves by its efforts, while also providing a vehicle through which local people can participate more fully in their community and its economy. The duality of private and public ownership stems from the historical realities of the agricultural and industrial ages, reflecting the deprivation and denial of potential of those times. Community ownership strategies offer one key to a fair and just economy, in keeping with the post-industrial need for everyone to achieve complete personal fulfilment and development.

The industrial age has been underpinned by traditions of banking, saving and lending which emphasise private gain at the expense of social or environmental gain. By transforming the underlying values of this tradition, and by creating initiatives which express new values, we begin to create a new kind of banking which is appropriate to our planetary, post-industrial needs.

Chapter Ten :
With nature, not against her

The next problem that needs to be addressed is the ecological one: how can we ensure that the economy we are building is ecologically sustainable, on a permanent basis?

The issue is a big one. Almost all our current economic activities are non-sustainable, whether through the toxic wastes we dump into the atmosphere, soil and waters and into our own bodies, the heat we emit from our energy consumption which is steadily warming up the atmosphere, the loss of the planet's cooling system with the destruction of the tropical rainforests, the way we are ravenously eating away at our non-renewable resources, or for a host of other reasons.

The overall problem is so broad that the growing environmental movement adopts a wide range of different approaches. Some people become involved in single-issue campaigns to save the rainforests or to stop the development of nuclear power stations. Others apply their imagination to developing such things as organic farms, 'greening the city' initiatives and bicycle tracks. Some adopt green politics, working either in the new green parties or to 'green' the existing parties. Others are seeking to change industrial consciousness itself, perceiving that one-off campaigns may be just 'cleaning the teeth of the dragon', as the German green politician Rudolph Bahro puts it; they seek to change our whole approach to consumerism, nature and life itself.

The trouble is that non-sustainability is deeply embedded in our entire economy and way of life. The urgency of the ecological issues facing the planet means that our goal must be nothing less than the achievement of complete ecological sustainability for all our economic activities.

There is growing evidence that this is what people want. In a recent Norwegian survey, 78% thought that their present standards of living were 'too high', 74% wanted a 'simpler life' and 69% were prepared to make personal sacrifices in order to help the world's poor. In West Germany, the number willing to accept material sacrifices in order to stop polluting nature has doubled to 80% since 1984. In the USA a recent Harris poll showed that 66% felt that we 'should break up big things and go back to more humanized living', against 22% who wanted to 'develop bigger and more efficient ways of doing things'. 61% against 27% agreed that it was 'morally wrong for the USA to consume such a large proportion of the world's resources'. In Britain, 80% feel that more should be done to protect the environment.[1]

To achieve the goal of full sustainability, we need to break it down into practical areas. There are many such areas, from 'toxic waste disposal' to 'river pollution', from 'animal cruelty' to 'greening the cities', from 'sustainable agriculture' to 'pollution-free transport', and so on. In each area, there are campaigns to run, people to see, books to publish, sustainable technologies to research, new initiatives to develop, meetings to hold, attitudes to change, a new consciousness to develop, new policies to draft, new practices to try out, new laws to lobby for and new international agreements to pursue. This chapter looks at the possibilities at local level, where the task facing local communities is to draw up and implement strategies that will ensure the sustainability of their local economies – ecologically, economically, socially and spiritually.

The basic approach of the rainbow economy development strategy provides the starting moves:

- form a partnership, drawing as many people in as

possible from every sector of the community;

• develop your vision and ideas, breaking up into working groups to study each area in depth using 'future workshop' techniques where appropriate (see Chapter Six);

• work with a win-win philosophy, trying to avoid casting anyone as 'enemies';

• use your full creative imagination; and

• set yourselves goals to keep your commitment boiling. The people of Basle, in Switzerland, spent the summer of 1988 participating in future workshops in each of their 14 city districts, asking the question 'How can Basle be turned into a model ecological city?'. This is the kind of question we need to be addressing in our villages, towns and cities.

This chapter addresses key areas – energy, resource conservation, agriculture, the greening of the cities, and cars, illustrating what is possible.

ENERGY

The problem with energy is that we are using far too much of it. The excess heat given off by our use of fossil fuels (oil, coal, gas and wood) is increasing the concentration of CO_2 in the Earth's atmosphere and creating the greenhouse effect:

> *'Widely cited projections conclude that by the year 2025 the world will need 4½ times the hydro power and 3½ times the coal used today, along with a total of 365 large nuclear power plants. Among the consequences of using so much energy would be greater risk of acid rain, carbon dioxide-induced climate change, species extinction, nuclear weapons proliferation, water degradation, human dislocation, and capital shortages and debt. The consensus forecasts would, within the next century, double the concentration of carbon dioxide (compared to pre-industrial levels) and cause an atmospheric temperature increase large enough to flood*

coastal cities and shift rain patterns all over the globe.'
Worldwatch Institute, 1985[2]
There are signs that the unusual weather disturbances we
are witnessing around the world, from the loss of rainfall
over the Sahel area of Africa to unseasonal snowfalls,
droughts, and floods may be the first signs of this warming. The changes are on such a massive scale that most of
us find them hard to believe. The evidence is solid, however: our steady increase in energy use is lining us up for
some unthinkable geo-climatic disasters.

Only renewable energy does not contribute to the
greenhouse effect at all.[3] The experience of Chernobyl and
the intractable problems of how to dispose of radioactive
wastes have done much to convince many people that nuclear energy is a 'genie' they would rather see put back in
the bottle. The development of renewable energy sources
from the sun, wind and waves while being an underde-
veloped and underfunded area with everything to offer us
in the way of long-term sustainability is increasing rapidly
every year. The greatest source of new energy at our disposal, however, comes from our own creativity:

'One of the best-kept secrets in the country is that since
1979, the USA has saved over 100 times as much energy
through such efforts as weatherizing houses and designing fuel-efficient automobiles and appliances as it has
gotten from the net increase in energy supplied by oil
and gas wells, coal mines and power plants combined.'
Amory and Hunter Lovins[4]
Rocky Mountains Institute

The arena of energy-efficiency represents the greatest
source of new energy available to us, and per dollar
invested, is three times more effective than nuclear power
in reducing CO_2 emissions.

Among the new devices available are fridges that use
only 260 kilowatt-hours per year (being marketed in
Denmark) instead of well over 1000; dehumidifying

clothes dryers that save two-thirds of the electricity; 18 watt light bulbs that deliver the same amount of light as 100 watt bulbs; new ballasts for flourescent lights that eliminate flicker, hum and 40% of energy use; microcomputer controls for heavy machinery; new devices in smelting and petrochemicals; improved heat-recovery devices; better controls, sizing and drive-trains for electric motors; and for the busy family, water-driven dishwashers that use no electricity at all.[5]

Data collected by the Worldwatch Institute shows that the world has hardly begun to develop the potential for energy-efficiency.[6] A single decision in the USA to raise the minimum permissible automobile fuel economy to 40 miles per gallon, or in the USSR to produce steel as efficiently as Japan would save as much energy as Brazil now consumes. Simply using the most efficient light bulbs in the USA would save a third of all US coal-fired energy. Using more recycled steel would enable producers to save up to two-thirds of the energy used to produce steel from ore. Making aluminium from recycled material allows energy savings of 95% on newly smelted ore. Upgrading electric motors would save the US over 7% of all electricity consumed and yield a 47% return on the investment. Whichever direction you look, the potential for more efficient, cheaper and better ways of using energy are so great that if we were to adopt existing measures we could cut the projected energy demand growth rate from 2% to 1.2% per year, cutting acid-rain-forming sulphur emissions from an expected 165% increase down to 35%.[7] This is good, but nowhere near good enough. The Third World will need more energy to further its own development even allowing for efficiency measures.[8] If we are to stave off widespread flooding, crop losses and environmental disasters, the industrial societies must reduce their levels of energy use by 50% by the year 2000.[9] If we deliberately foster energy-efficient strategies at both local and national levels, we can probably achieve this.

COMMUNITY ENERGY STRATEGIES

A community energy strategy is a 'win-win' affair. Using less energy:

• reduces the amount of sulphurous oxides thrown into the atmosphere (in America, each house heated with coal-fired electricity causes enough sulphur oxides each year to fill three times its own volume with acid rain);

• lessens the need for expenditure on pollution-control devices;

• saves local people's money, releasing extra spending power into the local economy (85% – 90% of money spent on imported energy leaves the local economy immediately, while 60% – 70% of that invested in efficiency and renewables goes on local employment, remaining within the local economy);

• keeps people warm, prevents death from hypothermia and helps preserve buildings from damp and decay.

A strategy starts with the formation of an energy task force drawing in key people from industry, local government, labour, community and voluntary groups, local colleges, environmental groups and banking/finance houses. The Energy Conservation and Solar Centre in London, for example, a company which does consultancy and training work in the housing and the public sector field, working both through commercial and charitable arms organizes 'Springboard Conferences' which bring together local people, council officers and energy experts to discuss ways of gaining energy savings in council houses. The next step involves carrying out a community energy study[10] to tell you how much money is leaving your local economy each year on energy importation, pin-pointing areas for saving and getting the people thinking about energy issues – an important step in obtaining widespread participation. A community energy study in Franklin County, Massachusetts, in 1977 found that every family in the County was spending $1300 a year on imported energy, and that the County as a whole was 'bleeding' to the extent of $23 million a year. This shocked local people into a major insulation and weatherizing effort.[11] In 1984/85, a Lewisham Energy Plan was carried out with funding from the Greater London Council, with two paid staff carrying out the bulk of the work.

A community energy strategy has three main targets: domestic users, businesses and local government. Community energy teams can deliver insulation programmes, advising families and companies on energy-efficiency processes and running training programmes. Consumers and businesses need information about the best available technologies, using energy-audits to show energy loss and potential savings. In California, by law, only fridges of a certain energy standard (for instance) can be sold locally.

In Boston, USA, the Citizens Energy Corporation obtained a large refund from an oil company for over-charging local people for their oil, and became the trustees for the money which they use as a loan guarantee fund to lever bank loans which enable landlords to weather-proof their properties. The tenants pay their same fuel bills to Citizens Energy, who pay the reduced bills, meet the repayment on the loans and give the rest back to the tenants to finance other low-cost energy-saving measures.[12] Cities can also sponsor their own municipal companies. 'Keeping Newcastle Warm' (a non-profit company employing 58 people) has insulated over 10,000 homes since 1982.

There is need for money and creativity in finding ways to finance energy loans. Banks will lend multi-million pound loans to build new power stations, but not to enable tenants and property owners to weather-proof their homes, which generates more energy at a lower rate of risk. In Seattle, USA, the Seattle Trust and Savings Bank will give you a better deal under their Conservation Loan Program if the house you are buying meets certain efficiency standards. Their reasoning is that since your fuel bills will be lower, you will find it easier to repay the mortgage.

In Britain, some building societies are considering similar arrangements.[13] The Tenants Heating and Installation Service in London arranges for the installation of heating and energy efficiency measures, funded by rent increases which are less than the savings on fuel bills. In California, the sheet-metal workers' pension fund arranges third-party finance for solar systems on schools and hospitals, hiring unemployed sheet-metal workers to do the installations, taking its pay-back from the cost-savings, and the schools get their installations for free. A local financial consortium needs to prepare a range of energy-loan options, to ensure that the investments needed to ensure the future stability of the world are not held up for a simple lack of finance.

Incentives can play a major role. The Milton Keynes Development Corporation (MKDC) has developed an Energy Cost Index, a target fuel running-cost for housing. All new housing must be better than (or meet) this standard, an arrangement which has led to much creative innovation and competition by builders and architects seeking new ways to better the targets. Public exhibitions are frequently held to show energy conservation in action. In Denmark, house surveyors are trained in energy efficiency techniques, and give energy audits and guidance. When houses are put up for sale, prospective purchasers expect to receive a list detailing which conservation measures exist, which are still missing, and the cost of installing them. The absence of key energy saving items frequently leads to a reduction in the sale price.[14] In Davis, California, it is not legally possible to sell an old, poorly insulated house without first retrofitting it.[15]

Local businesses have a critical role to play. In Newcastle, England, an Energy Task Force was set up in 1985 to give assistance to industry and commerce to help them achieve energy efficiency and increase productivity. Most local businesses start from a zero point of energy efficiency, so the assistance has a big impact.

Newcastle also has a
- strategy to insulate 20,000 council-owned homes,
- an energy information centre,
- a programme of work with tenants and community groups, and
- a research, development and monitoring unit.
- It has built low-energy business incubator units,
- set up a subsidiary bulk-buying agency and
- established a Community Building Insulation Project

which insulated 100 local halls and meeting places between 1982 and 1984.

In the case of the Central Library, gas consumption was cut through a package of measures by nearly 60%, with payback in one year. They have a long way to go before approaching the energy-sustainability goal, but they show a little of what is possible where there is a concerted will.[16]

Energy-efficiency measures represent one side of the equation. The other side involves the development of renewable energy sources. Combined heat and power (co-generation) units take the 65% waste heat from power stations and use it in local heating schemes, reducing the loss to 20% waste heat. A typical small-scale unit cuts energy demand in half and pays for itself in two to three years. Denmark meets 25% of her heating requirements in this way; Britain meets 1% of hers.[17] There are also many possibilities for the development of solar, wind, wave, micro-hydro, tidal, geothermal, biofuel and methane power.

As energy-saving strategies are implemented, this will affect the livelihoods of people who work (for instance) in nuclear power plants. Livelihoods are only threatened when change is a one-way process, however. A nuclear plant community faced with closure could, with appropriate support:
- run personal development workshops to help people identify their natural skills and devise positive career-plans;
- conduct future workshops to ascertain people's

needs, problems, hopes, ideas and dreams;
• set up a community development agency to pursue concrete development plans (see Chapter Six).

Until the 1960s, economic growth (Gross Domestic Product) and energy-use increased side by side. As we have discovered ever more efficient ways of using energy, this pattern has finally been broken. This is one expression of the drive within our consciousness to seek ever more subtle and refined relationships with the material world. *By consciously shifting to a high-intelligence, low-energy strategy, we are furthering this alchemy of matter and mind which underpins our evolution.*[18]

RESOURCE CONSERVATION

During the years after World War II, the industrial world grew accustomed to rapid annual growth, without stopping to think about the long-term consequences. An annual 4% rate of economic growth leads to a 50-fold expansion of the global economy within a century, and a corresponding increase in demand for resources. In terms of our evolutionary history, something very dramatic is going on. After millions of years of stable existence when we never touched our capital inheritance of natural resources, it seems that we are now consuming it all within just a few generations. At 1975 consumption levels, known sources of tin, lead, zinc and copper, will be exhausted by 2025. We are also consuming our topsoil, tree cover, oil reserves and wilderness areas at an alarming rate.

Perhaps we are using up our global capital as a massive investment in the future as we prepare to leap out of the age of matter, and into the age of intelligence, mind and spirit (see Chapter Twelve). Judging from the feedback we are receiving from the planet, we are reaching – or have reached – the end of the process. From now on, if we want to continue with economic growth, we must do so along lines that no longer consume ever greater quantities of natural resources.

> *'In a sustainable society, durability and recycling will replace planned obsolescence as the economy's organizing principle, and virgin materials will be seen not as a primary source of material but as a supplement to the existing stock.'*
>
> Lester Brown, Worldwatch Institute[19]

The issues of durability and recycling are very closely related. We need to start designing all our materials with durability in mind, so that they can be easily recycled or re-used, and we need tax incentives, policies and laws which encourage this.

The flip-side of our consumption of the Earth's resources is the steady accumulation of what we shamefully call 'waste'. The average North American generates almost a tonne of waste a year, dumping 97% in landfill sites.[20] The British produce around 300 kg each, dumping 88% in the same way. The value of the natural resources that we dump is immense – as is the energy involved in remaking things that could have been re-used or recycled.

In medieval Europe, we used simply to throw our garbage out of the window. When that got too smelly, the city authorities started collecting it and dumping it outside the city gates. That led to noxious odours and rats, so they began digging pits and burying it. This sometimes poisoned the water supply, so in 1874 the city of Nottingham tried incinerating it. When the air quality deteriorated, they returned to burying it.

There are limits to everything, including vacant sites for landfill. In the USA, 50% of all the available landfill sites will be full by 1990, and Britain faces the same situation 10 years later. What is going to happen to all the 'waste' we produce as we proceed into the twenty-first century and beyond? What will we do with it all? Will we simply try to float it around the world in barges, seeking countries that will buy it from us? We can no longer live by the philosophy which says 'nature will take care of it'. There is no longer any 'away' in the word 'throwaway'.

The main ingredients in the domestic 'waste' stream are glass (10%), paper and card (30%), metals (10%), organic matter (30%), plastic (8%) and miscellaneous (12%). When these are mixed together, you have an unholy mess. Treat them separately, and the problem begins to appear manageable.

The best thing to do with *glass* is to re-use it. The Danes banned the sale of non-returnable soft drinks containers in 1977, and are developing proposals to adopt five standard types of returnable bottle throughout the whole country. A national computerised inventory system would keep track of them and cut producers' transportation costs. In Holland, 95% of all soft drinks and 90% of all beer containers are returnable. New York brought in a soft drinks deposit law and within two years saved $50 – $100 million on energy costs, $50 million on clean-up costs, $19 million on solid waste disposal and generated a net gain of 3,800 jobs. California is now to follow suit. Reverse vending machines also help increase the return rate for bottles and cans – you put them in and get a deposit or voucher back. 12,000 are in use, a third of them in Sweden.[21] As a second-best option, glass can be recycled. Holland recycles 53% of its non-returnable glass, Japan 50%. Britain only recycles 13%.

Next comes *paper*. Almost all of this can be recycled. Britons consume about seven million tonnes annually, equivalent to a forest the size of Wales, some five million tonnes of which ends up in landfill sites. Recovering just one issue of the New York Times would leave 75,000 trees standing. While East Germany recycles 86% of its paper and card, using 50% in new paper and board, Britain recycles only 27%.

Metals are eminently recyclable. To obtain new aluminium, you have to mine bauxite, much of which occurs in tropical rainforest areas. Producing aluminium

213

from recycled material requires only 5% of the energy needed to make it from new bauxite ore. If the world rate of aluminium recycling doubled, a million tonnes of air pollutants would be eliminated. Austria has tripled her rate of aluminium recycling in the last 10 years, and Holland, Japan and some Scandinavian countries recycle more than 50%. By mixing metals, however, their value drops dramatically. Mixed-metal tin-plate cans, which account for about a half of the UK market, are only worth £10/tonne compared to £400/tonne for non-mixed metal.

Plastics are a real headache. There are at least 30 different kinds of plastic in use, needing separate treatment, but no laws demand that containers should state their composition. Making plastic 'biodegradable' just adds a dubious cocktail to the soil. In eight US states mandatory deposit legislation brings an 80% rate of return, as compared to only 5% – 10% with voluntary schemes. In Germany a deposit is imposed on every plastic PET (polyethylene terepthalate) bottle to encourage its return.

Organic waste can be composted, once it is separated. In France, 100 plants produce 800,000 tonnes of compost a year. Sweden composts a quarter of all solid wastes, and Heidelberg (Germany), which has composted a third of its waste for 12 years, is experimenting with the separate collection of organic material.

The key to achieving a high level of recycling is separation at source. The Japanese recycle 50% of their waste stream by practising separation at home into six categories: combustibles such as paper, light plastics and kitchen wastes; non-combustibles such as hard plastics and metals; newspapers; bottles; bulky items; and dangerous substances.[22] In Rockford, Illinois, a garbage lottery awards $1,000 each week to a resident whose trash bags are inspected and found to be free of newspapers and aluminium cans. Metropolitan Portland, Oregon (population 1.2 million), has determined that 52% of its waste stream shall be recycled or re-used. Communities in Portland can choose their own strategies, but after 1989, non-separated waste loads will not be accepted at waste disposal facilities.

By keeping the easily recyclable materials separate at source, householders can divert up to 50% of the total waste stream. Local voluntary groups, community groups and small businesses then take it away and trade it in for cash. In Britain, Friends of the Earth run over 100 community recycling operations, on differing scales. In Cardiff, South Wales, the Community Support Anti-Waste Scheme acts as a centralized collection and distribution agency for waste, involving 252 voluntary groups and 18,000 volunteers. In 1986 they were chosen by Cardiff City Council to act as their agents to develop all aspects of their recycling policy.[23]

Sharing our 'wastes' offers us further possibilities. The Manitoba Waste Exchange in Winnipeg, Canada, lists waste materials generated by 78 local companies, and offers them for sale to a mailing list of 1,100 people. In Britain, the UK Waste Materials Exchange was wound up in 1979, having facilitated exchange wastes worth £8.5 million for operating costs which totalled £187,000, because no one could work out a way of making it self-financing.

Markets for recycled materials need stable management to sustain demand. In Holland, the government has established buffer stocks for waste paper to stabilise the price, and in the USA, 13 states have passed state procurement laws regarding the purchase of recycled material. Oxford City Council uses recycled paper for all council committee papers, etc. In an integrated community economy, the needs of regional industry should be studied and ways developed to supply them using recycled materials. We have hardly begun this process – just think how many companies, offices or local government departments you know which do not use recycled paper.

Once it has reached the waste disposal depot, mechanical processing systems can sometimes recover up to 35% of the total waste stream by a variety of shredders, screens and air jets. The materials can then be sold on the secondary materials market. Alternatively, after appropriate screening for ferrous metals, the waste can be burned at high temperatures, turned into Refuse Derived Fuel (or RDF) and converted into useful energy. There are now nine such plants in action in Britain. The system is not without its problems, but by avoiding inefficient combustion in mass incinerators, dioxin, acid gas, heavy metal and ash pollution are greatly reduced.[24]

Resource-recycling also produces jobs. The Canadian Waste Management Board Study has shown that every 10,000 tonnes of garbage brought to landfill sites supports six jobs, while every 10,000 tonnes recycled supports 36 jobs.[25] The gain of jobs in small, labour-intensive work units far outweighs the loss of jobs in landfill or incineration operations.

Taken together, these measures could achieve an 80% rate of recycling. Nowhere in the world has yet achieved this, but some communities are heading in this direction. Pennsauken, New Jersey, boasted a 15% curbside collection rate only six months after starting their mandatory recycling programme.

'The inevitable global transition from dependence on extractive industries to reliance on recycled materials has already begun. Higher energy and materials prices, emerging environmental problems, and the development of new technologies are all slowly propelling the transformation.'

Cynthia Pollock, Worldwatch Institute[26]

A COMMUNITY RESOURCE CONSERVATION STRATEGY

An integrated local resource conservation strategy (as part of the wider rainbow economy development strategy) would need to include the following components:
- education;
- community involvement and organization (including

consumer awareness);
- community-wide resource-use planning;
- incentive systems to encourage the re-use of materials;
- community waste exchanges;
- source collection and separation at source;
- managed demand for secondary materials;
- integrated budgeting and accountancy methods to allow a proper cost-assessment for recycling (see Chapter Eleven);
- a cradle-to-grave management approach for all materials; and
- appropriate legislation.

As a starting point, local groups or individuals should study the literature, gain familiarity with different approaches and possibilities worldwide, and make contact with groups and organizations that are active in the field.

The next step is to meet with officials who are concerned with resource-management and waste disposal issues locally (some of whom may be suprisingly 'green') and to form a *resource conservation partnership,* involving people from voluntary, community and environmental groups, local industry (recycling, manufacturing and retail), and local and central government.[27] This partnership should engage in its own study-phase before drafting up a comprehensive community strategy. There are bound to be problems and difficulties along the way – no one said changing the world was going to be easy! The reassurance, however, comes from the knowledge that making this transition from living off our resource capital to living sustainably is an inevitable global process that every community must go through sooner or later. Someone has to start the ball rolling, to stop the garbage piling up. Cities, towns or regions which get going will benefit as the advantages of sustainability begin to show on the community's balance sheet.

AGRICULTURE

While our industrial way of living has been piling up the rubbish, it has also been destroying the land. It started quite innocently after World War II when Europe was in devastation, and required food convoys from the USA to keep starvation at bay. Science was young, and came to our rescue. We discovered that by applying chemical fertilizers to the land, crop yields could be increased. By spraying the crops, pest damage could be controlled. By keeping animals inside and feeding them high protein foodstuffs, they would put on more weight. By filling in the ponds, more acreage could be planted.

For centuries, farmers followed a tradition of sustainable agriculture involving crop rotation, fallow years, windbreaks, soil-improving plants, traditional breeds, mixed farming, and the return of manure to the soil. In the past 30 years, this tradition has been abandoned.

All seemed well until the late 1970s, when the problems associated with the new way of farming began to become apparent. By then, however, encouraged by their governments, farmers had grown used to and become financially and intellectually committed to the new methods. The agro-chemical industry was also well established. When a new fungus appeared that was resistant to the old sprays, they would develop a new strain of fungicide to sell to the farmers. When crop yields began to fall because the underlying fertility of the soil was weakening, they would publish new guidelines recommending the application of greater quantities of fertilizer. When pigs and fowl began to fall sick in their darkened iron pens, they would recommend new feedstocks and multi-purpose antibiotics to get them back on their feet.

Meanwhile, the problems have been mounting. By far the greatest of these is soil erosion. Once the soil is gone, it is gone forever. Up to 30 world civilizations have collapsed because they neglected to look after their topsoil.

At present rates of erosion, the world is losing 7% of its topsoil (25 billion tonnes) every year. The USA has lost 1.7 billion tonnes every year since 1977, and currently loses 500 tonnes of soil for every tonne of corn produced.[28] Soil loss is not quite so bad in Europe, but the underlying collapse of the organic soil structure, coupled with the removal of natural windbreaks and ploughing the land up and down are all playing their part. Every five years or so, when there is a really wet winter, the run-off carries the soil away from fields laid bare for winter wheat. Erosion rates of 20 or 30 tonnes per hectare per year are not uncommon. In the autumn of 1987 some fields on the lovely South Downs in England lost up to 100 tonnes per hectare – 10% of all the soil in the field. The natural renewal rate for topsoil is only 0.5 tonnes per hectare per year.

This is only the most serious of modern agricultural problems. The cruelty of factory-farming methods, the fall in quality of the food itself, the accumulation of toxic residues in the food, causing allergic reactions, the evolution of monster-bugs resistant to all known pesticides, the effects of residues in foods, the evolutionary weakness of genetically identical hybrid crops, the elimination of wildlife in the countryside and the loss of natural variety, the nitrate pollution of groundwater supplies, the energy-intensive nature of chemical farming, the massive unwanted food surpluses and tonnes of waste created by these methods, the loss of the beauty and mystery of the rural landscape, the increasing number of corporate landowners who care about little but profit, the growing mountain of debt brought on by the purchase of all the new technologies, the bankruptcies, and the stresses on the farmers and their families, all play their part in this cruel crisis. In Britain, farmers rate third in the suicide league, after self-employed people and doctors and dentists.[29]

Our post-war love affair with modern agro-industrial farming is over. We need to create a post-industrial way of farming which will nourish our bodies and our souls, and allow us to live again amid nature, while growing the food we need for a healthy existence.

The answers are within relatively easy reach. Methods of agriculture are being adopted by growing numbers of farmers which are less dependent on chemical and artificial input, and which are ecologically sustainable, profitable, good for community life, family farming and the local environment, and which produce high quality pollution-free food.

In September 1986, 1,600 delegates at a Farmer-Rancher Congress in St.Louis, USA, passed resolutions which backed a vision that involved decentralized ownership of the land, revitalized communities, rewards for preventing chemical soil and water pollution, rewards for building up instead of mining the soil, and appropriate tax, lending and pricing policies.[30] The State of Texas has changed to promoting low-chemical pest management, the development of a range of new cash crops, and the establishment of local marketing co-operatives and food-processing facilities. In Iowa, in a major policy turnaround, a new $64.5 million groundwater protection program funded partly by fees on chemical manufacturers and taxes on nitrogen fertilizers is supporting research into alternatives to chemical dependency, and the development of practices that require lower inputs and protect the soil. A similar clause to put a similar tax on pesticides was deleted.[31]

> 'The present agriculture system, unable to continue in its present form and unable to adapt, is starting to be scrapped. A new, more sustainable style of agricultural technology, shaped partly by farmers themselves, is poised to take over.'
> David Ehrenfeld, Technology Review[32]

Some 30–40,000 farms in the USA are now practising organic methods. This represents only 1.6% of the total 2.5 million US farms, but the number is growing. Small scale organic farming is not only proving itself to be more profitable and debt-free; it also marks a move back to the traditional values of rural life, lively local communities, a rich natural environment, and safe, wholesome food.

In Germany, the government of Nordrhein-Westfalen, a populous region with 100,000 farmers, has committed itself to enact a policy of soil protection and ecologically acceptable agriculture, emphasizing the need to protect the soil from toxic emissions, research into ways of applying sewage and animal wastes to farmland, the prevention of soil erosion, and the use of integrated biological pest control methods in place of pesticides.[33] In Austria, the government has brought in a package of measures for the whole country, assisting organic farmers to increase the quality of food, create new jobs on the land, help towards conservation and reduce the country's import bill for fertilizers. In the Alpine National Park, farmers and villagers in the region of Neukirchen am Grossvenediger have formulated an ecologically benign development plan, including low input farming, traditional crafts and waste recycling.

In Britain, applications by farmers to use the Soil Association's organic symbol on their food have increased from five a month in 1985 to 50 a month in 1987. Instead of attempting to fight nature, organic farmers work *with* nature, using the natural variety of her abundance to bring health and productivity to their farms.

Friends of mine have a 22-acre organic riding school in Yeovil, Somerset. Their pasture contains up to 70 different species of natural grass and herb, instead of the 20 – 25 that grow on scientifically stripped and reseeded pastures. When their horses get sick, they choose their own herbs, drawing on their own evolutionary 'horse-wisdom'. They need no antibiotics, and the vet's bills are very low. In a similar vein, docks are traditionally known as 'noxious' weeds which animals never touch. Yet on the organic urban community at Windmill Down, in Bristol, the farmer once saw a cow at a very particular stage of pregnancy eating docks. Nature possesses far more wisdom than we can begin to understand.

The shift to organic methods of agriculture generally involves a fall in yield that varies from 4% to 20%. This is less than the extent to which farmers are overproducing, using chemical methods. The yield that is obtained from good organic growing is the *ecologically optimum yield* around which plans and policies should be based. Increased yields from chemically-based farming are equivalent to the increased energy humans experience from amphetamines or sugar. They give an extra buzz for a while, but then lead to dependency and serious physical problems. In 1988, the people of the canton of Berne, in Switzerland, agreed in a referendum to provide a four-year transition subsidy for farmers wishing to move over to organic methods, to cover them while their fields regain their natural organic fertility.

The chemically-induced overproduction of modern agriculture is throwing agriculture in North America and Europe into a major crisis, and opening the doors to a complete rethink of our policies about food production, land settlement and the whole environment. Our need to use less energy, to farm in ecologically sustainable ways and to produce food that is safe and wholesome coincides with the need for widespread reforestation to help offset the greenhouse effect, with the wish many people have to live much more closely to nature in a rural or semi-rural setting, and with the need for wilderness zones where people can experience the wonder and mystery of nature.

The need for more tree cover is absolutely critical, both ecologically and spiritually – we need to double the number of trees on the Earth. Tree cover absorbs the excess carbon dioxide in the atmosphere created by our burning of fossil fuels, corrects the negative ion balance, cleans out pollutants from the air and nourishes us inwardly. Trees reach the parts other things cannot reach! For 11,000 years, ever since the ice melted, Europe was covered with trees, and in our unconscious ancestral minds the forest, with its canopy of beech, ash and oak, is still our spiritual home.

Possibilities for the future include the shifting of agricultural subsidies to encourage organic production, measures to stimulate and encourage organic farming, the purchase of land for forestry by local communities, the development of agro-forestry food-growing methods, and the repopulation of rural areas in ecologically sustainable ways. It is possible to imagine new human settlements dispersed among pasture woodlands where deer, cattle and sheep roam, and where a variety of local enterprise underpins a community economy. The romantic worlds of Robin Hood of Sherwood and the knights of King Arthur may become an economically viable, ecologically sustainable and spiritually nourishing way of life. Creativity, commitment, research, partnership and strategy – these are the methods needed to turn dreams into reality.

THE GREENING OF THE CITIES

The countryside is one thing – but what of the cities, where 89% of us live ? For many who are trapped in the wasteland of modern cities, where the air is dirty, community weak, where most relationships are impersonal and where loneliness and fear are common, life can easily seem a very grey and bewildering affair.

It is quite unnatural for humans to live apart from nature. Only in very recent times have we been herded together in metropolitan sprawls, locked up at night in flats and houses, alone or in tiny families. Only in very recent times have speeding cars and trucks stolen away from our children the streets and neighbourhoods and have soaring tower blocks become home to hundreds of thousands of people. Only in very recent years has child suicide become noticeable.

The cost of our lost connections – to nature, to the community and to ourselves – is hidden in the statistics for tranquillizers, alcohol consumption and the sale of security locks, in the budgets of our welfare and social services departments, in the costs of crime, prison and mental breakdown, and in the loneliness and distress of countless millions of people all over the world.

Since the mid-1970s, however, something very remarkable has been happening. Scraps of barren wasteland have been turned into urban nature reserves. Dirty old canals have been cleaned up by volunteers and have become homes for kingfishers. Concrete school playgrounds have been transformed into gardens. Urban farms with sheep, goats and pigs have been established in abandoned corners. In response to city alienation, people have begun a greening process.[34]

First it was small groups of enthusiasts meeting together at weekends to clear out the old bottles, brambles and broken prams that 'grow' on urban land that is neglected and unloved, and turning it into areas filled with butterflies, trees, shrubs, vegetables and children playing. Then the theme was taken up by others. In Birmingham, England, local naturalists, planners, teachers and landscape architects joined forces to form a partnership called the West Midlands Urban Wildlife Group, dedicated to creating a greener Birmingham. 'If urban greenspace could be used to sustain meadow flowers, skylarks, dragonflies and hedgehogs – to provide a "country experience" – then life could be far more pleasant for people living in towns.'[35] Out of this group grew new nature reserves, wildlife action areas and in 1984, a comprehensive nature conservation strategy for the whole West Midlands, the first of its kind in Britain.

A new vision is emerging of what a city can be, in which the magic of wildlife and rural life are restored in the midst of the noise and traffic. 'Green lanes' are being created as wildlife routes. New cycle tracks and pathways are being built which weave relatively silent paths amid newly growing shrubs and trees, away from the bustle of the High Street. This contrast between the noise, petrol fumes, police sirens and busy shoppers, and the quiet of an earthen path wandering slowly along the banks of a tiny cleaned-up stream is worth quite a few emergency social workers. Every hundred metres of such path may mean one less person in prison. Every town needs quiet spaces where one can wander and listen to the song of the birds.

One of the tasks facing green economists must be to quantify this contrast, and spell out the cost-benefit advantages of a way of life that builds community, gets people involved, nourishes the spirit, and is closer to nature. Horticultural therapy has been shown to be successful with offenders and prison inmates, and with the mentally disturbed. Wilderness therapy is practised widely by psychiatric hospitals and juvenile centres in the USA. An analysis of hospital records in Pennsylvania indicated that post-operative patients recovered more quickly, with fewer complications and with a two-thirds reduction in their drug-intake if they could see trees through their window instead of blank brick walls.[36] In a unique piece of research quoted by David Nicholson-Lord in 'The Greening of the Cities', it was shown that the children of the Abaluyia Bantu sub-clan in Kenya, who alternate between rural horticulture and city labouring work, were aggressive, threatening and disruptive in their city environment, but helpful, co-operative and sociable when in the country. The green economists need to find ways to spell out the cost advantages of living patterns that are in harmony with nature, and argue for this greater overall economic efficiency and wisdom in the budgetary procedures of government. It is crazy housekeeping to pay large sums of public money to run people-repair institutions such as prisons and hospitals, when smaller investments in community development, local economic development employment strategies, greening the city and local empowerment would remove many of the stress and alienation-related problems, and bring greater benefits to everyone concerned. This is a challenge that must be picked up by the coming generation of public accountants, policy-makers, managers and administrators (see Chapter Eleven).

The initiatives of the last ten years have shown the possibilities. For most urban dwellers, however, life is still characterized by too much concrete, noise and dirt. Wildlife paradises are few and far between, and far too many streets and open spaces carry an 'unloved' feeling which makes the heart tighten, and which sets the ambience for stress, fear and crime.

Local people need to be approaching their whole environment in a positive way, asking themselves. 'How could we turn this neighbourhood into a beautiful, loving, green environment?' By getting together, reading the literature, visiting projects to learn what is possible, and by using future workshops, community planning techniques and group walk-arounds, the latent creativity of a community can be awakened. By organizing partnership groups with the people in the public planning and landscape architecture departments, by calling on local companies to provide grants and sponsorships, by calling on local naturalists and ecologists for advice, and by involving local schools, colleges and hospitals, the energy can be mobilized and can achieve miracles. By holding a vision of what is possible at the very highest level, we can put an end to this way of life that gives no nourishment, which separates us from nature and which causes people to die inside.

It does not matter who starts things rolling. If it is left to local government, it may never happen. Anyone can form a 'Greening the City' group by writing an initial letter to the local paper and making a few posters to advertise a small initial meeting. Many local authority people will be delighted to help, and very pleased to see people in the community taking the initiative. You will find yourselves members of a growing movement of people who collectively possess the skills and experience to advise you further. Just start. Don't wait for someone else to.

CARS

It is hard to consider 'greening the city' without asking the question 'what about the cars?'. It is the car, above all (and the motorbike, coach, bus, truck and van) which fills the air with pollution and noise, which turns the streets into dangerous race-tracks, which kills 6,000 people a year in Britain (44,000 a year in the USA) along with huge numbers of birds, foxes, hedgehogs, cats and dogs, which cripples and injures countless others, and which prevents our neighbourhoods from becoming the wonderful pavement-culture places we love so much when we see them elsewhere (where are you, Montreal, Basle, Amsterdam?). It is the motor car which prevents young children from playing freely on the streets and keeps them locked inside their homes, making parenting an exhausting task, and is one of the reasons underlying the increase in cases of child-battering. Car exhausts kill trees, play a major role in creating acid rain, poison children and adults with lead emissions and cause psychic stress among pedestrians. We love the car for the convenience it gives us – but there are many reasons to hate it, too.

At a city-wide level, much can be done to encourage people to use buses and bikes instead of cars. The ancient city of Florence, in Italy, made its whole central area traffic-free in 1988, after decades of motorist-madness. Oxford City Council has had a 'Balanced Transport Policy' ever since 1972, when the local Labour government first came to power. Its aim is to make Oxford a 'liveable city', through an integrated transport policy, which aims to keep the cars out. Elements of the policy include:

- successful 'Park-and-Ride' car parks built on the edge of the city (Europe's only profit-making scheme) with 2,500 city centre car-parking spaces relocated on the periphery of the city;
- high parking charges in the city centre;
- traffic management schemes to slow traffic in residential streets (the 'Woonerf' model – see below);
- an extensive segregated cycle lane system;

- 1,200 cycle parking spaces in the city centre;
- rigid planning conditions which only allow essential city-centre parking;
- coloured street-bumps and chicane-effect bends to slow traffic on very busy streets;
- a deliberate mixing of housing and employment, making it easy for people to walk or cycle to get to work;
- major improvements for pedestrians; and
- 'company bikes' instead of cars for council officers going around the city on business!

It took seven to ten years for objections to die down and for people to get used to the new ways. After 15 years, even the traders and shopkeepers now praise the scheme. Traffic movements in the city are lower than they were 15 years ago, and 25% of all traffic movements across a main bridge into the city centre are now by bike. One result of the policy has been a massive rejuvenation of inner-city housing, with pleasant new residential areas appearing.[37]

The biggest impact can often be made on the immediate streets where you live. In The Hague, Holland, a scheme called 'Woonerf' has been running since 1981 in a residential part of the city. The streets have been obstructed by landscape features and the pavements removed, giving pedestrians, cyclists, children and cars equal rights over the entire road surface, with none being allowed intentionally to hinder the others. Cars which must travel there do so very slowly, and parking is restricted. Some cities in Britain are experimenting with closing streets altogether, filling them with trees, seats, small play areas and open-air seating. Others are closing them to all save residents, or closing them at one end, preventing their use by through-traffic. Without so many cars, people can breathe. Isolation and stress in the neighbourhood can be relieved, and communities can come together for street activities.

The only people who care strongly about the particular street you live on are you yourselves. If you wait until the local council or city government does something, you might wait until eternity. Form a small group with people on the street whom you know, and discuss your ideas together. Fix up meetings with your local councillor or representative in City Hall, with the local planning department, and if there is a local amenity or environmental society, with them too. Start a small campaign – it may take months (or years) to achieve anything, but once you have achieved it, you will enjoy the benefits for decades. The best place to start greening your city is right where you live, in your own neighbourhood.

Taken in conjunction with policies outlined in other chapters, these initiatives begin to add up to a completely new kind of city, recycling its own wastes, conserving its energy, nourishing its communities, creating havens of beauty and peace, fostering local self-reliance, developing user-friendly transport systems, encouraging local businesses to play their part responsibly in the local environment, and seeking health and wellbeing for all its people. The World Health Organization is currently supporting an innovative programme called 'Healthy Cities', which is exploring ways of achieving much the same goals.

Community architects have shown that when people are actively involved in the recreation of their local environment, the place is loved, and maintained with care. People take pride in its beauty. We can turn private artistry into community and environmental artistry, making cathedrals of the whole of our surroundings.

A STRATEGY FOR A SUSTAINABLE FUTURE

Our need to find a path that will lead to a happier, more balanced and sustainable way of life is critically urgent. For a hundred reasons, practically and spiritually, we must create a workable strategy for a sustainable future.

When people talk of a workable strategy, they normally think in terms of the 'they' of national or government action. The centralistic nature of our societies leads us into a vast mental error. We see government ministers and the heads of corporations on television, and assume that is where the power must be. Of course, they do have power – but nowhere near as much power as we potentially have within our own localities. It is locally, in our communities, and in our own hearts and minds, where the real power lies. It only seems as if someone else has the power as long as we fail to claim our own.

To claim this power and build the kind of world we dream of, we need to get together and form local ecological partnerships, drawing together people from all sectors of local life who share the vision, and who have the skills and commitment to work towards the goals of ecological sustainability.

The partnerships will need to establish special action committees to cover each of the areas where sustainability is needed, including planetary issues such as the development of alternatives to pesticides that are sold for export. In developing a strategy, eight main approaches can be used as follows:

1. *Education*, providing individuals, companies, schools and organizations with the information they need to change to ecologically sustainable ways.
2. *Consumer campaigns*, assisting people to become 'conscious consumers', avoiding CFC (chloroflours-carbons)-containing canisters and food-cartons, purchasing organic foods, biodegradable washing liquids, etc.
3. *Research* into technologies and social-economic arrangements which facilitate sustainability.
4. *Campaigns*, using whatever means are appropriate, including boycotts when other means bring no results.
5. *Transformation*, encouraging companies and organizations to develop policies of ecological excellence (see Chapter Eight).
6. *Creating new institutions and initiatives* to develop community participation in ecologically sustainable practices.
7. *Legislation*, creating new local by-laws and regulations,

enforcing national laws and international laws.
8. *Pursuing an integrated approach*, linking policies and using integrated budgeting approaches.

During the 1970s and 1980s, many environmental issues have been protest issues. As a strategy, this is necessary, but nowhere near sufficient. We must place the issue of permanent ecological sustainability on the agenda of all our local groups, companies, organisations and governments. In order to do so, there must be a widely-based ecological body which reflects the participation of the whole community. *The local ecological partnership is an idea whose time must, in some guise or other, come.*

In case you think this is too idealistic, read on . . .

In Germany, the symbol of the 'Blue Angel' is used to give products an environmental 'seal of approval'. Products seeking the symbol must be approved by a panel of independent judges appointed by the Environment Ministry. A separate 'Green *Which?*' magazine gives environmental appraisals to products. A similar idea is now being developed by the Canadian Government.

In the London Borough of Sutton, an 18-point Environmental Statement was produced outlining the council's commitment to pursue 'policies which reflect its concern for the quality of the local environment and the need to conserve the finite resources of the planet . . . [and] to establish a proper balance between short-term economic requirements and the longer term ecological needs of our community'. Sutton is backing its policy with initiatives to safeguard natural habitats and to create small woods, by involving the community through field days, voluntary action and special events, supporting local recycling initiatives, funding an independent Centre for Environmental Information, setting up an Urban Improvement Working Party covering energy conservation, transport, cycling and pedestrians, launching the umbrella Sutton Conservation Group, and setting up a special Policy Committee to ensure that the 18-point commitment is followed through

231

in every council department.[38]

Consider the following possibilities for action:

- Guidelines can be drawn up to help local companies develop ecological sustainability strategies, and encouragement given to the publication of annual ecological reports.

- Profit margins on many consumer goods are often as low as 10%. Thus it only takes 5% of consumers to change their choice of products to have a powerful effect – 'the 5% Effect'.[39]

- A score-chart can be created enabling individuals to work out the 'Sustainability Quotient' (SQ) of their consumer habits, with information-sheets telling where to buy locally produced goods, recycled paper and biodegradable washing liquids and how to invest money in a socially responsible way.

- Future workshops can be held to explore how different neighbourhoods can be developed environmentally, and competitions held in schools to encourage a constant flow of new ideas and activities.

- Communities can publish lists of relevant research which needs doing, enabling school and university students to use the opportunities their essays, theses and PhDs to serve practical local needs.

When a partnership works well, it will win local support, since surveys show that most people do support the goals of long-term sustainability: in Britain, 75–80% would pay more to protect the environment; 95% of housewives would be prepared to separate their household waste; 60% of consumers would be willing to pay higher prices for organic food if only they knew where to find it.[40]

In time, partnerships can evolve into regional ecological authorities, providing the long-term ecological governance we need to safeguard the unspoken needs of nature, of her rivers, fields, woods and creatures, and of the future generations as yet unborn. Over the next 30–50 years, we *must* learn new habits that harmonize with nature's ways.

To some, this might still seem like wishful thinking. Not so. In Canada, in the wake of the visit by the World Commission on Environment and Development, and the publication of the UN Brundtland Report, *Our Common Future*, the whole country is embarking on a process of strategy-building along similar lines using 'Round Table' groups to develop strategies (see Chapter Twelve). What we are witnessing are the first steps of a major process of change which will be affecting every community by the late 1990s. The ecological dimension of the rainbow economy development strategy is getting underway.

Objectively, the outlook for planet Earth is grim indeed. Already, however, the tide is turning. Many yearn for a different way of life, away from the greed and rush. Who could ever want this Earth to become an ugly wasteland, devoid of forest, peace or clear water? Most people, in their conscious or unconscious hearts, have strong beliefs that are on the side of life. The future is in our hands. It is simply up to us to take it, and create the paradise we want.

Chapter Eleven :
The evolution of community democracy

There are few limits to what can be achieved once creativity and initiative are awakened at the local level. But for this awakening energy to flow easily and smoothly, our systems of government must change, to reflect the desire for greater involvement which is coming up from the local level. The emerging rainbow economy needs an emerging rainbow politics and an emerging rainbow government to achieve its fullest goals.

Local government is smaller and more flexible than national government, so it is primarily within local government that these changes are beginning.

Local government in Britain is massive. It employs an eighth of the country's workforce and spends an eighth of the gross domestic product.[1] The City of Birmingham, with a population of one million, employs 50,000 staff and has an annual budget of one billion pounds. For many people, local government is distant, bureaucratic and tied up in its own machineries, delivering its services in a top-down way. That it manages to achieve what it does is a tribute to the dedication of some of those who work in it. For others, in the towns and cities where new approaches are being explored, local government is increasingly being perceived as open, democratic, flexible and as making a real contribution to local life.

Local government is evolving as younger (and women) councillors seek to realize the values that underlie the emergence of the rainbow economy. This chapter considers some of these changes.

SIX STEPS TO A PARTICIPATIVE FUTURE

Six political-administrative steps are needed to reflect the new values and give them expression. They are –
- decentralization;
- the evolution of community democracy;
- the shift from administrators to animators;
- the practising of integrated community budgeting;
- integrated policy-making; and
- 'transpolitical' co-operation.

Most of these developments are already under way, reflecting the wider process of evolution that is working through us in its constant search for ways to realize unity.

Decentralization

Local government, as currently organised, is too large, too impersonal and too distant to be able to function in a person-centred or a community-centred way. In Britain, an elected council governs through its service committees, which decide policy in areas such as housing, social services, education, planning, leisure and recreation. The committees meet once a month, and deal with matters for the whole area, which may include from 100,000 to one million people.[2] Each committee is served by a department with paid staff who concern themselves (for instance) with the housing problems of the whole borough or district. The departments are large, usually housed in separate buildings, and rarely have the time to plan co-ordinated approaches to the issues with which they deal.

Over the last seven years, there has been growing interest in decentralization. One of the first councils to commit itself to change was the London Borough of Islington. In May 1982, the new Labour council adopted a policy of decentralization in order to improve the delivery of their services and to increase local democracy. They divided the borough into 24 neighbourhoods, each with an average population of 6,500 people, and created 24 Neighbourhood Offices, each equipped with office space for the key local government departments, and with a children's area and community meeting room. Instead of having to wander all over the borough in search of different departments, local people can now find solutions to most of their local government-related problems in this one building.

The decentralization did not go through without its share of fears, resistance and difficulties, but by organizing staff trainings and holding detailed discussions with trade unions and with public meetings in every neighbourhood, the timetable was upheld. The new offices are open-plan, designed to be true community offices where local people feel welcome.

On both personal and organizational levels, the new system works well. Local people like it, as they have a Neighbourhood Office within ten minutes walk of where they live. The staff like it, because they have closer working relationships with people in other council departments, and better contact with local people.

Islington's second goal was to spread the process of democracy to the neighbourhood level, and to this end they are creating 24 Neighbourhood Forums which will involve local people in practical decision-making. In some neighbourhoods, the first elections have been held and the Forums set up.[3] In the next section, 'The evolution of community democracy', the potential of these Neighbourhood Forums is discussed.

Three miles south of Islington, the Liberal council of Tower Hamlets has carried through both political and administrative decentralization.

Tower Hamlets is a traditional working class community of 140,000 people who used to work in the docks and the surrounding factories. These are now mostly either abandoned, or undergoing rapid upmarket development. The borough is made up of seven 'hamlets' — the Isle of Dogs, Bethnal Green, Wapping, Globe Town, Poplar, Stepney and Bow. It is one of London's poorest boroughs, and includes some of the city's worst housing conditions.

For fifty years, the borough was ruled by the Labour Party in a traditional way. After each election, councillors were allocated to one of the committees which serve the whole borough (as elsewhere). Councillors tend to be parochial, however, and unfamiliar with problems outside their own patch. Much of the agenda at the meetings would concern areas they knew little about, so the council officers ended up making most of the decisions, with the councillors just toeing the line. The different departmental offices were large and far apart, and local people often felt very frustrated.

In the May 1986 local elections, the Liberal Party won control on a platform of full political and administrative decentralization designed to restore control to the elected councillors and to improve the delivery of services.[4] The borough was immediately divided into seven separate neighbourhoods, each with around 20,000 people. The old departments were abolished, along with their service committees. In their place, seven new Neighbourhood Committees were set up and seven new one-stop Neighbourhood Offices opened. There was again much resistance from local government staff and officers who felt threatened by the change, but in the end most of the changes went through on schedule.

For local government, the change represents a real revolution. Each neighbourhood is now governed by a single Neighbourhood Committee, consisting of the locally elected councillors. Instead of trying to make decisions for the whole borough, the councillors' attentions are fully focused on the patches they know and represent. The Borough divides the income from the rates (local taxes) and from central government among the seven neighbourhoods, and Neighbourhood Committees can spend the money in any way they like. There are no central budgetary controls except in issues which concern the borough as a whole, such as the Canary Wharf development in the old docks.

As in Islington, once they got used to the changes, the council staff found they much preferred the new system, which brings them increased responsibility and more contact with local people. Inter-departmental communication is much improved. Everything is now on a smaller and more personal scale, though not as small as in Islington. There is a new ability to deal with needs within their local context, which leads to appropriate decision-making. Staff loyalty is now primarily to the neighbourhoods, not to the departments, and the old sense of 'them' and 'us' is gradually dissolving, along with the sense of battle it engendered. While 10% of the staff either left or took early retirement in the change-over, new staff are being attracted by the new approach.

Councillors now feel they have the power to achieve something. A proliferation of innovative housing schemes has started, with wastelands that have lain empty for years being developed. A critical blockage in the area's energy-system has been removed, and with the flow of new energy comes a new sense of life. The neighbourhoods are free to develop their own ways of extending democracy to the local community, and in some areas, Neighbourhood Forums are being established, with their own elected representatives.[5]

In Tower Hamlets, both political and budgetary power have been decentralized. There are only a limited number of councillors who can be elected in any one borough, so if Tower Hamlets had divided itself into 24 neighbourhoods, as Islington did, there would have been only two councillors per neighbourhood to constitute the Neighbourhood Committee. Islington has avoided this problem by decentralizing only the administration, not the political and budgetary power (but see below).

Tower Hamlets and Islington have shown that in Britain

at least, if you have vision and determination, local government can decentralize itself without need for any new laws.

The evolution of community democracy

Tower Hamlets and Islington have gone a long way, but they have still only made half the journey towards a fully participative local democracy, serving the needs of local communities.

Local government is a top-down affair, even in its decentralized state. The Tower Hamlets 'top' simply reaches down to 20,000 people instead of 140,000. That is a seven-fold improvement, but it still leaves a long way to reach. The 'bottom' must also have a way to reach up.

The essence of the bottom-up approach to government is that local people can meet together, develop their ideas and start their own initiatives. Their vitality is awakened and their latent power released. This book has been full of examples of this vitality.

To create the extra level of community democracy needed to reflect this vitality, the Bow Neighbourhood Committee in Tower Hamlets divided its area into 18 natural localities and set up the Bow Neighbourhood Forum, with representatives elected from each locality. In Islington, the Neighbourhood Offices are establishing Neighbourhood Forums in a similar way. The new Islington Forums have advisory control over £180,000 of the Neighbourhood Office's annual budget, and it is intended that this figure will steadily increase to £3-4 million per annum.

When local government is decentralized to a scale small enough to be properly personal, something critically important happens.

People tend to identify with their local communities. Their relationships with local people are personal and direct, not official, abstracted from real life. They grow to love and care about the place where they live, and often develop effective ideas about ways in which local life could be improved. When the steering mechanisms of local government are far away they hardly ever act on their ideas, however, as no channels exist to allow them easy expression. When the steering mechanisms come within reach, creating these channels, local people suddenly find that they can act on their ideas. An initiative from one of the new Islington neighbourhoods illustrates what can happen next.

The steering group for the Clocktower Neighbourhood Forum decided that unemployment was a key issue, and set up an Employment and Youth Sub-Group to explore what might be done. Islington has an unemployment rate of 19%, which means that one person in five of working age is out of work, a total of 650 people in the Clocktower area.

The sub-group commissioned a survey of job opportunities among 91 local businesses, which pointed to many areas where action could be taken, from the provision of literacy and numeracy courses to the establishment of a 'compact' between the local schools and colleges and employers (see Chapter Eight). Altogether, 22 proposals were made for local and regional action, which the sub-group is now working on. There is no one answer to the problems of unemployment. There are instead a hundred separate answers, which require integration in a coherent strategy. Probably half of these answers can be achieved by local action, while the other half require national action. When the local community has no way of organizing itself, the local components remain undone, and people are left hoping that someone else will do something about the rest, which adds to their sense of helplessness. In the Clocktower neighbourhood, the way is now open for the new Forum to set up a Neighbourhood Development Association (see Chapter Six) and establish an integrated strategy to tackle unemployment, in conjunction with Islington Council.[6]

Unemployment is just one area where a community can devise its own strategies, once it has the means of working together. The same is true for housing, for greening the neighbourhood, for drug-abuse, for work-sharing, for holistic business development, for preventing crime, in fact for every area where local life does not measure up to people's dreams. Building a sustainable rainbow economy simply requires a multitude of actions, of which half are local. Once local people have the structures to organize themselves, the essential local work can be tackled.

Oxford City Council, which has fewer powers than the London boroughs, is pursuing its own path to decentralization and community involvement. This entails a major £800,000 p.a. grants programme to voluntary groups; the widespread co-opting of local people on to council committees (with at least 170 co-optees outnumbering councillors by four to one); locally-based working parties which span different committees, where the majority of the membership consists of local co-optees; the establishment of local offices and Neighbourhood Councils on some estates; the abolition of the Policy and Resources Committee through which the chief council officers normally seek to control the other committees, the rotation of committee chairs (a practice introduced by the Green Party in Germany), and a rule which says that the leader of the Council may not chair a committee. The introduction of Parish Councils into inner-city areas is also being actively considered.[7]

In the USA, many cities have ways of making democracy more answerable to the electorate. Some have established the right of recall, making it possible to remove a locally elected official before the end of his or her term. Some cities enable citizens to initiate or enact legislation directly. Others have referendums, permitting citizens to vote on legislation. Each of these is a valuable addition to the tool-kit of democracy. In Hawaii, every city uses each of the three methods. In California, the three methods are practised by 96%, 90% and 93% of cities respectively. In Indiana, the figures are 14%, 6% and 36%.[8] In Britain, home of 'the mother of parliaments', the equivalent figures

are 0%, 0% and 0%. At the national level, British democracy has become completely stuck and ceased to evolve, a
condition which contributes in a major way to the political
sickness that characterizes British life. It is at the local level
that democracy is beginning to find new life.

All this requires work. New community organizations
don't spring into being overnight. They require careful
nursing into existence by a new breed of community mid-
wife – the community worker, or 'animateur'.

Shifting from administrators to animateurs

Animateurs are people whose skills are not in delivering,
but in awakening. The French use the word 'animateur' –
'she or he who breathes life'. They are community
development workers, people who have been trained to
help local people meet together, share their concerns and
organize themselves to do something positive. Their attention is set on helping local people do what they want to do
– not on undertaking specific tasks themselves. The 'Esperance' initiative provides a good example (see Chapter
Seven).

Many animateurs are already at work in the communities of Western Europe, North America and
Australasia. They are helping people start up businesses,
co-operatives, community businesses, credit unions, community associations and self-help groups. Some are
unpaid, and some are paid by grants and fund-raising
efforts, and increasingly by local government. In Islington,
the new Neighbourhood Offices each employs a community worker who helps local people organize themselves
around their rights and needs.

Local government is gradually evolving – and needs to
evolve – from being a 'provider' to being an 'enabler'.
Instead of providing housing, social services, parks and a
hundred other things, its role is becoming one of providing
the supportive structures which will enable people to meet
their needs themselves.

In the mountainous Isère region of France, near Grenoble, a development project paid seven local farmers to hire part-time helpers, so that the farmers could work part-time as animateurs among other local farmers in the region. By meeting together to discuss their problems, the farmers were able to develop a wide range of new initiatives, including new agricultural co-operatives, a flour mill, a homeopathic veterinary training course, a training programme in agrobiology and a stock breeders' support group. These home-grown measures are helping to stem the rural exodus. In Austria, a development agency in the mountainous Bergland area employs animateurs to achieve very similar goals.[9]

This enabling approach works for problems of loneliness and mental disturbance, to help local people work out a strategy to cope with the closure of a factory or the retooling of an arms factory, or to help people develop strategies for ecological sustainability. In a 'post-crash' context, community animateurs will help local people organize self-help financial circles, form housing trusts to purchase the houses of people whose mortgages might have been foreclosed, set up community agriculture co-operatives, establish LETSystems (see Chapter Four), and so on.

There are seven ways in which local government can speed up the evolution from providing to enabling, from administrating to animating. (We haven't got forever to get these changes made.)

• The *first* is by setting up a working group to examine council practices to ensure that they encourage community initiative.

• The *second* is by organizing training sessions for staff and officers so that they understand what 'enabling' is all about, and rethink their modes of operating where necessary.

• The *third* is by decentralizing.

• The *fourth* is by co-opting local people onto council committees, so that the divisions between 'government' and 'the people' become blurred.

● The *fifth* is by employing paid animateurs trained in the process of enabling (community workers, development workers) to assist in the development of community initiatives. The more a community does for itself through its own initiatives, the fewer top-down administrators are needed.

● The *sixth* is by funding courses in the techniques of community development, group facilitation, teamwork skills and personal counselling, so that local people acquire the skills needed to start initiatives and lead self-help groups themselves.

● The *seventh* is by providing grants and loans to assist in the development of community initiatives, starting off with small start-up and feasibility study grants, and the assurance of continuing support for initiatives which meet community needs.

On their own, community initiatives often have difficulty in sustaining themselves. They need help from people closer to the top who can open doors, share professional skills, write cheques and sign important bits of paper. Without this help, the leadership of a group changes, the grants run out or something else happens to weaken a group's resolve, and all of a sudden the initiative collapses. It happens tragically often. Without a deliberate policy to support and nourish them, community initiatives are like steam engines trying to move across open land without any tracks to run on. The going is difficult, and many engines end up on their sides in the mud.

Taken together, decentralization, the organization of neighbourhood forums and initiatives, and the development of policies geared to serve the needs of community groups give the flow of power from the grassroots upwards real meaning. Local politicians and government will then have something solid to concern and involve themselves with. An integrated system is created which permits the organized energy of community initiative to achieve whatever it wants, needs and dreams of. At last, our creative human energy can flow freely, and our evolution can move into a higher gear.

Integrated community budgeting

Behind local government's traditional approach of providing for people's needs lies an inadequate analysis of community problems, and a consequentially inadequate budgetary policy. The same applies to national government. Although it has never been seen as such, social expenditure should always be treated as an investment, just as business expenditure is. There should be sound investment analysis and an approximation of the likely rate of return before each investment is made.

The usual emphasis in both local and national government has been on accepting the social order (or disorder) much as it is, and endeavouring to meet the human needs that arise in consequence. Homelessness has been met by building council houses, family problems by creating and staffing children's homes and problems of crime by building prisons. These are band-aid responses which deal with the symptoms, not with the underlying causes of the problems. As investments, their rate of return ranges from 0% to a heavy loss.

Tackling the symptoms of a problem by providing band-aids is the least effective (and least cost-effective) way to tackle it, but the practice continues year after year because the different departments in charge of administering the solutions are never asked to apply their resources to the solution of a problem as a whole. They have separate budgets, and pursue separate paths.

To contain crime, for instance, we pay enormous sums of money every year to maintain prisons, courts and lawyers, and to cover a whole list of crime-related costs. In Wolverhampton, the local authority spends £100,000 a year replacing broken school windows and more than £1 million pounds cleaning graffiti from the buses.[10] Little of this expenditure actually reduces crime – it just contains it. As an investment, it is a non-starter. In communities where there are strong social networks, where young people are given responsibilities from their teenage years onwards, and have role-models who are engaged in meaningful work, where the diet is balanced and where young people have fulfilling work to look forward to in adulthood, juvenile crime is practically non-existent. The social factors which create a low-crime community can be listed, as can the social factors which create a high-crime community. Quite simply, investments in the former will earn a high return in the shape of a reduced annual crime-bill.

The present system, because it approaches breakdown in a fragmented, symptom-related way (like much western allopathic medicine) instead of in a holistic, cause-related manner, addresses only the surface needs, not the deep ones. The frustration of having to implement band-aid remedies with families whose real problems may be poverty, capital-deprivation, bad education, internalized self-oppression or awful housing has been the bane of many a social worker's life. Schemes which address the deeper needs through community organizing, forming neighbourhood self-help groups, greening the cities or personal counselling have to fight for funds as pilot projects, while the prisons and graffiti-washing operations receive regular finance from the main budgets. As a cost-effective way of governing a country, it is sheer madness.

There is at present no way in which the financial savings on prisons, law-courts and graffiti-cleaning which would result from investment in preventative initiatives can be offset against the initial cost of the investment. The two budgets have no relation to each other, and the resulting mess is a grand waste of public money. Governments which pride themselves on 'good housekeeping' persist with such folly because their own personal and social prejudices make them prefer to believe that crime is simply caused by criminals, and poverty by laziness, and because they want the votes of people who enjoy holding the same views. It is a shame that the natural intelligence of government ministers and civil servants should be so wasted, when a clear-minded approach would quickly tell them that a different pattern of investment would bring the results they sought. Furthermore, as a psychological response to having to implement policies which they know can never work, the officials responsible lose their motivation, and focus their energies instead on rules and procedures, forgetting the human distress their actions so easily cause.

The same financial mismanagement applies to areas such as hospitals, social services, debt collectors, doctors, welfare, mental hospitals and pollution clean-up. Disintegrated social investment analysis and budgeting leads to a dis-integrating society.

One answer to this muddle is the application of greater intelligence in the social analysis of breakdowns like crime, homelessness, family assault, sexual abuse and environmental collapse, and integrated or holistic community budgeting in the pursuit of their solution.

All the costs relating to a particular problem should be analysed in a single integrated procedure, and an accountancy system set up to relate investments to results, providing the information needed to enable investments to be made in the most cost-effective way.

Taking crime as an example, the first thing that is needed is the gross annual crime cost for the whole country.[11] A formula can then be worked out to calculate the average cost for each type of reported crime, and using a city's annual crime figures, an annual crime bill could be arrived at for that city. In Britain, in 1988, 50,000 prisoners each cost the tax-payer around £300 a week. A further £105 a week per prisoner goes to support dependants and to cover for lost taxes and revenue generated from spending power. Leaving aside the costs of maintaining the police service, the total cost of crime in Britain comes to around £43 million a week, without the cost of maintaining the police, £100 million a week including the police. For a city such as Leicester (population 280,000) this comes to £220,000 a week, or £500,000 a week if the cost of policing is included.

These figures represent part of the yearly social repair bill which British taxpayers pay to cover the costs of the social breakdown which is resulting from many years of bad social investment. Any further investment in social control is simply good money thrown after bad. Investment in social renewal, however, by financing initiatives which increase the level of social well-being in a community, yields a good return by reducing the gross annual bill for crime and other forms of social breakdown. Careful social investment analysis should be able to relate the investment cost of particular initiatives to the ensuing reduction or increase in personal and social breakdown, and give a likely rate of financial return for each initiative. By investing in initiatives which yield the best rates of return, government and local authorities can reduce social breakdown, along with its associated social repair bills.

As examples of different investment policies, in 1972 the head of the prison systems in Massachusetts, USA, closed down all the State's juvenile prisons and released the inmates. Instead of rising, the juvenile crime-rate in the area fell, and has remained low ever since. In Britain, 70% of all prisoners are non-violent offenders who have been convicted of offences such as theft, burglary or the non-payment of fines. The cost of imprisonment is nearly 20 times greater than the cost of keeping someone on probation or on a community service order, but imprisonment seems to serve no useful purpose, with 60% of ex-convicts re-offending within two years.[12] Magistrates should be made to consider the cost-effectiveness of their punishment policies, and be asked to follow formulae for punishments which relate the investment in a punishment which the magistrate is making to its likely rate of return. Similarly, the public's investment in police salaries might be linked to productivity agreements which pegged police pay to reduced crime rates (as ascertained by local surveys as well as by reported crime figures). That would give them an incentive to start thinking holistically.

Under existing budgetary procedures, there is no incentive to practise holistic policy-making or budgeting, since the return on an investment hardly ever returns to the department which makes it. If Leicester City Council invests £1 million in an integrated programme of community-based social repair initiatives, the return on the investment in reduced crime-costs will accrue to the Home Office and the insurance companies, and to the Area Health Authority in reduced road accident and mental breakdown costs. Only in reduced need for social services intervention will it accrue to the local authority. Under integrated budgeting procedures, for every £1 million fall in Leicester's annual £26 million crime/law-and-order bill which resulted from the investment, the City Council might receive £750,000 (the rest being needed to service standing capital costs which cannot be eliminated overnight). In this way, Leicester would receive a proper return on its investment. If this type of policy were applied to the whole country, the capital costs of new prison building could be eliminated and existing prisons gradually closed down. Investment in social efficiency programmes removes the need for prison-building, just as investment in energy efficiency programmes removes the need for new power plants.

The same approach can be taken regarding the costs of hospitals, mental hospitals, social services and all the other social breakdown and repair industries. Where fragmented social expenditures occur within a local authority's own budgetary frontiers, the approach can be applied without need for governmental agreement.

The same approach should be applied to private sector activities where a product or service is known to incur social and ecological costs which have to be born by society as a whole; for example:

• the costs of facilitating self-help groups for people addicted to valium and similar drugs should be added to the market price of the drugs, and paid to agencies running such groups;

- the cost of running debt advisory services should be added to the fees charged by companies offering credit loans and credit cards;
- the disposal-cost of bottles, cans, paper, toxic chemicals, etc., should be added to their market price and transferred into a collective waste-disposal fund;
- the cost of cleaning polluted rivers (etc.) should be added to the cost of the items whose production causes the pollution;
- the cost of subsidies needed to enable farmers to make the transition to sustainable farming should be added to the price of chemical fertilizers; and so on, under the label 'integrated social and ecological costing'.

The holistic social analysis which underlies the need for integrated community budgeting reflects the arguments presented in the earlier parts of the book. As individuals, for evolutionary reasons, we tend towards personal wholeness, especially when self-empowerment and personal expression are encouraged. The wholeness or the disempowerment and defeat that we experience in our personal lives is reflected in our social lives. Society itself is a whole, which reflects the state of our inner consciousness.

By adopting budgetary principles which mirror the integral nature of society, and by investing in policies which encourage our emerging wholeness, the foundations can be laid for social, economic and ecological harmony and stability.

We know that the application of intelligence to commercial and industrial affairs can yield a good return on an investment. We need to apply the same intelligence to our pursuit of social and ecological wholeness, aiming to achieve a similar return through sound and intelligent investments. Most people hold this vision in a dusty corner of their brains, telling themselves that it's just a dream which can never be realized. We forget that we once held dreams of flying machines, and that everything we dream of is within our command to achieve.

Investment in seven fundamental processes will bring a

good financial return in terms of reduced social repair bills, and yield progress towards these goals. They are processes and initiatives which:

(a) encourage our personal sense of direction and purpose;

(b) develop our practical and enabling skills;

(c) increase the empowerment and self-control which a community exercises over its own future;

(d) foster the growth of participatory self-help initiatives;

(e) strengthen the web of neighbourhood and community connections;

(f) enrich our relationship with nature, and

(g) give personal and community access to capital.

The best social investments foster increased personal and community empowerment, leading to purpose, hope, inspiration, action and love. These are the wellsprings of creative action in humanity, which enable us to realize the visions we hold.

Integrated policy-making

You may feel overwhelmed at the number of tasks, goals and strategies that are involved in the building of a full rainbow economy. How can we ever achieve all that is needed?

The keys are *integration* and *organization*. Nature consists of a myriad of different molecules, cells and organisms, but the overall effect is one of harmony because she uses self-integrating systems. Can we copy nature, and create a self-organizing social, economic and political system which will provide us with the integration we need to achieve the multiplicity of tasks ahead? It means moving right away from our normal ways of organizing, which depend on the lower social levels doing what they are told and not thinking for themselves. The more our personal consciousness is liberated, the more we need organizational systems that model themselves on nature, which has to be the world's expert in the area.

The first key is *participation*: every human must be able to play his or her part. In a healthy organism, there are no redundant cells.

The second is *vision*: every cell in an organism has a built-in programme of its own growth and purpose. When we can see clearly what we want and where we are going, we discover the motivation to realise our dreams. Future workshops and community development associations meet this need by awakening people's vision.

The third is *bottom-up organization*: nature is self-organizing from its smallest participating cell up to the body and spirit as a whole. As our wholeness emerges, human society needs to do the same.

The fourth is *top-down facilitation*: nature provides an organism with an overall grid, or energy pattern, which facilitates the growth of its many parts. A linked need is *communication:* nature's organisms use a network of bio-electronic information which enable the different parts and levels to keep in touch and to co-ordinate, and know what each different part is doing.

The fifth is *integrated planning and co-operation*: the local cells participate in a wider plan which is shared collectively, knowing that their efforts will be supported by other cells, and by the higher organizational structures.

The sixth is *appropriate scale*: nature always places a natural limit over the size of her living forms. The basic unit of human self-organization should be similarly limited in scale to optimize the participation of the parts.

The seventh is *celebration*: nature celebrates spring as a whole, and so too should a community, coming together to celebrate the greater purposes of life and to recommit to the realization of the dream. By gathering together, divisive egotism can be dissolved and our deeper unity reawakened.

To achieve everything that needs doing to build a full rainbow economy, a fully integrated policy needs action at seven levels as follows:

1. Within our own individual lives, as we increasingly take the responsibility for creating our own realities, changing our values and consumer habits, developing new skills, and establishing goals that will encourage our growth, fulfilment and wholeness.

2. Within businesses, schools, colleges, trade unions, churches, community groups, political parties and other organizations.

3. Within the new local and other forms of democracy – the community initiatives, community development associations and neighbourhood forums.

4. Within local government, through integrated policy approaches within its committees and departments, and through working in partnerships with other actors in the community – the private sector, banks, other financial institutions, community and voluntary groups, ecological groups, health authorities, colleges, trade unions and government agencies.

5. At the regional level, through cooperation with other local governments, through larger regional partnerships, and through Enterprise Boards and Regional Development Agencies.

6. At the national level, through policies designed to support developments at local and regional levels, to pursue the development of social, economic and ecological goals within society as a whole, and to support the emergence of planetary unity.

7. At international and global levels, through the development of co-operative treaties and agreements.

The key to much of this is partnership – working with other people to achieve a common goal. Integrated policies and partnership go together.

Oxford City Council is developing an integrated City Health Strategy in conjunction with the Health Authority, community groups and employers. The strategy includes participation by various local authority departments; community involvement in measures concerning health and fitness, holistic medicine, food quality, smoking prevention, occupational health, cervical cancer and AIDS testing; cycle routes; community fitness programmes; smoke-free offices; air pollution control; heating policy; home safety; health promotion events; employer health contracts, and a wide range of other activities. 'This process of joint work is not without its fair share of conflict, professional jealousy and personality difficulties',[13] but without that commitment to joint work, an integrated approach would not be possible.

The higher the commitment to integrated policy-making, the more can be achieved. In Vermont, USA, there is growing concern about the threat that development is bringing to Vermont's social fabric, village culture, environment and sense of community. Alarmed by increasing congestion, housing costs, failing public services and fiscal inequities, Governor Madeleine Kuhn appointed a commission in 1987 to consider Vermont's future. Meetings were held around the state which showed that many shared her concern, and the commission recommended that all towns and regions, as well as the state, should draw up comprehensive plans for development. This initiative is still in progress, so the results cannot be told. However, it is likely that ecologically sustainable development and other goals in sympathy with the outlook of this book will be on the agenda.[14]

Launching a major initiative at this level is one way to set the ball in motion. In past years, various US states and cities have run similar initiatives under such names as 'Hawaii Commission on the Year 2000' (1970), 'Goals for Georgia' (1971), 'Alternatives for Washington' (1974) and 'Atlanta 2000' (1977). Together, they have pioneered a wide range of techniques for involving the community in planning its future.[15]

Transpolitical action

The final step concerns some of the political realities

involved in making change happen. The term 'transpolitical' has its origins in Sudbury, Ontario, where I was
attending the annual conference of the Canadian Institute
of Planners in 1985. Sudbury was an appropriate city to
choose, since the City Planning Department has conducted
a major participatory exercise to lift Sudbury out of its
metal-smelting industrial past. Over a five year period, the
entire city plan was reviewed and rewritten, building in
post-industrial policies and setting the city on a new path.

I was in conversation with Jim McCormack, who was
working to create an integrated approach to community
economic renewal in the island jewel of Cape Breton,
Nova Scotia. Walking round a city block, he said: 'So
many different people are involved – it's not really political, it's apolitical.' 'No', I said suddenly, 'it's not apolitical
– its *transpolitical*. These people are working in a very
political way – but they are ignoring political boundaries.'

If you look closely at what is happening, you will
observe that local and community economic development
initiatives in Europe and America are drawing on:

- the best aspects of current left wing thinking,
emphasizing concern about social issues such as
unemployment, poverty and housing, a desire to help the
weakest members of the community, and concern for the
well-being of the community as a whole;

- the best aspects of current right wing thinking,
emphasizing a concern to stimulate new enterprise, to
encourage initiative and responsibility, and to build an
economy that works; and

- the best aspects of current green thinking, emphasising concern for the environment, holistic approaches to
life, and an insistence on human-scale, participatory
approaches to sustainable development.

A major invisible shift is happening. Growing numbers
of people are discovering that the shared wish to get something done outweighs the political differences they have.
The old political divisions no longer make sense, except to
those who put ideology and dogma before people. Rather

than focusing on what divides them, they are focusing on what unites them, and working together in this transpolitical way.

Integrated approaches to development and partnerships necessitate the transpolitical approach – when so many people are working together, emphasizing political differences gets in the way of action. In Sheffield, the solidly Labour City Council has established a strong working partnership with the local business community in order to achieve economic development for the city. Lancashire Enterprises Ltd, the Labour Council's arm's-length economic development agency, which is doing so much to build a new future for some of Lancashire's most polluted areas, is likewise committed to an integrated approach:

> *'What is especially pleasing is that the project . . . has bridged all the political divisions along its route in a real team effort.'*
> Louise Ellmam,
> Leader of Lancashire County Council[16]

When Marion Dewar (Member of Parliament and past president of Canada's New Democratic Party) was Mayor of Ottawa, she found that in the debating chamber the male politicians would line up behind their party flags and attack each other, emphasizing their differences. When she got the same people round a table to tackle a common problem, however, they would forget their differences and get on with the work at hand.

The transpolitical way of operating emphasizes four qualities:

1. Going beyond domination, and beyond having power *over* others.
2. Actively seeking the empowerment of everyone, both personally and in communities.
3. Respecting the 'I' in everyone, the emerging self.
4. Working together for a greater goal.

The transpolitical approach extends to areas where traditional ego-based approaches to power, life and work can play havoc:

• The rivalries and power games that arise in departmental politics can ruin a good day's development work. Problems of this kind often stem from personal insecurities and bottled up grievances and conflicts. Participative management techniques and greater teamwork are being used to overcome them, with appropriate trainings and facilitation by management animateurs.

• In many meetings and committees, proceedings are dominated by whoever speaks loudest and interrupts most often. Quieter men and women need to demand that meetings be run in more sensitive ways so that everyone can speak and be heard. Trainings in co-counselling skills and in group and teamwork skills help here.

• Traditionally masculine and traditionally feminine ways of relating to other people can also obstruct progress. Many boys (and some girls) grow up in a fiercely competitive environment where to show weakness or vulnerability invites ridicule. They learn to shield their emotions and wear a front which can underlie depression, loneliness in adult life. People's difficulties in sharing their feelings in an open and honest way underlies the creation and maintenance of many organisational problems. Similarly, women who were taught as girls not to assert themselves easily slip into playing secondary roles, which supports and encourages the habits of dominance and disempowerment we need so much to change. Appropriate trainings can help us change old patterns.

• Many people will be threatened by the goals of planetary and ecological sustainability, from pesticide manufacturers to weapons producers. Jobs, incomes, security, power and positions may all be felt to be at risk. In these situations, the transpolitical approach means not falling into the old 'enemy' games. There is need to come from a loving place, separating the role and the job from the person who occupies it, and work to build relationships, not destroy them. We can't afford the luxury of fighting – there is too much to be done. The first lesson of all effective development work is to start from where people are. When conflicts arise, we need to learn to use the skills of 'aikido politics' to remain centred and inwardly clear, while using the contradictions of the opponent's own situation to wear down his or her resistance.

Women are playing an increasingly important role in the emergence of the rainbow economy. Lacking the forced upbringing in aggressive-defensive styles of relating, and the unconscious archetypal heritage of centuries of waging conflict and war, many women slip into a trans-political way of relating with greater ease than men. It is not entirely coincidental that Oxford City Council, which is working in an actively participative and integrative manner, has 21 women on it out of 44, and that the leadership of the Council is all-female.[17]

We will need 30 years to realise the main features of a rainbow economy – to achieve a planetarily just, ecologically sustainable, environmentally beautiful, economically stable, materially secure, socially rich and spiritually nourishing community. These six steps show some of the processes we need to get there. With every passing year, young people are coming of age carrying a more passionate concern and a stronger commitment to build a different and a better way of life on Earth, prompted by what they see around them. There is no time to delay.

Chapter Twelve :
Global evolution

For millions of years before our present time, we were fully a part of the animal world, living without tools or language in the forests and plains of Africa and Asia. Without knowing it, we were the inheritors of 15,000 million years of steady, gradual evolution. Somewhere within our being, far from awareness, we are also the inheritors of whatever consciousness preceded that event, when time started ticking and the universe as we know it began.

Once we had evolved into human form, we continued to evolve for hundreds of thousands of years, living in small clans or tribes, drawing our security from our own people, our traditions and our familiar territory. Outside this territory the world was unknown, full of danger and possible death, where people spoke strange languages and worshipped even stranger gods. Always within us, the quiet pulsebeat of unfolding evolution beat away, step by gradual step, drawing us on to seek, to enquire and to explore.

In making our evolution towards settled agriculture, we gradually expanded the frontiers of our security as the processes of travel, trade and conquest slowly opened up the world. It was only 500 years ago that Europeans first sailed around the Earth, discovering it really was round.

In this most recent period of evolution, the processes of change have advanced with self-increasing acceleration. We have plunged into the world of science, unravelling the secrets of matter and creating miracles of engineering in their wake. We have created the nation states and power-blocs of the present world, widening ever further the frontiers of security, and learning to co-operate and trust within these frontiers. We have developed ways of communicating with anyone on Earth just by tapping out some numbers on a telephone. We have shot into space, seeing our Earth as a whole for the first time. We travel further every year, exploring every corner of the Earth, marvelling at the beauty and splendour of the mountains, lakes and valleys. In the late twentieth century, we are falling in love with Earth itself. Perhaps we have never really *seen* its full beauty before. For the first time we are extending the frontiers of our security to embrace the whole. This is not just another step. When we embrace the Earth as a whole, we move beyond enemies, and beyond war. We no longer exclude anyone from the embrace of consciousness.

TROUBLES GALORE

When viewed with this perspective, it is clear that something astonishing is in progress. We are in the midst of an awesome awakening into some new kind of reality, of which we have but vaguely dreamed. We are on the verge of a whole new level of existence.

In the process, we have run into some massive problems, some of which have been outlined earlier in the book. If you still have any doubt about the seriousness of the crises, I recommend the annual *'State of the World'* report from the Worldwatch Institute, which keeps abreast of the changing storms and the indications of change.[1]

These problems transcend all our national, political and religious differences, and make our various wars and squabbles irrelevant. They force us to think and act in global terms, or face disaster. We must match our growing love affair with the Earth with urgent action to stop abusing her, and develop new ways of relating to her.

We are in the midst of a single, multi-faceted crisis of planetary evolution. The greenhouse effect, the rising ocean, deforestation, rainforest destruction, debt, financial crash, soil erosion, social disintegration – these are different facets of the same single crisis, which is a crisis of change caused by the evolutionary leap we have begun. This leap is taking us from nationhood to planethood, from a struggle against nature to a partnership with her, and from limited to a more complete and open awareness of what life is all about. Growing numbers of people know in their hearts that this is true.

While writing this book, during 1988, awareness has grown (at least in Canada) of just how serious a threat to the world the greenhouse effect presents. Heat from the sun is becoming trapped within the Earth's atmosphere because of the ever-increasing levels of carbon dioxide produced by our burning of refined petroleum products (petrol, gas, aviation and diesel fuels), our burning of coal and our clear-cutting and felling of forests. The CO_2 absorbs solar radiation, preventing its escape back into the stratosphere, causing the global temperature to rise. The problems are exacerbated by the destruction of the ozone layer by CFC gases released in the manufacture of styrofoam, fire retardants, refrigerants and aerosols.

The prospects for the next 50 years include temperatures rising by 5 degrees, melting icecaps, sea-levels rising by 4–5 feet, low-lying plains and river deltas becoming flooded, forest areas turning to grasslands and grasslands turning to desert. In Canada, the *Vancouver Sun* and Victoria's '*Monday*' have both produced major multi-page spreads on the crisis, warning British Columbians of the crisis to come as beaches disappear, agricultural areas are flooded and over-heated forests experience an increase of forest insects, diseases and fire. The solutions lie with concerted efforts to cut back fossil fuel consumption, and with widespread re-afforestation. Cameron Young, writing in '*Monday*', proposed that every town and city keep a 'carbon budget', to record the balance of how much carbon is emitted and absorbed locally, with the objective of balancing the budget.

> 'What is required is sincere and concerted international action on a scale the world has never seen before. The alternative is a planet spinning into chaos'.
>
> Cameron Young

As in most things, our personal consciousness has got there first. Our growing awakening to the disasters we are courting by our pre-planetary, pre-unitary conduct on a small and vulnerable planet has not yet changed our social, political and economic behaviour. In spite of the warnings, we are still acting for the most part as if nothing was wrong.

We already possess most of the answers we need to change our ways, and to adopt a more holistic and planetary model of growth and development. This book has focused on local development and not on national or international change, but such a book could be written, based on what we know. The models already exist in Africa, Asia and Latin America for locally-based development strategies based on the rainbow approach, bringing healing to the chronic crises of poverty, unemployment and ecological destruction. Other models exist within the intelligence of bankers, stockbrokers, politicians and business leaders. None of these global problems is insoluble, however huge.

When we approach the chaos and crises of the world with despair, saying 'Oh no, not another famine or disaster we've got to do something about', we can get bewildered. The prospects for change begin to seem very far away. That is not the way to approach the work of change.

When we touch the place within our consciousness that feels the love, that sees the beauty and bleeds with pain for what is happening, then we start to want these changes more than anything else we want on Earth. The hope for change becomes a fact, not an ideal. We know that we are going to do it.

The means, the tools, the examples to follow already exist. All that we need is the *will* to make it happen, in a committed, global way.

TAKING THE LEAD

In 1986 people could rightly ask 'Who is going to give the lead?', and receive no answer. While ever-growing numbers of people were committing themselves to healing the Earth and birthing the dream, no single nation was making a move (although New Zealand's anti-nuclear stand gave encouragement to many throughout the world). In 1988, there may be an answer to that question. There are many signs that Canada is about to emerge as the first nation in the world to take a clear stand on planetary, ecological and economic issues, saying 'Our loyalty as a people lies not with the North, or with the West, but with the Earth as a whole'.

Canada's concern for a global perspective goes back some way, and has found expression in the policies of people like Lester Pearson and Pierre Trudeau. Canadians have a deep love of the huge open spaces of natural wilderness, and are well placed to extend their concern to a global perspective given that their neighbours are the USA and the USSR, and that they share in both the Atlantic and the Pacific oceans. They are a quizzical people, often asking themselves 'Who are we?' and finding very few answers other than 'We are not American'. Canada is a consciously multi-cultural society, embracing the differences of French, Ukrainian, English, native Indian, Metis, Filipino, Chinese, African, Indian, Pakistani, South American, Thai and many other racial groups, shunning the American melting-pot approach to national identity. This is not to say that Canada does not have reason to be ashamed for the racial oppression which has wounded the lives of so many native Indian and Inuit people, or for her own share of environmental monstrosities such as acid rain production, and the logging of the exceptional beauty and grandeur of the Pacific coast. In spite of these things, or perhaps because of them, something deeper is emerging within the Canadian soul.

During 1986, in the wake of the UN World Commission on Environment and Development's visit to Canada, a National Task Force on Environment and Economy was set up by the Canadian Council of Resource and Environment Ministers to consider what could be done to foster environmentally sound economic growth and development in Canada. In 1987, the Task Force published its findings.

The report expressed major concern about soil erosion on Canadian farms, and about forest depletion, toxic chemicals, acid rain, hazardous wastes and other issues which had become 'woven into the fabric of Canadian society'. It stated that 'despite the value of the new ideas and approaches to harmonizing economic development and environmental concerns, there is evidence that we are in a desperate race against time. Many experts and credible institutions argue that things are becoming much worse'.

It went on: 'It is the responsibility of individual nations to initiate domestic institutional reform. A coherent national strategy and action plan to solve domestic concerns and realize the benefits of the growing interest and need for global environmental management is within Canada's grasp. This opportunity must not be lost'. It called for a major effort throughout Canada to integrate environmental and economic planning and decision-making, and urged both national and provincial governments to embrace the concept of sustainable development based on private and public sector co-operation.

The Task Force's recommendation was that multi-sectoral 'Round Tables' on Environment and Economy be set up in every province and territory, and at national level. These Round Tables will develop conservation strategies for every province and territory, which will serve as blueprints for development 'to ensure today's resource utilization does not damage the prospects of future generations'. The strategies are to be in place by 1992, and a national strategy will integrate them, linking them to the international scene.

The report went on: 'In a new era of environmentally sound economic development, a full partnership of governments, industry, non-government organizations and the general public must guide us through an integrated approach to environment and economy'. Round Table members are therefore to be drawn from various sectors of Canadian society, including industry, environmental, labour, academic and native organizations, with government representation including environment, resource and economic development ministers.[2]

Where Canada leads, New Zealand, Australia, Norway, Sweden, Denmark, Finland, Holland, Austria, India, Kenya and Ireland may follow, with the Soviet Union and Japan being possible surprise applicants to join a new 'global ecological alliance'. The process of change which has begun in the Soviet Union cannot be stopped now, and many surprises will be coming from that quarter yet. If for some reason Canada falters before the finish, New Zealand or Norway will share the responsibility, and take the lead in developing new, planetary and ecologically sustainable patterns of conduct and relationship.

As the changes begin to develop more solid form in the shape of practical development strategies and real reforms, there may well be other surprises. Within the USA, individual states such as Massachusetts, Oregon, Wisconsin, Florida, California, Vermont and Hawaii may come on board in their own right without waiting for national changes stemming from Washington. In several of these states, initiatives have been started aimed at establishing a basis for ecologically sustainable development.[3] In Eastern Europe, where economic and ecological problems combine with social and political impatience to create conditions ripe for change, the 1990s may also see some surprising new adherents to the ideals of environmental awareness and globally sustainable economic conduct. The more youthful socialists may find themselves at home with the holistic framework of values beyond 'left' and 'right' which community-based economic development encourages.

The only step which is required for a country to embark on the path to sustainable development is the willingness to make it a top priority. By bringing the issue to the top of the agenda, it gets attention – it's as simple as that. But what happens then?

When the members of the Canadian Round Tables sit down they will confront a complex agenda of issues. Ecological unsustainability is deeply woven into the whole fabric of industrial life.

Each province will have to consider how it can involve people in the cities, towns and farms of its territory in the development and implementation of its strategy.

To create a strategy that is far-reaching, detailed and thorough enough to achieve the necessary goals, widespread participation will be required. A 'Strategy for Sustainability' must contain many components, including mini-strategies covering:

- energy efficiency measures;
- resource-use reduction, materials re-use and recycling;
- agricultural sustainability;
- local community economic development strategies;
- worksharing strategies;
- pollution elimination; etc.

By involving people in the communities where they live, and getting them thinking, studying and drafting strategies for action in their own communities, schools, companies and farms, a spirit of involvement and commitment can be created which will assist the Round Tables to become truly effective and powerful in their work.

MILITARY EXPENDITURE

Environmental instability is only one dimension in the complex of issues which make up the multi-crisis of our global evolutionary leap. The issues of military expenditure, of footloose global finance and of Third World debt must all be resolved if the leap into a planetary existence is not to become a painful fall into distress and confusion.

The USA, USSR, Europe, the Middle East and the other countries of the world spend $1 trillion a year ($2.7 billion a day) on military purposes ($10,000 a second in the USA). These are the very resources which we need to start stabilizing our planetary existence. Consider the following:

● Half a day's military expenditure would be sufficient to implement the Action Plan for Tropical Forests developed by the International Task Force set up under the World Resources Institute. (Cost is $1.3 billion a year over five years.)
● Ten days' military expenditure would finance the goals of the UN Water and Sanitation Decade which aim to bring clean drinking water to everyone on Earth. (Cost is $30 billion a year for 10 years.)
● Ten hours of military expenditure would supply contraceptive materials to all women already motivated to use family planning in the world, in addition to the $2 billion per annum already being spent today. (Cost is $1 billion per annum.)[4]

The high priority which military defence receives is partly an expression of the pre-global consciousness which has dominated the minds and emotions of the world's leaders, and partly the consequence of the material needs of our pre-global, unsustainable economies. Research by staff at the Rocky Mountain Institute in the USA has shown that:

> 'at least a fourth, and perhaps a third, of the entire US
> military budget is for missions chiefly meant to obtain
> and keep access to foreign resources, most of which can
> be more cheaply (and far more safely) saved or substi-
> tuted by specific energy-saving and resource-saving
> technologies'.[5]

Just *one year's* budget for the US Rapid Deployment
Force, for instance, if spent on home insulation, would
about eliminate the need for all US imports of Middle East
oil, which the Deployment Force exists to protect. There
are also many examples where modern materials such as
new polymers, composites, ceramics, carbon and boron
fibres, amorphous metals, supermagnets and other synthe-
tic materials can displace the need for 'strategic' minerals
such as cobalt, chromium, tin, industrial diamonds and
oil, the requirement for which is used to justify military
operations overseas. It is important to grasp the close links
between our unsustainable economies and our military
expenditure, and that the development of sustainable
economies plays an important role in strengthening overall
global security.[6]

The origins of the conflict between East and West lie
with the battle between the twin dreams of capitalism and
socialism in the nineteenth century (see Chapter Two).
The part in us that said 'I!' went down the capitalist path,
and the part that said 'We!' went down the socialist path.
In separating, each side turned away from its shadow, and
then turned against it. This splitting of our inner nature
underlies the massive duel which threatens to end all life
on Earth. The reality of the separation, however, is that
without the creative energies of the individual 'I', an
economy can never really build up steam and generate
prosperity; and without the caring energies of the collective 'we', a society loses its sense of community, and individual suffering and distress increase. The joy of community economic development is that it re-unites these twin
aspects of our being and puts them back together, healing

the wound, and laying the foundations for long-term peace between East and West.

Once we accept that *security* is the primary aim of defence policy, not plain aggression, military dominance or the defence of strategic mineral resources, a totally new analysis can be applied, which reveals that military expenditure is the least effective and most cost-ineffective option. Wherever two countries are engaged in conflict (such as the USA and USSR), investment in an integrated security-building programme of youth exchanges, scientific and environmental exchanges, sporting and artistic visits, commercial trade, peace-making initiatives, personal group sharing workshops, verification processes and joint projects will yield a much better return on the investment in generating a deeper sense of trust, love and security. One of the overpowering realities of the global era is that there will be *no winners* from a major war; the only true security that is now possible is security based on the growth of friendship, mutual understanding and love. Governments which are truly serious about achieving security will invest in security-building programmes while carefully negotiating their way to disarmament.

A factor that plays into the hands of those who want to see global disarmament and peace is that neither the USA nor the USSR can any longer *afford* the arms race. Both economies are being crippled by the cost of maintaining their armies, missiles, air forces, navies and research establishments. The sheer logistics of paying for the arms race are undermining the economies of both countries and forcing them to the conference table. Throughout the 1960s and 1970s there was not the political will to make disarmament a priority. With the arrival of Mikhail Gorbachev in the Kremlin, the inevitable process of disarmament has finally begun.

WORLD FINANCIAL INSTABILITY

The next dimension of the global crisis concerns the danger of a world financial crash, and subsequent depression. If there is a crash, it will be partly the result of the craziness of the huge sums of money which, because they have no secure home, rush from one short-term purchase to another, seeking immediate gain. As a result of this hyper-nervousness, the index of global instability (if there were such a thing) is extremely high.

One reason why the money can find no secure home is that the US economy is burdened by problems of instability which stem from its non-sustainable economic policies. In May 1988, the US journal 'New Options' listed 12 proposals from innovative economic thinkers who share a commitment to building a sustainable society which, when put together, would cut government expenditure and raise extra revenue enough to entirely eliminate the projected $220 billion budget deficit forecast for 1992, while *at the same time* fostering a sustainable society.[7]

Among their proposals were ideas for health and well-being incentives (paying people who kept well and did not need medical treatment), energy-related measures, eliminating the subsidies for non-sustainable farming (combined with a five-year transition strategy), encouraging worker democracy (generating extra revenue from their higher productivity – see Chapter Eight), a 10% cut in military expenditure (starting the process gently), increasing the gas/petrol tax by 50 cents a gallon, a stock market tax to discourage financial speculation, a tax on inheritances over $100,000 (while leaving family farms and homes secure), a merger tax to discourage the speculative fever which is divorced from anything real, a fair income tax to surcharge people in the higher income brackets, and by cutting the national debt itself, cutting interest payments on the debt. If the integrated approaches to budgeting, policy-making and investment outlined in

Chapter Eleven are included, the resulting fall in expenditure will create an even rosier balance-sheet.

During the industrial period, in keeping with the psychology of material gain, we assumed that the way to get something was to pay for it. Better health ? Build more hospitals. More secure farming ? Increase farm subsidies. More security? Built more missiles. Less crime? Hire more police and built more prisons. Less child abuse? Hire more social workers. Better education? Build more schools. If you wanted a better society we assumed you had to pay for it.

We are now realizing that this approach does not always produce the results we seek. In the examples given above, traditional expenditure has become an investment which often performs negatively, bringing no guarantee of more security, better health or less crime. Meanwhile, government expenditures soar, and when taxes are not increased proportionally, deficits accumulate quickly. When the one-off economic windfalls of North Sea oil and the sale of public assets are removed from Britain's finances, major budget and trade deficits are revealed here, too.

By operating on different principles, sustainable economic development produces policies that are more cost-effective, reduce deficits, and create sounder investments. By emphasizing a holistic approach to 'wealth', including human, social and economic development, to policy-making and budgeting and to the biological economy which underpins the human economy, sustainable development is able to draw both on the self-renewing resources of our own emerging wholeness and on nature's own self-renewing processes. The result is a sounder, more stable, and sustainable economy.

These few comments do not provide 'answers' to the world financial crisis, but perhaps they point the way towards an economic order beyond crisis, without which the changes and reforms needed to steer a path through the chaos will be meaningless.

THE WORLD DEBT MUDDLE

The final dimension of the world's crisis which needs healing is the debt crisis. (Enough has already been written in the course of the book to indicate the way to heal the crisis of community collapse.)

The $1 trillion debt which the Third World countries owe to the countries of the North is not repayable in any normal way. That must be our starting point. It is also intolerable, for a host of reasons. It is impossible for Brazil, Poland, the Philippines, India or Mexico to pursue development policies which will aid their people and their environment and contribute to overall global stability as long as they are weighed down by such a massive financial burden of debt.

Everyone wants to get out of the hole – the banks as much as the Third World countries. The solution the banks would most like – full repayment – is simply impossible; and the solution the Third World countries would most like – full default – would mean that a defaulting country's credit status would slump to zero, making it impossible for that country to borrow any further money on the foreign markets. It would also cause the banks' major customers to rush to move their money into safer keeping, resulting in the likely collapse of the banks themselves. The chief difficulty with the debt crisis is that there is not yet the *will* to create a solution to the problem. If this continues, a solution will impose itself in the form of outright default by one or more countries, which will ring the panic bells in banks and governments all over the western world, and soon produce the necessary will to do something.

Once the will is there, solutions can be created. A formula for debt write-off over a period of five years could be devised, on a country-by-country basis, which would allow the banks to appear to remain solvent while they adjusted their books. The formula would need several components, including the following:

● First agreeing how much each country actually owes, erring on the low side to facilitate negotiations. It may be astonishing, but no one really knows the total debts for any one country.

● Discounting from the total debt the amount of 'flight capital' which has already found its way back to the West's banks, albeit under private names, leaving the banks to make whatever arrangements they like with the customers in question.

● Recalculating the total amount of debt owing at an assumed lower rate of interest, from the date of the first loans, and relabelling all interest payments above that level as capital repayments.

● Involving lender governments in the purchase of substantial quantities of discounted debt on the secondary debt market, which would then be written off in exchange for agreements by the debtor countries to set aside areas of natural habitat as conservation parks. This requires some explanation.

The 'secondary market' is where debts that are unlikely ever to be paid back in full are bought and sold at a percentage of their face value. In 1987, the US group Conservation International bought $650,000 worth of Bolivia's debt from a Swiss bank, and then negotiated with Bolivia (with whom they had some good connections) for the setting aside of four million hectares of precious environmental habitat, an area the size of Wales, along with associated laws, agreements, and a $250,000 endowment fund in local currency for the management of the new area. Two weeks later, the World Wildlife Fund negotiated a similar agreement with Costa Rica.[8] A World Conservation Bank has now been set up to collect money to finance further deals.[9]

As part of the global write-off process, governments, companies and other organisations would buy the debt from the banks at discounted rates and donate their purchases to the Conservation Bank, or a similar body. Deals could then be negotiated whereby Brazil, Indonesia and the Philippines (for instance) set aside their rainforest areas as national parks, in return for the debt being written off. Since one of the prime reasons why the rainforests are being destroyed in the first place is to raise the foreign exchange to pay the debt, either through the sale of timber or through the sale of cash crops grown on cleared ground, or both, the arrangement has a very compelling logic to it.

• As a variant on the 'debt-for-trees' swap, secondary debt purchasers should ask debtor countries to establish their own national and regional *sustainable development funds*, and pay money into these funds in their own currencies in exchange for agreed amounts of debt being written off by the owners of the debt. These funds would then be used to finance locally-based sustainable development initiatives, based on models which have already established a sound track record – the Third World equivalent of the development initiatives described in this book, of which there are many.[10]

• Where debtor countries require essential goods which must be imported, the purchase of these goods would count as debt repayment, and the creditor countries would sort out for themselves re-imbursement between the suppliers and the banks.

As part of the negotiated settlement, Third World countries would be able to apply for new loans from the World Bank and private banks approved by the World Bank, to which a new kind of condition would be attached, designed to foster sustainable local development and eliminate corruption.

• No new loans would be given for a project in a particular region until a local Grameen-type bank (see Chapter Nine) had been set up in that area, to guarantee that community-based economic development proceeds alongside top-down development.

• Loans would only be given for projects that related to an overall economic development strategy founded on criteria ensuring ecological sustainability, open community economic development and planetary co-operation. Loans which would entail dependency on the continued import of foreign goods would not be allowed. In other words, future loans would have conditions built into them which maximize the chances of commercial success, and hence of repayment. There is nothing inherently wrong with lending, as long as the prospects for repayment are good.

AN INTEGRATED GLOBAL STRATEGY FOR SUSTAINABLE DEVELOPMENT

When they are put together, the various components outlined begin to add up to an integrated global strategy, including:

• The development of locally-based strategies for ecologically sustainable community economic development.
• The development of equivalent regional and national strategies (as Canada is now beginning).
• The stabilization of world financial markets through the development of new approaches to investment and speculation, new controls or taxes on purely speculative investments, and the development of more permanently stable and sustainable local and national economies.
• Negotiated reductions in military expenditure, linked to the development of more self-reliant economies and to sustainable development strategies entailing planned reductions in the use of energy and scarce resources.
• A carefully negotiated write-off of all Third World debt, tied to development agreements designed to ensure the preservation of the world's rainforests, and future development along locally secure, sustainable lines.
• International strategies to reduce energy-use, to prevent deforestation and to reverse the greenhouse effect.

All that is needed is the will to do it.

275

Something is happening on our Earth. When we first began our evolutionary journey, all those billions of years ago, very little was formed. Only a vast potential was there, a hidden mystery veiled in matter.

In the centuries since, that potential has steadily unfolded, at first with infinite slowness, now with immense speed. Where are we going? What are we doing? We are certainly not here just to grow potatoes and pay mortgages. Where is our evolution taking us? These are huge questions.

Long, long ago, a tiny germ of consciousness implanted itself in matter, somewhere in the midst of space. Since that time, that consciousness has steadily progressed and grown, gradually pulling the different parts of matter together, uniting cell with cell, creating living organisms which breathed, connected, and colonized the Earth.

After many years, humans appeared. We learnt to think, to work, to use our hands our brains and our dreams. We started to shape reality ourselves, using our consciousness and our dreams to guide us.

In this generation, we have reached the limits of material expansion and resource exploitation. We have used up most of our resources, investing them in the great leap of consciousness which we are making. The Earth is no longer available for us to consume like jelly at a children's party. Our task now is to come together and heal the wounds between east and west, north and south, between humanity and nature, and all her creatures, and between women and men. Creating a stable, sustainable economy in which all our needs are met is just a matter of good housekeeping. In doing this, we lay the foundations for the future. The whole of heaven awaits us.

Chapter Thirteen :
Seven Years On

It is now seven years since this book was first published –
seven years in which we have seen the end of the cold war,
the collapse of communism and the Soviet bloc, the birth
of new nations, the end of apartheid in South Africa, the
beginning of independence for the Palestinians, a possible
end to hostilities in Northern Ireland, an expanded role
for the UN in dealing with world conflicts, a surge of
economic growth in eastern Asia, and the final arrival of
the information age.

It has also been seven years in which the alarm bells have
been ringing continually about the state of the world's
environment, and in which governments, businesses, communities, non-governmental organisations and ordinary
people have moved into action in a thousand different
ways to address the environmental problems that face us.

It has been seven years in which the levels of
unemployment in industrialised countries have risen to
historical highs, bringing a tidal wave of distress; in which
Third World debt has continued to climb, increasing the
pressure of hunger and poverty on countless millions; in
which many western governments have realised that they
cannot repay their debts without major cutbacks in
programmes and services; in which the wealthy have
become wealthier still; and in which increasing numbers
of people, especially in the USA, are clamouring for
simple, right wing solutions to the sea of troubles which is
besetting them.

There are a thousand reasons for being depressed about the state of the world in the late 20th century, if you want to be. The thrust of this book, however, is that underneath the multiple symptoms of breakdown and collapse, a new society and a new economy are emerging, expressing themselves through initiatives based on values which recognise the importance of personal, community and environmental wholeness. To the outside world, these initiatives may seem small and insignificant; but to those who are involved in them, and who commit their days to them, they represent a new way of living, a new way of doing business, and a hope for the future.

> *It is better to light a candle,*
> *than to curse the darkness.*

These final two chapters have been added to the 3rd edition in order to revisit some of the initiatives covered, bring them up to date, and to add some new thoughts, seven years on. What has happened to the various projects and initiatives described in the book? Are they succeeding – or have the candles sputtered out? Are we still heading towards a crash, as the book's title suggests? What would it take for initiatives such as these to blossom and prolif- erate all over the world? And finally, how are we to address the profound and desperate clash between the material needs of the world's economy and the biological needs of the world's ecology?

Community currencies

First, let us consider the progress of the LETSystem (Chapter 4). The Courtenay LETSystem closed down in 1990, fundamentally due to management problems. It re- opened in 1993, and by 1995 350 members were trading around $8,000 a month. There are now 500–600 LETSystems operating worldwide. In Britain, Liz Shephard set up a LETS development agency called LETSlink from her Wiltshire kitchen table. She had

30,000 enquiries in the first 3 years, and over 300 LETSystems were established, serving 30,000 people. Each system has its own unit of currency, so depending on where you live, you can trade in Bobbins (Manchester), Acorns (Totnes), Olivers (Bath), Anchors (South London), Links (West Wiltshire), Fromes (Frome), Stones (Sheffield), Trugs (Lewes), Cockles (Exmouth), Currents (Cheltenham), Thanks (Bristol), Newberries (Newbury), Beaks (Kingston), Sutts (Sutton), Brights (Brighton) or Buzzes (Findhorn).

The LETSystem is being taken seriously at quite high levels. In Manchester, the City Council loaned £10,000 to the local LETSystem, to be repaid over ten years in 'bobbins'. In Haverfordwest (south-west Wales), the LETS group is negotiating with the local authority to run a daycare nursery with the fees payable 80% in LETS, allowing parents to trade their skills for childcare. In Halifax, Calderdale Council has formally joined the local LETSystem, and allows LETS members use Council facilities for photocopying, postage and printing; in return, Council uses its LETS credits to top up grants to local charitable organisations. Scarcely a week passes without a new group forming or some new LETS initiative developing. Liz Shephard is now developing links with credit unions, coops, and sustainable food production, and a spin-off initiative called 'Lets Eat'. At the time of writing, most LETSystems are still small, but growing. The Manchester LETSystem is the largest with 500 members (1995), who trade 120,000 Bobbins a year. One of the problems yet to be resolved concerns the ability of unemployed people to trade in the system without fear of losing their benefits. A progressive government decision is urgently needed. LETS has blossomed in other parts of the world, too, including Spain, Switzerland, Denmark, Germany, France, Holland, Canada, Australia and New Zealand. Australia has over 200 groups, started initially by Jill Jordan, who went to Canada in 1986 and spent 3 weeks learning the system, and then went back to form the Maleny system (trading in Bunyas). Other Australian systems trade in Rays and Beams (Sunshine Coast), Eggs (Crows Nest, Queensland), Swans (Cygnet, Tasmania), Wellingtons (Hobart), Auras (Dandenong Valley, Victoria), and Locals (Richmond Valley NSW). The government of Western Australia in Perth produced a start-up manual, and gave A\$50,000 to encourage and support LETSystems in the Blue Mountains, where three women have been jobsharing a very wide-ranging LETS development programme. Faced with the problem of people on welfare being taxed 100% on everything they earn, Peter Baldwin, the Australian Minister for Social Security, said 'LETS credits will not be counted as income for the purpose of the Social Security income test. LETS-type schemes are a useful community initiative which should not be artificially discouraged by Social Security arrangements'. Jill and other Australian LETS members deposit LETS units in special tax accounts, hoping the government will use them by hiring people for community enhancement projects – but so far, there have been no takers. In New Zealand, the government gave active support to help get groups started (via various trusts and funds), once the idea had been introduced into the community. By 1995, there were 50 active groups, with around 50 active members in each. Wellidun Exchange and Barter System (WEBS), founded in 1989, is one of the larger and more successful of New Zealand's LETSystems. In 1993, average monthly trading among WEBS members was around W\$30,000, composed of 1700 transactions.

In the USA, the development of community currencies is moving in a different direction. In Washington, the 'Time Dollar' was invented by Edgar Cahn, a lawyer, as a unit of currency which could be paid out to community volunteers, and be spent on similar services available from other volunteers. You can pay your medical bills in Time Dollars in El Paso, Texas, while earning your dollars by volunteering as an adult literacy tutor. In 1995 there were Time Dollar systems running in 38 states; the Miami Time dollar system has 3000 members.

In Ithaca, New York, the 'Ithaca Hours' community currency was founded by Paul Glover in 1991. Ithaca Hours are printed notes worth $10 each which can only be traded in Ithaca. By 1995, 1500 people (including 250 businesses) were using the currency, including plumbers, electricians and chiropodists. The Alternative Federal Credit Union in Ithaca accepts Hours for mortgage fees, loan repayments, lines of credit and overdrafts, and its employees have agreed to accept part of their salaries in Hours. Similar systems are being developed in 18 other US cities, and in Nova Scotia, where a 'Maritime Hours' system was launched in 1994. In St. Paul, Minnesota, there are moves to develop a local credit card which can keep track of conventional dollars and local currencies at the same time.

Community currencies have clearly taken off, and unless some unforeseen problem occurs which causes people to lose faith in the systems, they are probably destined to become a standard aspect of life for people throughout the world. If you want to start your own system, you'll find a contacts listing in the Appendix.

Jobless growth

Rapid though its expansion might be, no-one is suggesting that community currencies should replace national currencies, or that the work and trade made possible through the new currencies will ever provide anything more than a partial solution to the continuing problems of poverty and unemployment. In fact, except in Australia, the bureaucratic rules and regulations which curtail the lives of unemployed people have been shown to discourage unemployed people from using the LETSystem, undermining one of its main purposes.

The number of people suffering from the confusion and poverty of unemployment has continued to rise throughout the industrial world. In Europe there are now 30 million people without work; 1 in 10 of the working population is unable to support a family without government assistance. The figures are much the same in Canada, Australia and New Zealand. In America, the official figures show an unemployment rate of only 5% or 6%, but you have to add in the enormous number of 'discouraged' workers who do not show up in the statistics, and the 900,000 men who spend their days in prison. Young people are particularly hard hit, as are people over 50.

Traditional economists continue to believe that the problem of unemployment will be solved by economic growth: as the economy grows, companies will hire more people. It happened in the past, so they expect it to happen in the future. For the short-term ups and downs of an economy, the view holds some truth. Since the late 1970s, however, there has been a steady long-term trend towards higher unemployment, which is the critical problem we have to deal with.

The long-term increase is caused by two new factors. The first is that women have been joining the workforce in huge numbers, instead of staying at home; in Canada, 70% of two-parent families have both parents working. The second is that information age technologies are steadily taking over the work, giving us the phenomenon of jobless growth. From 1975 to 1990 the Gross World Product per person increased by 20%. In the same period, the level of employment per person dropped by 1.2%.[1]

> *The more the economy grows,*
> *the fewer jobs it needs.*

This is a radical departure from everything we have known before. By any natural instinct, we should be welcoming the promise of less work. This is the dream of millennia ! Before we can enjoy the fruits of the change, however, we have to sort out the mess in which it is the unemployed who have all the additional leisure, while the rest work as long as ever, paying taxes to support those who do not. As a system, it just doesn't make sense.

One part of me says that given the natural resistance with which people embrace change, it will be a long time before we resolve this problem. Another part, however, reminds me that we are living in an age of miracles, when all kinds of unexpected problems are finding resolution. At present, there are three strategies most likely to bring results: community economic development, worksharing, and protest.

Community economic development handles the practical matter of putting community economies onto a strong, permanent, ecologically sustainable footing. Worksharing enables working people to work fewer hours, and start sharing the new leisure-time. Protest makes people's lives uncomfortable, so that they wake up and start thinking about the need for change. So far, the protest has been unforthcoming. The stigma of personal shame stifles the voices of those who are unemployed, making them believe that if only they looked a little bit harder, they would surely find a job. Those with the leadership abilities find it easiest to get work, leaving the unskilled and vulnerable to suffer alone. Nonetheless, there must come a point when protest erupts in a determined, organised effort to produce change.

Protest has been unforthcoming so far because the unemployed have not known what to ask for. Anger can express itself in street riots and looting; but organised, long-term protest needs an objective and a set of goals. The suffragettes organised their anger around the right to vote; the labour unions organised around the right to decent pay and working conditions. So what should the unemployed be demanding? This brings us to worksharing.

Worksharing[2]

When the agricultural revolution of the 18th and 19th centuries displaced millions from the fields of Europe, they found work in the new industrial factories, and in

North America and the colonies. Between 1846 and 1930 over 50 million Europeans sought a new life overseas. The industrial age has now given way to the information age, but it comes ready-automated, and its jobs are insufficient to replace the disappearing industrial jobs. At the same time, a growing number of people want more time to enjoy life, instead of more money to buy more things.

Bruce O'Hara, a Canadian from Vancouver Island, has spent twelve years promoting the idea of the shorter working week. His book *Working Harder Isn't Working* argues the case for national legislation to phase in a 4-day, 32 hour week. Studies show that a shorter working week would bring an average 5% increase in productivity, along with reduced sick-leave and absenteeism. Companies would hire extra staff to maintain their previous level of production or service, and some would move to 7-day operating, to make better use of their plant and equipment. The 4-day week would result in an 8% increase in jobs, and an 80% reduction in unemployment (leaving aside the need to provide appropriate training). By taking the increased productivity into account and eliminating the costly unemployment contributions that employers have to pay, existing employees would take an average 5% reduction in pay, in exchange for a 20% reduction in time worked. To most people, this is a pretty good deal.

A study by Pradeep Kumar, of Queens University, Kingston, Ontario, has shown that if the workweek is reduced by 10%, unemployment will only fall by 1.5 percentage points, since employers will make up the slack by changed working methods, rather than hiring new staff. It is the shift to 4-day working that signals the real breakthrough, as far as new jobs are concerned.

In the early 1990s, when Europe began to come to grips with the stubborn nature of its unemployment problem, the debate on worksharing heated up. The French national plan (the Larrouturan plan) called for a 4-day, 33 hour working week, which would create 2 million new jobs, increase the overall workforce by 10%, and involve an average 5% cut in pay. The state was to assume payment of unemployment insurance, and eliminate the 8.8% payroll tax to compensate employers for their added costs, and companies were to be required to introduce profit-sharing plans to allow workers to participate in future gains in productivity. The measure was approved by the French Senate, but defeated in the National Assembly. It will hopefully be brought forward again soon.[3]

> *'Lavorare meno, lavorare tutti'*
> *Work less, and everyone works*
> Italian slogan

A similar debate has taken place in Italy and Germany. In Denmark, a government Leave Scheme allows people to take up to a year off work, provided that their employer fills their place (or an equivalent place) with someone from the pool of long-term unemployed people. From 1993–1994 some 120,000 people took advantage of the scheme to enjoy their children, to travel or to retrain. Those who retrain receive full unemployment insurance (UI) benefit, while those who take parental or sabbatical leave receive 70% of UI.

Various companies have been creative in response to the demand for more flexibility in working life. When the French company Digital offered a 7% salary cut to staff who would choose a 4-day week, 530 out of 4,000 workers made the choice, saving 90 jobs with no loss of productivity. Still in France, Hewlett Packard put its workers on a 32 hour week for 38 hours pay, in return for an agreement to adjust the shift-work arrangements, which increased productivity. In Germany, the BMW Regensburg plant has been operating a 4-day, 36 hour week since 1990, with productivity gains more than offsetting the cost of hiring new staff. In 1994, when Bell Canada went to a 4-day week to weather a financial crisis, and then returned to 5-day working, 79% of their staff chose to stay on the 4-day week. In Montreal, the Outside Workers signed a contract for a 4-day, 35 hour workweek. The Quebec Federation of Labour found that 63% of its members preferred a 4-day week, and that 31% were willing to take a cut in pay to get it.

In the USA, the situation is somewhat different. Even though a Hilton Hotels survey showed that a majority of Americans would be willing to trade a day's pay for an extra day off work, and a US Department of Labor study found that the average American worker is prepared to give up 4.7% of his or her earnings in return for free time, the direction is towards longer hours, increasing stress among workers. In US factories, hours of work have increased by 3.6% since 1981, and the number of workers employed has steadily declined. Employers are expected to pay huge medical insurance contributions for their staff, which encourages them to squeeze more out of their existing staff, rather than shorten the week and hire more staff. The San Francisco-based New Ways to Work organisation negotiates with employers, encouraging flexible work options, as described in Chapter 5.

In both Europe and North America, there is resistance to the change. Employers argue that a reduced working week will interfere with traditional practices; economists argue that legislated worksharing schemes are an undue interference in the economy; unionists argue that worksharing will reduce their members' standard of living. The logic of worksharing is undeniable, however – it offers greater productivity, less stress, less absenteeism, less sick leave and reduced unemployment. At a deeper level, choosing to get off the treadmill of endless working and spending is a key step towards achieving ecological sustainability for the world as a whole. Bruce O'Hara believes governments should legislate the move to a 4-day week; Jeremy Rifkin, author of *The End of Work*, thinks governments should legislate tax credits to businesses which move to a 30 hour week, with further credits to businesses which instate profit-sharing schemes, which are known to increase productivity.

The central demand around which unemployed people and others should organise their campaigns and their protests, therefore, is the 4-day week. History tells us that people threatened with losing their benefits never surrender them easily. Women needed seventy years of prolonged, organised struggle before men agreed to let them have the vote. Today, the status quo is those who are lucky enough to have full-time work. Only when groups of people start picketing factories, offices, schools and union offices, demanding a 4-day week, demanding the right to share the work, will we start to see change.

The Growing Underclass

Meanwhile, something very disturbing is happening to the social fabric of many developed nations. In Britain, France, the USA and Canada, in the words of Christopher Smallwood (British Sunday Express, 17/7/94), 'nothing less than a social and economic timebomb is ticking away, as it has been for much of the past generation. What is this timebomb ? It is a huge a dramatic widening of income differentials'. This is not just a new version of 'the poor will always be with us'. This is something very specific and identifiable that has been happening only since 1978. Between 1978 and 1992, in Britain, the average income of those in the top 10% increased by 50%. For those in the middle range it increased by 35%, but for those in the lowest 10% it fell, and remains stuck at the 1974 level. (Institute of Fiscal Studies). When the city of Nottingham undertook a city-wide survey in 1993, councillors were shocked to discover that almost half the city was living in poverty, dependent on welfare of one kind or another. In Britain as a whole, the Child Poverty Action Group estimates that 1 person in 4 is living in poverty, 1 child in 3.

The story is repeated in Canada, where 1 child in 5 lives in poverty, and the USA, where a 1992 Carnegie Corporation study found that almost one child in four is living in poverty and social deprivation, and the number of poor children under 3 rose by 26% during the 1980s. Poverty in the USA is defined as being an income of $14,763 for a family of four (1994 figure). In 1993, 39.3 million people fell below the poverty level, the highest since 1961. Meanwhile, during the 1980s, people earning over $1 million in the USA saw their salaries increase by the astonishing figure of 2,184%. (Philadelphia Inquirer, Nov. 3-8, 1991).

With poverty and unemployment come increases in illness, family breakup, single parenthood, suicide and crime. A British study showed parallel month-by-month changes in the youth unemployment rate and the youth crime rate. A US study (Merva and Fowles, Economic Policy Institute, 1992) showed that a 1% rise in unemployment results in a 6.7% rise in homicides, a 3.4% increase in violent crimes, and a 2.4% increase in property crime. When you are young, bored, unemployed and full of hormones, car-theft is a good substitute for the challenge and risks of adulthood.

What are the reasons behind this increasing gap between the rich and the poor? Various causes have been suggested, including government policy (squeezing the poor and pandering to the rich), the impact of free trade (threatening the jobs of unskilled workers), the development of new technologies (eliminating lower-skilled jobs), the failure of governments to invest in educational and training systems, and the more brutal explanation that the rich have simply won control of the taxation system. Through a variety of tax-exempt family trusts and off-shore tax havens, the argument goes, and guided by financial lawyers for whom this is a full-time occupation, individuals and corporations all over the world are finding ways to move their money out of the tax collector's reach.

At the same time, advanced countries are struggling with increasing levels of government debt. In 1995, interest payments on Canada's outstanding debt ate up 33% of the government's entire annual income – and the government had to borrow $35 billion to balance its books. Nor is Canada alone. By 1993 OECD figures, Canada's debt represented 73% of its Gross Domestic Product (GDP); Belgium's represented 145%, Italy's 113%, Sweden's 83%, Holland's 79%, the USA's 63%, Germany's 48% and Britain's 46%. A parallel process is underway: while the rich get richer and the poor poorer, governments are heading for fiscal melt-down.

What is going on? It is affecting all governments, not just those with generous social programmes. A clue can be found in Canada, where an analysis by the auditor general showed that out of Canada's accumulated 1995 debt of $575 billion, only 9% had been spent on actual government programmes or services. The other 91% went on interest payments. In the years before the 1980, when economic growth rates were high and interest rates were low, governments were able to stay ahead of the game. When the tables turned, economic growth rates fell to a steady average of 2-3% per year while interest rates rose to 10%. From this moment on, governments which failed to balance their books were inviting the devil of compound interest to sup at their tables. With each year of deficit spending, the devil's feast grew larger, and many countries now face a situation such as Canada's, where a greater percentage of government income is needed each year to pay the interest on the debt. For governments all over the world, the debt is taking control.

Needless to say, the overall story is much more complicated. Each country has different tax-laws, different balances between the rich and the poor and different political factors to take into account. The economist who can give us a proper analysis of the changes, apportioning blame, highlighting the long-term trends and recommending appropriate solutions, has either yet to leave college, or is still staring at a computer screen, trying to figure it all out.

For our own part, frustrating though it may be, this book leaves the big picture to one side, and focuses on the smaller but very profound changes represented by new initiatives around the world, especially at the community level. One unintended virtue of the first-world debt-crisis is that it will lead to government downsizing, which in turn will raise the importance of endeavours at the community level. Out of these small initiatives, the argument goes, a new economy can emerge.

The Progress of Community Initiatives

Whatever goes on in the international world of high finance and currency speculation, it is within our own local economies that we must look to create the stability, the meaningful jobs, and the social and environmental integrity.

The Dean Clough centre in Halifax, Britain (pp.119-120), which grew like a phoenix out of the ruins of a collapsed carpet factory, has continued to grow from strength to strength. In 1987, the centre was home to 180 varied businesses, employing 1,800 people. By mid 1993, 200 businesses were employing 3,000 people, representing an incredible turnaround for this small Yorkshire mill town, which had been in a state of deep despair only 11 years before. In keeping with Sir Ernest Hall's dream of building a 'practical utopia', the centre has become far more than just a workplace. As well as businesses, there are 6 art galleries, an international sculpture studio, a major theatre company, a composer in residence and an artistic community of 20 painters, sculptors and print-makers who have made Dean Clough their home. An Enterprise Campus operating with the local college, a Design Trust working in primary schools and a language laboratory have all been added. As Sir Ernest Hall puts it:

We see these developments as a virtual renaissance in Calderdale – a restatement of our commitment to local regeneration....a commitment to provide the broadest range of experiences for as many people of Calderdale as possible, and to satisfy the need for

> *individual achievement against a backcloth of civic*
> *culture and pride in the local community .... We*
> *believe that individuals are potentially powerful*
> *beyond limit, and that with motivation, they can*
> *make progress towards any goals they set themselves.*

Dean Clough has made a huge contribution to the revitalisation of Halifax, the Calderdale town where pay rates were once the lowest in Britain, where infant mortality in 1989 was 50% above the national average. The whole town has picked up the spirit of Dean Clough, discarding its dirty, smoky image and restoring many of its old Yorkshire heritage buildings to join the renaissance that Sir Ernest talks about. When Sir Ernest first came to Halifax in 1982 to buy the carpet factory, many local people assumed he was an asset stripper. The only asset which has been stripped away is a negative one – the cynicism itself.

Across the water in western Ireland, Connemara West (pp.99-102) has continued its journey towards community self-empowerment. In 1992 the community-owned development company enjoyed its 21st birthday with a big celebration attended by Mary Robinson, President of Eire. The 1500 residents of this rural area, 70% of whom live below the poverty line, have continued to support their company. The woodwork and furniture-making course has graduated into a full-time Furniture College with 70 full-time students, an international reputation, and a satellite training programme with colleges in Wales, Portugal and Denmark. There are plans to build 6–12 houses for young low-income families and elderly people, and the community radio station is now broadcasting – and this leaves out a host of other initiatives. What is it that enables a tiny place like Connemara to achieve so much, when other communities fail to get a grip on the issues of poverty and unemployment ? If a city of 180,000 people, 100 times the size of Connemara, were to achieve 100 times what Connemara has done, there would be astonishment all round.

First, it isn't easy. As President Mary Robinson said at the 21st birthday party, 'Consensus does not arrive, alas, like the Holy Ghost upon a meeting! There is a great deal of cut and thrust, bruised egos and bruised feelings that go on in arriving at agreement on how to progress an idea in a local community'.

Right at the beginning, when the idea came up among a group of people that they should build the Thatched Cottages as a source of local income to the community, the group decided they should raise a portion of the money locally. They decided not to allow anyone to invest more than £100, and they also decided that shareholding would be restricted to members of the local community (the same principle that keeps the Mondragon credit union in a healthy condition). The local priest put in a lot of effort, and 14 teams of two each took to the doorsteps one Sunday afternoon in January, 1971, seeking investments. 80% of the households in the area subscribed, and with this commitment, a solid sense of ownership was born. Right from the beginning, it was decided that financial dividends should be retained and invested in new projects. There have been some complaints, but local people appreciate that they have received their dividend ten times over through the activities their company has brought them. It is hard today to imagine a group starting out on a building project, and asking local residents to pay for it themselves. The discussion would be around who to apply for grants to. Two other essential lessons are firstly the emphasis on inclusiveness, with everyone being invited to get involved; and secondly, the merit of building on a philosophy that draws on a higher belief, such as the quest for excellence, fulfilment, or the potential for human wholeness. This lays a sound foundation which many want to build on.

Across the water in Scotland the Community Business Movement (pp.105-6) has moved steadily ahead. In 1988 there were some 100 enterprises owned and managed by local communities; by 1992 there were 170, supporting some 3,300 jobs and training places, plus additional jobs created by the tenants of community-run workspaces. Govan Workspace, one of the earliest and best known community businesses, has grown to occupy 3 sites in Govan, providing 120 workshops, and work for over 450 people. They have opened a workspace cafe and outside catering business, and run trainings for entrepreneurs and unemployed people who want to return to the workforce. The Barrowfield security and decorating business ran into problems. At its peak, the community business employed 100 people in commercial projects and 150 in government training and employment programmes. A management failure coincided with a change in policy over government training programmes and a cash crisis. The local government sponsors refused to judge the business on anything except purely business criteria and refused a loan, so the business went into liquidation. It was a sad day for the many who had invested so much hope and hard work in a worthwhile dream of community renewal. These things happen, in both the community business and the capitalist business realm. Meanwhile, 200 other community businesses are continuing to succeed. The Castlemilk Group in Glasgow employs around 100 people, 90% of whom are Castlemilk residents; one of their main activities involves an imprinted concrete franchise called 'Creteprint'. Possil Community Business, north of Glasgow, runs a security guard operation with 80 guards and an annual turnover of £1million.

South of the border in England, community enterprises do not have the kind of support the Scottish businesses receive. The Eldonians in Liverpool (p.91), having built the biggest housing cooperative in Europe, have become involved through their Development Trust in training programmes for young unemployed people, and a range of business ventures, including a garden centre, a children's nursery and an old people's home. Another leading initiative, not mentioned in the book, is Coin Street Community Builders Ltd. In 1984 a group of local

293

community groups managed to buy a 13-acre site in the heart of London, which was about to be turned into Europe's tallest skyscraper. They built low-cost co-operative housing, a new park and riverside walk, and a workspace street occupied by restaurants, food shops, craft shops and clothing manufacturers and retailers. The group has plans to build homes for 1,300 people, a River Thames Museum, and exhibition and performance space. Their slogan 'There is Another Way' proudly proclaims that we do not have to sit back and allow our future to be determined by high financiers and other property moguls: we can win control and determine it ourselves along small-scale, human lines.

The Workers Co-operative Movement in Britain built its strength through the work of the Industrial Common Ownership Movement (ICOM), and through local co-operative support organisations such as CDAs (Co-op Development Agencies). CDAs are very important to the spread of new co-ops (p.117), but their funding has been drying up, and the number of CDAs fell from 60 (1988) to 46 (1995). The growth of the late 1980s has stopped, and the overall number of worker co-operatives is holding steady at around 1,000, with new co-operatives balancing failures. In Sweden, 18 CDAs were formed during the 1980s, based on the successful British model; in Gutteborg, on Sweden's west coast, the local CDA has helped 300 new co-ops to get going since 1988. The model works – it just needs to be supported, or to find a way to be self-supporting.

Leaving Britain, we travel south to Mondragon, in the Basque country of northern Spain. When we left in 1988, 20,000 people were sharing in a closely woven network of 100 different mutually owned co-operatives (pp.126-131), making and distributing everything from automotive parts to sewage treatment equipment, semiconductors and bicycles. The late 1980s saw continued success and expansion, but in 1992–1993 Mondragon had to weather the worst recession since

World War 2, when economic demand tumbled throughout Europe. The recession gave Mondragon its worst crisis for a decade. To keep in good shape they were forced to bring in a 2-year wage freeze and lay off 500 workers. By the end of 1994 Mondragon had bounced back, however, rehired the 500, and hired an additional 400 workers who became members of the Mondragon cooperatives by investing $12,000 each, bringing the number of owner-workers to 26,621. Mondragon is currently Europe's No 1 exporter of machine tools, Europe's leader in the field of domestic appliance components, and the third largest supplier of car components. They own 300 co-op food stores and 30 hypermarkets, and are engaged in establishing new hypermarkets across France and Spain at the rate of two a year. The Entrepreneurial Division of the Caja Laboral (the credit union) provides venture capital for the new starts, with almost 100% success. By contrast, venture capitalists in the USA expect to lose 80% of their new starts within 5 years. At Mondragon, the riskier the loan, the lower the interest rate, to maximise the chances of success.

Mondragon has proved beyond question that co-operative ownership, co-operative banking and co-operative networking between businesses bring a level of success, stability and employment that can be matched by very few privately owned companies. If a community can pull it off, this is without doubt the formula to follow.

This success, however, (especially the move into hypermarkets) raises profound environmental questions. Mondragon has always existed squarely within the traditions of the industrial way of life, successfully riding the waves of growing consumer demand. Along with other leading companies in Europe, Mondragon has accepted the need for change and begun to address the green agenda. In 1993 a major ECOPlan was finalised, and 1994 saw environmental action in the areas of CFCs, water, energy and paper efficiency, and campaigns to collect materials such as used batteries, motor oil and glass. An ecological fair 'Ekokonsum' was held, aimed at making consumers more ecologically aware in their own lives, and an environmental guide was published. ECOPlan will be extending its activities to include Mondragon's suppliers of products and services, too. As Mondragon continues to apply its pioneering social consciousness to the environmental realm, we can look forward to an entire new chapter in the history of this remarkable experiment.

On the other side of the world, in San Francisco, the Briarpatch Network (p.121) had 150 active members in 1995. During its life, over 1,200 businesses have drawn on its various skills and services. During the Briarpatch's first decade their business failure rate was less than 5%, but in the second decade, as a result of the recession, the AIDS epidemic, and an influx of younger, less experienced business people, the 5-yearly failure rate went up to 40% (still only half the national average). Several Briars have been instrumental in launching a new Master of Arts in Business programme within the California Institute of Integral Studies, based on the Briarpatch experience of what does and what doesn't work, and focusing on training highly skilled professionals in socially responsible business management methods.

Further up the coast in northern California, the residents of the Mattole Valley (pp.93-4) have continued the enormous task of restoring their watershed. The task has been underway for 17 years, but (writes David Simpson) 'the impacts of the past 45 years of intensive road-building and logging cannot be easily reversed, and will only be mitigated through natural healing processes'. The Mattole Restoration Council and the Mattole Watershed Salmon Support Group have attempted almost every restoration technique available to them, protecting and rebuilding miles of streambank, armouring dozens of streambank slides, creating new in-stream salmon and steelhead habitat, planting hundreds of thousands of Douglas Fir, Redwood, Alder and Willow trees, implementing erosion control work on roads throughout the drainage, maintaining educational programmes in the valley's schools, and providing restoration programmes to valley residents and landholders. In 1990, a painful polarisation occurred over logging and timber issues, which had people in neighbouring valleys almost at war with each other. Out of this conflict, the Mattole Watershed Alliance was set up, composed of representatives from every economic interest and each geographic reach of the valley. The Alliance has been meeting monthly since 1991, and has taken unified stands on critical resource issues such as sports, fishing regulations and ocean salmon harvest. 'When the Alliance makes proposals to government', David writes, 'government listens and responds, substantiating the premise that when a combined citizenry speak with real knowledge about the place they live in, government must follow their lead. The alliance process has been truly empowering'.

On a practical level, there has been a small resurgence in the numbers of king salmon spawning in the Mattole Valley, but not of the coho salmon, which have continued to decline throughout the US Pacific North-West. The critical factor is the loss of the cold-water pool habitat which they need for spawning, due to greedy and careless logging practices. Local timber harvest regulations still do not offer enough riparian (riverbank) protection. The watershed protection groups go over the timber harvest plans with a toothcomb, and the Mattole Restoration Council has managed to negotiate a series of voluntary measures with timber companies and individual landowners to mitigate the negative aspects of their management practices. On the arts side, the theatre group has written a show called 'Queen Salmon', a 'biologically explicit musical comedy for people of every species' and toured the Pacific North-West, generating much amusement.

Continuing north, we come back to Vancouver Island. I moved to the Island in 1990 and settled in Victoria, within easy reach of the oldgrowth forests and the wild west coast. Much of my time has been devoted to working with a progressive community development company on plans to build a new town at a place called Bamberton, on the site of an abandoned old cement works, 20 miles north of Victoria. The town is designed on principles of ecological, economic and community wholeness, and funded by four labour union pension funds. As an example of sound community financial investment, ecologically sustainable planning, detailed planning for a strong local economy, and a commitment to recapture the spirit of small-town community life, Bamberton represent the potential fulfilment of many people's hopes. Population growth is a hot issue on Vancouver Island, however, with 33% of the existing population wanting to pull up the draw-bridge and say 'no more'. As a result, the project ran into strong local opposition, and is currently going through a hefty layer of further studies and assessment.

All across Canada, in cities, towns and on native reserves, people are at work to improve people's lives and build stronger local economies through community economic development. From Vancouver to Nova Scotia, local groups and organisations are building up community economic strengths, creating businesses, teaching new skills, getting unemployed people back to work, and extending the reach of community ownership. There are many initiatives in Ontario and Quebec. On Cape Breton Island, overlooking the Atlantic Ocean, New Dawn continues to grow in strength (pp.103-4). In 1990, the nearby Canadian Forces radar station closed down, creating a widespread sense of disappointment and loss. The County of Cape Breton approached New Dawn and asked if they could help find an alternative use for the site, which consisted of a lot of duplex housing and some workshop sites. New Dawn jumped at the opportunity, and converted the duplexes into special care homes where a family lives in one side of the duplex, a doorway is cut in the wall, and 3 seniors live in the other side. Under a contracted care arrangement, the seniors pay New Dawn to provide a range of services, which New Dawn contracts out to the family, and everyone benefits. New Dawn spent $3.5 million to renovate the site, and converted the workshops into successful business incubators. A good working partnership with the local municipality and the availability of research and development funding from federal and provincial agencies were essential components of this success.

We now move on to financial issues, starting off with the bad news.

Third World Debt

In 1988, third world countries owed $1.2 trillion to the world's banks and governments, a figure that is hard to conceive when many people in the poorer third world countries earn less than $1 a day. In the late 1980s, British banks began to get the jitters, and 'wrote down' 40%–80% of their loans, receiving a $3.5 billion tax write-off for doing so. They did not write the loans off, however, and for every year that has passed the debtor countries have continued to pay interest. By the end of 1993, $1.4 trillion had been painfully repaid – but like a drowning man trying to swim against the tide, the overall outstanding debt had risen to $1.76 trillion.[4] Sub-Saharan Africa only manages to pay 37% of its annual debt servicing costs, and consolidation has led to a tripling of the overall debt over ten years. The cost of servicing the debt costs third world countries $240bn a year, while foreign aid brings them just $70 billion. In 1990, Britain received $3.5 billion more in debt repayments than it paid out in aid.

During these years, some countries have managed to improve their situation (Latin America, Thailand, Philippines), while for others the situation has got worse (Sub-Saharan Africa, India, Indonesia). To take just one country (while remembering that the same misery is happening all over the world), Zambia owes its foreign creditors $725 for every Zambian citizen, double the average wage of $310. This is equivalent to Canadians or Americans owing $80,000 each – four times the level of indebtedness of their own very indebted governments. Debt repayment is still a major problem for 44 severely indebted countries. As a condition of receiving new loan extensions to cover for defaults on interest payments, the International Monetary Fund imposes strict economic conditions on countries, designed to help their economies grow and maximise the income they can earn by growing cash crops for export – which are used to pay the debt. When more countries grow more of the same products, however, prices falls, so overall earnings fall too. During the 1980s, the prices of tea, coffee and cocoa fell by more than 30%. Overall, African exports rose by 4% in 1991 – but their value fell by 9%, resulting in a 6% drop in earnings. The faster you run, the more the ground turns into quagmire. The Philippines grows and exports 100 million pineapples a year, covering 5% of its debt service bill – but it can't afford to grow enough rice to feed its own people. The Philippines is still paying $350,000 *per day* in interest payments to the banks on the failed Morong Nuclear Power Station, built at a cost of $2.1billion on the advice of western nuclear engineers. The Philippines total debt is $27billion, of which $9 billion is owed to commercial creditors. In Latin America and the Caribbean, between 1983–1989, these countries paid $111billion to their creditors in the wealthy nations, of which the banks received 91%.

In Britain, Lloyds and the Midland Bank own more than £3 billion in third world debt. In 1993, Lloyds made £498 million in profit, 33% of which came from interest payments on the third world debt holdings for which they had already received a tax write-off. The Midland Bank went one better – the interest on their debt brought them fully 95% of their profits. From that year on, the bank stopped reporting where their profits came from. The National Westminster Bank decided to get out of the game. They sold off their debt on the secondary debt markets (where the debt can be bought for a discount), and arranged debt-for-nature swaps in Madagascar and Peru.

In Europe and North America the debt crisis is seen as old news, and seems to have been forgotten, at least until the next international crisis. Writing about the debt crisis in *The European* (5 Sept 1993), Paul Vallely wrote:

'The danger is that Europe will slip into a spiritual and economic solipsism which will not do credit to a continent which claims to spread a civilising influence throughout the globe'.

The solutions are relatively simple and straightforward: * outright cancellation of loans owed by the poorest countries; * sufficient reduction in the debt for the other countries to allow for sustained economic recovery; * debt for Social Equity swaps, in which debts are converted into local currency and used to finance local development projects, micro-enterprise programmes and environmental restoration projects; * co-operation by the banks in disclosing information that could help identify illegal flight capital – loan money which leaves the country in unmarked suitcases the same day that it arrives, destined for private bank accounts overseas; * legislation to prevent banks from receiving tax-breaks until they write debts *off*, and obliging banks to convert bad debts into local debt-for-social-equity arrangements.

So far, no-one is lifting a finger. The system is cruel and corrupt, but as it was with slavery, those who benefit from it are unwilling to give up their benefits. So far, since the public does not seem concerned, national governments are unwilling to legislate. Slavery was awful, and was eventually abolished. This debt-slavery is equally awful, on ten times the scale, and ought equally to be abolished. Where is today's Wilberforce?

While the capitalist banking economy continues to wreak this kind of cruelty on the world, in the world of microlending, small institutions continue to demonstrate that socially and ethically responsible banking is an enormously better way of dealing with the need for development capital in a growing economy. Women's World Banking (p. 193) has continued to grow; by 1995 WWB had provided loans to 200,000 of the world's poorest women entrepreneurs through its affiliate organisations in 51 different countries. The Grameen Bank in Bangladesh (pp.195-6) is also flourishing. In 1987, the grassroots bank had 347 branches, serving 290,000 people through peer-bonding loan circles in 5,600 villages, 75% of whom were women. By 1994, the bank had 1,044 branches serving 1.9 million borrowers in 34,000 villages, 95% of whom are women.

Prior to the Grameen Bank's existence, villagers had to borrow money from money-lenders, often at outrageous rates of interest. When they were unable to repay, they would forfeit any land they owned and make their way to the misery of the cities. It is mostly women who take out the loans, since they are better able to form the 'circles of trust' which substitute for collateral. Upon joining, they have to agree to the Bank's 16 Resolutions, which include commitments to 'keep our families small; educate our children; live in well-built houses; and grow vegetables year round'. The effect is astonishing. 'We've never seen anything like it', one villager said, 'we're all getting money, and we're all taking up projects of our own'. A study has shown that at one Grameen Bank branch, 46% of the borrowers escaped poverty after ten years in a savings group. Muhammad Yunus' next goal is to reduce that time to five years.

The bank is also going one step further. Every borrower is obliged to buy one share, and as a result of this policy, the government's holding in the bank has fallen from 60% to only 15%. The bank will be soon owned by its own borrowers, following the credit union model. In 1993, the World Bank came up with a $2 million grant to help spread the Grameen concept. By 1995 there were Grameen-type micro-lending projects in 40 countries, including Indonesia, Malaysia, the Philippines, Nepal,

Pakistan, Sri Lanka, Ethiopia, Nigeria, Lesotho, Chile and Bolivia. There are also many peer-group lending projects in North America modelled on Grameen, including projects in Maine, Vancouver, South Dakota, Oklahoma, Chicago, Arkansas, Boston, Arizona, LA, and among the Cherokee Indians.

> *'My aim is to eradicate world poverty. In the Middle Ages the great scourge was the plague. That was eradicated and is now just recorded in history books. We could do the same today with poverty, if we really want to.'*
>
> Dr Muhammad Yunus

If the Grameen Bank had been invented ten years earlier, and if the world had channelled most of its Third World lending through Grameen type community banks instead of through governments, there would be no Third World debt crisis today. There would be far less poverty in third world villages, and the divide between the world's rich and poor would be much reduced. The Grameen Bank is probably the single most important social invention of the twentieth century. It demonstrates the power and vitality of community economic development with extraordinary success. Recognising this success, in 1995 the World Bank established a $200 million microloan fund, 75% of which is earmarked for institutions that lend mainly to women. One day, every low-income community in the world will hopefully have access to a community-controlled Grameen-style bank for its capital needs.

The other big banking story covered in the book, the South Shore Bank in Chicago (pp.188-192), has continued to develop. In the bank's words 'Worldwide, low-income communities share three needs: decent housing in which families can be nurtured, enterprise expansion to create jobs, and labour force preparation to increase job skills'. Since beginning, Shorebank's loan programmes have facilitated the rehabilitation of 13,000 homes in Chicago's low-income South Shore and Austin neighbourhoods. In the area of enterprise expansion, 12 different programmes are now in operation. In 1988, Shorebank launched the Southern Development Bancorporation in Arkansas, with job creation as its primary focus; they also operate a micro-loan service (under $25,000) for the self-employed and less credit-worthy firms in Chicago, Arkansas and Michigan. In 1994, they launched a new initiative in the Austin area of Chicago called the Austin Initiative, which combines job-training support for local people in the fields of manufacturing and health-care, while providing information services and non-bank financing to local manufacturers with growth potential, backed up with business loans. The intention is to link 'two adjacent but isolated worlds', so that local manufacturing business owners, who normally hire their own friends and family, will consider local Austin residents as friends and family too.

Shorebank's success in neighbourhoods treated as 'no-go' areas by the mainstream banks has generated a huge amount of interest. In 1992, the bank was awarded the Princeton Peace Award, and in response to demand, Shorebank has stretched out to form various new subsidiaries, including business development programmes in Poland and in five Russian cities.

The bank recently launched a new initiative called EcoDeposits in conjunction with EcoTrust, which works in the Pacific North-West of the USA, integrating conservation and development by building on the cultural and economic traditions of local communities, as an alternative to logging the last remaining fragments of oldgrowth forest. When people invest in EcoDeposits, their money is used to finance conservation-based developments. Working through the Willapa Alliance in Washington State, EcoTrust assessed the needs of dozens of local businesses, and the EcoDeposits were used to start a revolving loan fund, which will become ShoreTrust,

'The First Environmental Bancorporation', serving the needs of sustainable development in the area. ShoreTrust will also be working with the natives of the Haisla Nation in British Columbia's Kitlope forest region. By 1995, $2.5 million had been raised, using word of mouth contacts.

> *Some day, in a greener future, each region will have financial institutions founded on both ecosystem and market realities. With the proper support, entrepreneurs may find that their ecological business practices actually help them compete in the marketplace.*
>
> *In Business Magazine, December 1994.*

When we look at initiatives such as South Shore, Women's World Banking and the Grameen Bank, we are looking at the possible future. The new models have been invented, just as merchant banks were invented in the 17th century, and limited companies in the 19th. The future will be different: in time, it is to be hoped that these new models will displace the ethically challenged banks and corporations that rule the world today.

There is good news also from the other alternative financial initiatives described in the book. The socially responsible investment movement has continued to grow. In Britain, Mercury Provident, 'the little ethical bank that could', has had a 54% annual growth rate since 1990, and accumulated a base of 1,700 customers who provide loan finance guarantees for the wide variety of schools, organic farms, bookshops and environmental initiatives to which it lends. In 1990, Shared Interest opened its doors for business as a lending partnership with the people of the Third World. A Christian-based group, Shared Interest gathers its capital from individuals and groups in Britain who care about poverty and injustice, and lends it to co-operative producer groups in the third world. By 1995 they had raised their first £5million, and set course for £10 million. Also in 1995, after five years planning, the Aston Reinvestment Trust (ART) was launched, designed to serve inner-city Birmingham in much the same way that Shorebank serves the South Shore neighbourhood of Chicago. ART consists of 3 separate companies – a community loan guarantee fund, a public/private sector investment fund, and a community development loan fund, They will use the funds to invest in social housing ventures, energy efficiency projects, local businesses and not-for-profit organisations in Birmingham.

The UK now has 24 specialist ethical funds. As an example of what is possible once you have the will, the London Borough of Sutton (famous for its green initiatives in other areas) now requires that every company in which the local government superannuation (pension) fund is invested must explain how it is complying with Sutton's environmental charter. Still in Britain, the Co-op Bank broke ranks with the mainstream banks in 1992 by actively promoting itself as an ethical bank, with policies to screen investments against repressive regimes, arms production, animal experimentation, factory farming, the fur trade, tobacco manufacturers and organisations linked to blood sports. They also took a proactive stand against unethical financial services linked to currency speculation, money laundering, drug trafficking and tax evasion. 84% of their customers thought the ethical stance was a good idea and 78% endorsed the policy statement. The new stance led to a 13% increase in the bank's deposit base as customers left other banks to sign up with the Co-op, and profits climbed from a £5.9 million loss in 1991 to a £10 million profit in 1992.

In the USA, $800billion US is now being screened for various social and ethical factors. A number of new socially responsible investment funds have opened their doors, along with two new community-based, ethical banks – the Community Capital Bank in New York, and the Vermont National Bank, which uses its resources to support local housing, agriculture, education, environmental projects and small businesses in Vermont.

Community Development Loan Funds have continued to expand too: by 1994, there were 42 in the US (p.178), managing over $140million. In 1994, the US Congress approved a $382 million federal programme to increase the capitalisation of community loan funds up to 1997, by making equity grants available on a matching basis to community loan funds, credit unions, microenterprise loan funds and community development banks. This represents a culmination of many years of steady growth in the community development loan fund movement, spearheaded by groups such as the Institute for Community Economics.

The credit union movement continues to grow in Britain. In 1987, there were 50 credit unions; by 1995 there were 400, with a combined membership of 120,000 people. The credit union movement in Britain is still very young, and represents just 1% of the population. In Ireland and the USA, credit unions represent 25%. It should be said that credit unions in Britain, and the vast majority elsewhere, still only lend for home mortgages and consumer spending: they do not engage in active business development, or other forms of community economic development. In the USA and Canada, a minority of community development credit unions offer finance for small business and co-op developments as well as for home loans. The Clinton administration's support for this sector will hopefully help it grow. In Vancouver, VanCity Credit Union (p.176) has expanded into a range of new community and environmental initiatives, including Community Investment Deposits, which channel members' investments as loans to affordable housing and environmental projects.

In Quebec, the Credit Desjardins credit union invests $56 billion of Quebecers' money in Quebec, and the National Bank invests a further $40 billion. In 1992, these two got together with various other Quebec financial institutions to set up a $100 million risk capital fund to help ailing Quebec companies, and provide start-up capital for new companies. The Mondragon model of community-financed business development may be simmering just beneath the surface. The chartered banks did not contribute a cent, and nor did they in neighbouring Ontario, where the banks hold $160 billion of Ontarians' money, compared to just $12 billion with the credit unions. Faced with difficult economic times, and not sure how to invest for the future, the banks are pulling their lines of credit from small businesses and shifting their attention to $5 million deals, investing in foreign markets, and buying up American banks and trust companies. We have seen how Barings Bank, a supposedly stable pillar of the British banking community, can collapse into bankruptcy by abandoning whatever ethics it might have once had and indulging in the high-finance gambling of derivative trading. How many more banks may follow in their footsteps?

'In future the question will not be are people credit-worthy, but rather, are the banks creditworthy?'
Muhammad Yunus, founder of the Grameen Bank

A new British organisation, Bankwatch, associated with the New Economics Foundation in London, said in its first report that 'While barely the tip of the global financial iceberg, (these new initiatives) represent the arrival of a new set of banking values which accept that finance can be embedded in a broader social and environmental context, and that banks can viably pursue social and environmental aims'. There is a long way to go, but the models are being successfully created. As much as anything, what is now needed is that ordinary people shift their accounts and investments into the new ethically screened funds, banks and credit unions – and tell their pension funds to do likewise.

Not all the news from the last 7 years is good. The Tower Hamlets experiment in government decentralisation in London, England (pp.236-8), survived a major electoral test in 1990, and seemed to have become established as a model that had everyone interested. The Liberals turned their wafer-thin majority into a solid 10-seat majority (30 seats to 20), and overnight, the Tower Hamlets experiment emerged as a blueprint for local government decentralisation. In the 1994 elections, however, a national anti-conservative Labour landslide swept the revolution away; the new Labour government is scrapping the neighbourhood councils, and re-establishing the status quo. The wider movement towards decentralisation in local government has become too-well established to be turned back, however, in spite of Tower Hamlets' loss.

In Chapter 12, I wrote with enthusiasm about Canada's commitment to multi-sectoral Round Tables on Environment and Economy (pp. 263–5), which were set up with the intention to develop conservation strategies for Canada and for every Canadian province and Territory. The commitment was sincere, and Round Tables were set up, with leaders from major sectors of the economy, environmental groups, and society as a whole. The Round Tables agreed to operate on the basis of consensus, which was a very new experience. After many meetings and much voluntary commitment, sustainability strategies have been produced, but much of what they recommended lingers on the shelves of government and other bodies. With the exception of Manitoba, where the Premier sits at the Table, those Round Tables which have not been wound up have seemingly fallen into the status of junior think-tanks. The process of turning a society based on the pursuit of affluence to one based on the principles of global sustainability is a truly massive task, which offers a direct challenge to many profitable vested interests, and the Round Tables, while doing much valuable work, have been unable to address this fact. In the USA, the President's Commission on Sustainable Development has been modelled on the Canadian Round Tables. It would be wrong to hold out great hopes for it;

but it would also be wrong to dismiss it as useless. Life works in mysterious ways, and you never know when a simple conversation on an aeroplane or in some meeting might lead to a sea-change in the way a corporation or city runs its business.

MAINSTREAMING THE RAINBOW ECONOMY

What would it take for initiatives such as these to become mainstream, widely supported by people, businesses and governments ? Here is my 'wish list' of things that would help mainstream the rainbow economy.

One is that university departments of economics, management and social and environmental studies should integrate this material into their course-work, so that students become aware of what is happening on the front line of change. Another is that governments should support community-based banking and loan funds, as the Clinton administration did in 1994. A third would be the decentralisation of welfare, unemployment insurance, education, training, career counselling and job-seeking support and community economic development to the community level, along with their integration under one roof, and the devolution to the community of budgetary control for each of these seven areas. Combined with local community democracy, this would enable a community to make intelligent decisions about the wise investment of funds, maximising investments in training and business development, while minimising the tragic waste of human energy and financial resources through welfare and UI. This is what Mondragon does, and the effect is almost zero unemployment. A fourth is that governments should encourage the shift to the 4-day week, as the critical step towards eliminating the scourge of unemployment. A fifth would involve a legal redefinition of 'fiduciary trust', so that the social and environmental bottom-line became an institutional imperative for pension and investment funds, alongside financial profitability. A sixth would be the development of national 'Green Plans' similar to those in Holland and New Zealand, widened to include sustainable community economic development, coupled with legislation to mandate the screening of all major national expenditures for social and environmental goals. A seventh would be an educational revolution that strengthened the shift from passive to action learning, encouraging young people to engage in real projects, where they would learn by trial and error, eliminating 'failure' as a heavy personal and social judgement, making it instead an ordinary part of everyday life.

The list could go on. There is so much that can be done: we just need to step into the light of our own enthusiasm, and get on with it.

Chapter 14 :
Building an Eco-Sustainable Earth Economy

Since this book was first written many things have changed in the world, some for the better, some for the worse. Most of the initiatives described have gone from strength to strength, justifying the hopes and hard work many people have invested. During these years, however, one over-riding question has risen to the surface of our consciousness : *How can we reconcile our desire to pursue our economic activities with the paramount need to protect Earth's ecological integrity?* The problem is profound: almost all economic growth is accompanied by an equivalent ecological shrinkage. What actions, initiatives and policies will shift our restless, consuming society onto a foundation that is ecologically sustainable? For our civilisation, this is a critical intelligence test. Unless we can find practical solutions, our progress towards higher goals will halt as the ecosystems which support us collapse. The stark realities of population growth, the collapse of food and fish-stocks, soil erosion, global warming, ozone depletion, and the toxification of our skies, waters and ecosystems do not bode well : the curves are almost all heading in the wrong direction. So what are the solutions? How can we make this critical transition?

Many people despair for the future. They see our widespread addiction to material accumulation, how global corporations are trampling the earth, and how global problems are getting worse day by day. All change takes time, however. It took the women's movement 70 years from the 1850s to finally win the vote for women in 1919. It took decades to end the slave trade. The industrial revolution itself, which lifted so many out of the mire of hunger and poverty, took 200 years to deliver its results. The men and women who worked so hard for change must often have despaired – but with persistence, change came. The environmental revolution, like the industrial revolution, is a huge historical process. Try as we may, we cannot achieve such a shift overnight. It consists of a billion interconnecting changes, each of which requires individual effort.

Among those billion changes, I have come across 15 major pieces that show real promise in resolving the economy/ecology puzzle, at least for the developed world. None alone will be sufficient to secure the shift in consciousness and practice that is needed, but each is a key part of the puzzle, and put together in an organised manner, they may help create the whole.

1. UNDERSTANDING THE DILEMMA

On the surface of things, it is easy to assume that it is the very process of economic growth which is at fault. Ecology is the primary reality, and ecology operates within the limits of a finite world. If economic growth breaks a primary law of ecology by assuming that growth can go on for ever, then the growth itself, surely, must have to stop. The argument seems persuasive, and many ecologists and environmentalists accept it as fact.

On deeper analysis, however, the argument is flawed. As humans, we stop growing physically around the age of 18. If we were to continue to grow physically all our lives, we would be 25 feet tall by the time we died, and our teeth would be 5" long. Luckily, nature has designed us so that once we reach physical maturity, our growth continues on the inner dimension, at the level of mind, spirit and heart. An economy too must cease physical growth once it reaches maturity, and shift its development to the realms

313

of knowledge, quality, and wholeness (see Fig. 1). To continue to grow physically beyond the limits of Earth's capacity to absorb the growth is eco-suicide.

Fig. 1   Curve A   Curve B   Curve C

In Curve A, the young economy starts to grow, consuming ever-increasing amounts of material resources as its people discover the usefulness of timber, plants, animals, coal, oil, minerals, land and a thousand other natural resources. Most economies on Earth have grown this way, with the exception of aboriginal and stone age societies, which are either still on the flat part of the curve, or have chosen to adopt the wisdom of self-limitation and simplicity.

Curve B addresses the simple but profound question : what is an economy really made from?

Take a watch : what is it made from? Is it metal? Is it silicon or quartz? Yes – but on its own, the metal would still be metal, the quartz quartz. What makes it a watch, and not a steam engine or an artificial heart is intelligence, which turns the metal into a watch. Curve B shows that Curve A actually consists of two curves, illustrating the parallel growth of material resources and human intelligence – quantity and quality. When an economy is young, the quantity curve meets few problems. Life is an adventure of physical discovery, in which the economy takes, consumes, discards, grows, and continues on its way. Before long, however, the quantity curve begins to run into Earth's ecological limits. The forests run out; fish-stocks are exhausted; the atmosphere can no longer purify itself. We hit the limits to growth. Disaster and collapse stare us in the face unless we can achieve a rapid turnaround, placing the economy on a new footing, shifting the growth to the upper curve, the curve of quality and intelligence, and stabilising the lower curve into what must be, for all natural purposes, a steady state economy.

Curve C illustrates the process of turnaround. The upper curve, representing intelligence, quality and other invisible (including spiritual) factors, can grow forever, since it is constrained by few physical parameters. This is the realm of knowledge and spirit that Descartes put to one side back in the 17th century (see p.19) because he had no way to measure it. The lower curve, representing matter, must be rapidly turned around. In the language of Herman Daly, co-author of the key ecological economics book *For the Common Good*, the turnaround must shift the economy from *growth* to *development*[1].

The shift can also be described as one of 'decoupling'. Ever since the industrial revolution, economic growth has been accompanied by an equivalent growth in the use of energy, resources and raw materials, and in the accumulation of wastes and wasted lands. As Earth's economy grew, Earth's ecology shrunk. Decoupling means shifting our economies so that they embrace methods, technologies and energy sources which are renewable and sustainable, allowing the material aspect of the economy to operate on a sound ecological foundation, while enabling the non-material aspect of the economy to continue to grow without ecological harm. The shift actually has to go further, so that every action on the material plane becomes (in Paul Hawken's terms) a *restorative* act, which helps restore the richness and diversity nature used to have before the industrial (and agricultural) ages began[2]. Organic farming and holistic medicine are good restorative models, where the economic realm reinforces the ecological, instead of exploiting it. Decoupling requires energy and materials efficiency, renewable energy, solar aquatic sewage treatment, permaculture, ecoforestry, renewable fuels, recycling technologies, and social technologies such as car-share co-operatives, cohousing and ecovillages. The information age is made in heaven for the shift from quantity to quality. Telecommuting, home-based businesses and the Internet allow us to abandon commuter lifestyles by using technologies of light, which is free and abundant, instead of oil, which pumps pollution and carbon dioxide into the atmosphere.

In the language of Amory Lovins of the Rocky Mountain Institute and Ernst von Wieszacher of the Wuppertal Institute in Germany, we need to build a 'Factor Ten' economy, which uses 1/10th the energy and materials it did before, and is ten times more efficient[3]. Once we have achieved this, we will have made the permanent shift to a mature, steady state economy, while continuing to grow in the realms of mind, creativity and spirit. It is achievable. All over the world, individuals, communities, businesses and governments are hard at work on the shift.

2. CLOSING THE LOOP

A good place to see decoupling technologies working in synergy is San Francisco, California, where the state passed legislation in 1992 to set up Recycling Market Development Zones (RMDZ), and Oakland and Berkeley set up a joint zone. The goal of the zone is to establish strong connections between recyclers and enterprises using recycled feedstock, closing the materials-use loop. By giving businesses assistance with site selection, permit processing, loan and grant packaging and other financial services, and actively promoting the markets for recycled products, by November 1995 the zone had helped create 155 new jobs in businesses using recycled materials, while diverting over 100,000 tons of material from landfills[4]. Another place is Kalundborg, in Denmark, where over 15 years, a group of adjoining industries (including a coal-fired power plant, a refinery, a plaster-board factory, a pharmaceutical factory and the city of Kalundborg itself) have been building a system of industrial ecology, modelling nature by using each other's waste materials. In their most recent accounting, the companies at Kalundborg have invested approximately $60 million on making the exchanges possible, and returned $120 million through cost savings and new revenues[5]. Several eco-industrial parks are being planned in the USA, using the same principles. Every industrial country is experimenting with different ways to close the loop, from Germany's innovative packaging laws to Berkeley's and Oakland's Source Reduction and Recycled Product Procurement Policy[6].

3. GREENING EVERY BUSINESS, AND EVERY SECTOR OF THE ECONOMY

It may sound like a big task, but there's no avoiding it. We need to move way beyond the patchwork greenery of a few, committed businesses. In the USA, the 265 members of Vermont Businesses for Social Responsibility (with 9,000 employees and over $1 billion in collective turnover) are a good example of businesses joining together to achieve social and environmental goals[7]. VBSR's mission is 'to foster a business ethic in Vermont that recognises the opportunity and the responsibility of the business community to set high standards for protecting the natural, human and economic environments of our citizens'. Together, they educate and learn from each other, assist each other with environmental initiatives, and work to achieve progressive social and environmental legislation in Vermont. In 1995, they succeeded in creating and winning legislative approval for the Sustainable Jobs Fund, which helps smaller companies work together on eco-sustainable projects they could not have achieved on their own[8]. A group such as VBSR

317

provides the ongoing dynamic and organisational clout to make sure the overall 'greening' initiative has persistence, reach, and vision. In Anchorage, Alaska, the Chamber of Commerce runs another lively 'green-up' programme, and in Austin, Texas, the City itself, in conjunction with a local non-profit society, runs a Green Builder Programme which has put Austin in the leading position for green building practices across the USA[9]. Business by business, the change has to be made.

4. INTRODUCING INTEGRATED, COMPREHENSIVE, LONG-TERM PLANNING

The process is complex; the number of issues that have to be addressed is enormous; and the temptation for governments to deal with them one by one is huge, prioritising whatever has the media's attention. Most governments deal with environmental issues in this way. As a strategy or long-term game-plan, however, the method is hopeless.

Luckily, the Dutch government has taken a lead in developing a comprehensive, integrated long-term plan, known as the Green Plan, and is putting major government resources behind it[10]. The Plan takes a 25-year time-frame, establishes target groups in key sectors of the economy, and sets clear goals for problems such as pesticide use, CO_2 emissions, the discharge of industrial waste-water, the emission of acidifying substances, reforestation, and the restoration of wetlands. The target groups are able to determine their own methods for achieving the goals; honest and full monitoring is part of the ongoing commitment. Elsewhere in Europe, the Swedish, Danish and Norwegian governments are developing comprehensive approaches to ensure that ecology is thoroughly imbedded into most government decision-making, and many local governments are using 'Local Agenda 21', developed out of the 1992 UN Rio environmental conference, as a vehicle to drive comprehensive reforms. New Zealand brought in the comprehensive

Resource Management Act in 1991, and rewrote the country's internal district boundaries so that they are defined by watersheds, rather than political inventions. When you live in a country such as Britain or the USA, where there is no overall planning for eco-sustainability and no sense of shared purpose or direction regarding the environment, it is hard to believe that this kind of planning is possible, like the child who has been raised in a foggy valley who does not know that everyone else lives with fresh air and clear views. But it is possible.

5. REDUCING CO_2 EMISSIONS

Carbon dioxide emissions are just one among many global environmental problems, but the problem is so embedded in our economy and lifestyle and the need for stabilisation and reduction of global CO_2 levels is so urgent that it merits a heading all to itself. The industrial age has been fuelled by the release of ancient sunlight, locked up in coal, oil and gas; its release is now destabilising our atmosphere, oceans, climate, and all the associated ecosystems. The increase in tropical hurricanes and typhoons, the break-up of the Antarctic ice-sheet, the disappearance of zooplankton from the California ocean, the melting of glaciers, the increase in floods, droughts and forest fires – all these can be attributed with a reasonable degree of certainty to the increasing level of CO_2 in the atmosphere.

Before the century is out, world opinion will probably have accepted the need for a 20% cut in CO_2 emissions by the year 2005; in reality, what is needed is a 60%–80% reduction now, if we want to stabilise the atmosphere. This will require a major commitment to energy efficiency investments, the development of renewable energy sources and the removal of subsidies which encourage oil-based energy; a revolution in transport which effectively banishes carbon-fuelled vehicles; and a revolution in the design of our settlements focused around ecologically-based land-use planning, and the development (and redevelopment) of urban and rural ecovillages with internal pedestrian travel and their own local economies[11]. Far from crippling the economy, as many traditional economists and politicians claim, reducing CO_2 emissions will force businesses to become more efficient, improve the quality of community life, and give the whole economy a globally competitive edge[12].

6. WORKSHARING

There's something wrong with improving the economy and making it eco-sustainable, if 10% of the working population is excluded from the economy due to unemployment and forced to live in poverty, while everyone else is overworking. After spending 20 years looking at the problem of unemployment from every direction, I am convinced that there is only one fundamental solution to the problem, which is also empowering to those who feel trapped in jobs they have no wish to sacrifice their lives to: and that is worksharing (see Chapters 5 and 13). I am also convinced that only when unemployed people themselves finally start getting angry, and hanging by ropes from the roofs of the offices, factory-buildings and union headquarters where others are working, will worksharing finally arrive at the top of the political agenda. It may seem like a separate issue, but worksharing is a fundamental part of the eco-sustainability agenda.

7. ESTABLISHING COMMUNITY TRUSTS

The years of unemployment have left many regions and city districts mired in poverty and depression, with all the negative consequences that follow. Other regions suffer from depopulation or geographical isolation; and all regions need greater support to build strong local economies, with greater internal resilience and cultural strength. The history of community economic development has demonstrated (see Chapters 6 & 7) that community trusts have the best long-term ability to bring results. To achieve the turnaround that is necessary, I would give community trusts responsibility for the management and distribution of unemployment and welfare funds, for coordinating all local adult education and training, and for establishing local community banks and community currencies to assist them in their work of building a strong local economy and encouraging local businesses. Only when these functions are coordinated will communities really be able to pull themselves out of their difficulties[13]. This too is part of the eco-sustainability agenda.

8. EXPANDING LOCAL FOOD PRODUCTION

We are heading into a global food crisis, triggered by China's economic growth. Always a steady exporter of grain, China became a food importer for the first time in 1994, as millions of Chinese people used their new found wealth to eat more ducks and pigs, which need more land since they eat 3 lbs of grain for every pound of meat they deliver to the table[14]. As the floods and droughts of global climate disturbance bring agricultural disorder, and world food prices rise, famine will bring more tragedy to the world's poorer countries, and low-income families in developed countries will see their money evaporate before their eyes at the supermarket check-out. At this point, the high price of food will prompt many people to dig up their back yards to grow food, along with any corner of boulevard, park or rooftop they can get their hands on. Food that has been grown locally without use of chemicals will be in demand, and growers who set up systems of Community Supported Agriculture will benefit from a secure and stable market. The development of permaculture, urban farming, co-operative electronic marketing, heritage seed varieties and local pesticide bans (as in

Hudson, Quebec) will all play a role in what will hopefully be an agricultural and permacultural revolution[15].

9. DEVELOPING NEW TECHNOLOGIES

Technology has an essential role to play in the process of decoupling and the evolution of a Factor Ten economy. The evolution of technology involves the embodiment of a progressively higher level of intelligence into matter. When that intelligence is used purely to maximise profit, without any other guiding purpose, it can give birth to very selfish or destructive technologies. When the intelligence is guided by the principles of maximum resource efficiency, renewable energy or closed-loop recycling, however, we can develop solar-voltaic roof-tiles, and build a culture of industrial ecology. When intelligence takes nature as its model, instead of trying to impose human intelligence onto nature, we get the brilliance of a solar aquatic 'living machine' system of sewage treatment, which uses the natural microbiological processes of plants, fish and snails to turn a soup of raw sewage and industrial chemicals back into what is almost drinking water. During the agricultural age, we powered our technologies with the simple energies of wood and water. In the industrial age, we shifted to the energies of coal, gas and oil. As we enter the ecological age, we are moving to the energy of light, the ultimate renewable resource, with solar energy, fibre-optics, and the Internet. Every kind of tax-break, incentive and support is needed to speed the shift, and get our planet off its chronic dependency on the energies of matter.

10. ENSURING A STEADY FLOW OF INVESTMENT

All these changes cost money and need investment. Once a socially responsible fund or community bank is set up, experience shows that the money is generally there, ready for its owner to invest in a socially and environmentally responsible way (see Chapters 9 & 13). At present, the spread of community banks and eco-sustainable financial institutions is about as thin as ecological understanding in the World Bank: learning from its founding spirits in Bangladesh, Chicago and Vermont, it needs to grow enormously, so that people in every region of the world have access to socially and environmentally motivated banks where they can store their savings knowing their money will work for the benefit of the planet and the local community, not their destruction.

11. ECOLOGICAL TAXATION

Traditionally, governments have taxed whatever was simplest and politically easiest. At present, we tax personal and corporate incomes, consumer goods, various 'sins', and jobs themselves, through employer contributions. Over the past ten years, a body of consensus has developed within environmental and governmental circles which believes that we should be shifting taxation from jobs to ecological resources such as water, energy, pollution, and scarce resources such as timber, so that the full environmental cost can be incorporated into the prices we pay at the counter. For the Dutch, the system is seen as a 'closed money stream', in which an extra tax on fuel-inefficient cars (for instance) is used to subsidise a rebate for more fuel-efficient cars, or a tax on pesticides is used to subsidise more sustainable agricultural practices[16]. By taxing water, energy and carbon, we send a price-signal that encourages people to conserve. In California, an organisation called 'Redefining Progress' has completed a report which details how California could shift its whole tax structure from work and enterprise onto the use of finite resources, including land[17]. Their preliminary calculations suggest that such a shift could wipe out all federal taxes for families earning under $75,000 a year – which could prove quite acceptable, politically. Alongside the shift in taxation, we need to change the way we measure our economies, packing away the old systems of GNP and GDP and replacing them with indicators that measure a country's human, social, ecological and productive wealth, not just its economic development, such as Hazel Henderson's Country Futures Indicators – a kind of GDQ (for Quality) instead of GDP[18].

12. ESTABLISHING WATERSHED STEWARDSHIP COUNCILS

We must not get lost in the world of ecological economics, and forget the needs of mushrooms, mice and mountain lions. Our existing land-planning traditions have grown up around human needs such as forestry, urban settlement or agriculture. We clear the trees off a mountainside, and then wonder why the salmon runs are disappearing. We spread agricultural fertilisers on our farmland, and wonder why the rivers have strange blooms of algae on them, and the fish are vanishing. The missing key is integrated, ecologically-based watershed planning, which enables us to see the watershed (or catchment area) as a whole, and plan our human intrusions accordingly (see pp.93-94). This is well expressed through the idea of the Stewardship Council, a gathering of human stakeholders who meet together to find the best ways to meet their needs within the overall context of the watershed itself, and its natural inhabitants, from fungi and micro-organisms to eagles, bears and downstream inhabitants. Some watersheds are small; others, such as the Mississippi, are enormous. But with the collective industrial and agricultural run-off from the Mississippi basin causing an annual 'dead zone' in the Gulf of Mexico some 18,000 sq. km in size[19], the need for holistic, integrated management is clear.

13. CONTAINING THE GLOBAL CORPORATIONS

Around the world, global corporations are often out of control, as they operate in spaces unregulated by international agreement, and unrestricted by social or environmental laws. The damage that is being done in the name of corporate progress, from the Indonesian and Malaysian rainforests to the Ogoni oil-lands in Nigeria, is just too painful. We have developed national democracies, but we have not yet developed global democracy; in the gaps where legislation and penalties do not yet exist, corporations are acting with impunity. The challenge is not to stop the corporations, but to control their conduct, and constrain them within the standards of socially and ecologically acceptable behaviour.

One option is being explored by the Community Environmental Defense League in Pennsylvania, which is mounting a legal challenge to revoke the corporate charters of two US corporations which are constantly breaking the law, and acting like ecological psychopaths[20]. Another approach is taken by CERES, the Coalition for Environmentally Sound Economies, whose CERES Principles spell out a detailed commitment to sound ecological conduct[21]. By 1995, 81 companies had endorsed the Principles, including the Sun Company, Polaroid and General Motors. Locally, grassroots community and environmental groups can also succeed in overturning harmful corporate decisions, although as with everything, the work of campaigning is expensive and exhausting. The real challenge is to develop a working system of global democracy, with a binding UN Charter of Social and Environmental Conduct, under which offending corporations could be taken to justice at the International Court in the Hague. David Korten's 1995 book *When Corporations Rule the World* provides the best single coverage of this critical piece in the eco-sustainability puzzle.[22].

325

14. BUILDING AN ECO-SUSTAINABLE WORLD ECONOMY

The corporations represent just one aspect of the overall confusion that rules at the global level. It sometimes seems that the entire world economy has been set up to encourage grab-it-while-you-can economic greed and ecological piracy. On any day of the year, $1 *trillion* (a thousand billion) is traded in 'virtual securities' – derivatives and future options on stocks, bonds, commodities and currencies. Not a cent of that money supports any actual business, farm or forest: it is a gaseous froth which hovers over the real economy like swamp-gas with indigestion. When it comes to real trade, the European Union has a strong environmental policy statement within its free trade agreement, but neither the North American (NAFTA) nor the world trade treaty (GATT) contain any meaningful conditions for ecological or social protection[23]. Major reform of these agreements is needed to incorporate the conditions needed for local, regional and planetary eco-sustainability. In the meantime, we can encourage fair trading by supporting organisations such as Co-op America, Bridgehead, and Shared Interest[24].

The United Nations struggles with constantly inadequate funding, but there is a growing voice for various forms of global taxation which could be used to fund the UN and support sustainable development initiatives such as a tax on foreign exchange trading (the Tobin tax), a carbon tax on international air flights, user fees for the global commons such as the oceans, Antarctica and non-coastal fishing, and a tax on arms trading[25]. A tax of just 0.003% on foreign exchange transactions would bring in $8.4 billion annually (the UN's total budget including peacekeeping and relief work is $6.6 billion)[26].

15. LIVING SIMPLY – AND DEVOTING OUR TIME TO CHANGE

The final piece comes back to us, as individuals, with the way we live, and the purposes we devote our lives to. By any standard of sufficiency, most people in Europe and North America consume too much. With every decision we make to buy another something, we place an additional burden on the region that has to yield up its resources. In recent years, a simple but powerful movement has come out of the Pacific Northwest region of the USA, known as voluntary simplicity. Through the movement, people are taking time to analyse their purpose, their income and their expenditures, and to reorganise their lives so that they spend less, earn less, work less, and have more time to spend with their families, and to travel, study, and work on things they find meaningful[27].

Another way in which the movement expresses itself is through the decision to live in a more co-operative, sharing manner. By choosing to live in cohousing, communities or ecovillages[28], we can share many material resources, instead of needing to own our own separate kitchens and garages full of equipment. At another level, the change is about improving the spiritual and emotional quality of our lives by choosing a richer involvement in the lives of others, and the communities we live in.

Finally, this last piece in the puzzle is about the power of personal commitment. Behind every positive initiative I have shared with you in this book, there is someone who at some point has stood up and said 'I'm going to do it'. This is the power of one.[29] There is nothing more powerful, except for the power of more than one.

Never doubt that a small group of thoughtful, concerned citizens can change the world. Indeed, it's the only thing that ever has.

Margaret Mead

In every country on Earth, there are people who have heard the sound of a different drum. They have sensed a vision, and chosen to become involved in a field of commitment that speaks to their heart. Often isolated, not knowing the existence of others around the world who are motivated by a similar vision, they press on. Sometimes they forget, and give up. Sometimes they are defeated. Sometimes they are even killed. But often they succeed, and create something new and beautiful. Fundamentally, it is through individual people such as you and me saying yes to their vision, and acting on it, that the world is changed.

The Power of Love

There was once a mountain, and if you stood on top of the mountain at dawn, you could see the most beautiful sun rising over an incredible land, full of grace, full of peace and meaning. On the plains between you and the sunrise, however, there was a great black barrier, acting like a huge hedge, full of people fighting, tearing at the Earth's resources, acting selfishly. It was clear that the barrier blocked any possible road to the sunrise, and this dampened the hope that one day you might be able to live in that beautiful place, and share it in peace with others.

Everyone on the mountain saw the sunrise, but everyone saw the barrier, too. Some started to walk towards the sun, but they soon fell under the shadow the barrier cast, and began to be influenced by its ways until they were behaving like those in the barrier, becoming absorbed in their own survival and their own needs and pleasures, forgetting the sunrise. Some remained on top of the mountain, creating great theories about how to overcome the barrier. 'If only everyone would give up sin we would all be in paradise now', they said, or 'If only people would rise up and eliminate capitalism these problems would disappear', or (more recently) 'If only humans would catch some terrible disease and die, nature would restore itself to paradise'. They wrote about their philosophies, and attracted followers who sat on the mountain with them – but the barrier remained in place.

Over time, however, growing numbers of people saw the sunrise, saw the barrier, and decided to walk towards it, holding onto the memory of the sunrise and the beautiful land beyond just that little bit more firmly, knowing in their hearts that they could not go on living without the sun, without love. As they walked, the barrier became larger, blocking out the sun for longer each day. When they started to get close to it, they could see that the barrier was made of a mass of separate barriers, called Hunger, War, Injustice, Environmental Devastation, Ignorance, Greed, Hatred, Cruelty, and so on. But they kept on walking – for there was nowhere else to go. Now because each person had only two feet, and because it was physically impossible to be in more than one place at a time, people started walking towards that small part of the barrier they felt attracted to, until they found themselves standing next to a piece of the barrier called 'ozone depletion', 'kids who know nothing about nature', or 'poverty in the Chicago slums'.

And so they started working away at that part of the barrier, remembering the sunrise, and learning all they could about the area, working to overcome the barrier in that particular place. After a short while, they sometimes became so immersed in the tiny piece of the barrier where they were working that they became overwhelmed by the difficulties, and began to feel depressed at the scale and complexity of it all. When this happened, someone working nearby would come over to give them encouragement, and tell them what a good job they were doing, which made it possible for them to continue some more. Then gradually they began to realise that they were slowly getting on top of whatever it was they were doing, and that if you bent this bit of the barrier this way, and tied that bit back, fixed those bits together and untangled those other bits, it was possible to remove the barrier bit by bit, and work a way through to the sun.

At this point, however, they remembered that they were only working on one tiny piece of the barrier, just six feet wide, and that there was so much more to be done. How ever would it be possible to transform the whole barrier? And then they remembered that on either side of them there were many other people, fifty thousand on one side, fifty thousand on the other, each looking after their own six foot section. And they knew that together, it was possible to transform the entire barrier, and open the land to the sun of love.

The End[30]

Chapter references

CHAPTER ONE

1. Paul Kennedy, *The Rise and Fall of the Great Powers* (Hyman, London, 1988).
2. Susan George, *A Fate Worse than Debt* (Penguin, 1988).
3. As reference 2, p.20.
4. James Henry, 'The Great Third World Debt Caper', *The New Republic/Utne Reader*, Oct/Nov 1986.
5. As reference 4.
6. As note 2, p.139
7. John Seymour and Herbert Girardet, *Far from Paradise* (Green Print, Basingstoke, 1988).
8. Barbara Bramble, *Debt-for-Nature Swaps* (National Wildlife Federation, Jan 1988).
9. *'The mass of extinctions which the Earth is currently facing is a threat to civilization second only to the threat of nuclear war . . . the current reduction in diversity seems destined to approach the great natural catastrophes at the end of the Paleozoic and Mezozoic eras, the most extreme for 65 million years.'* US National Academy of Sciences pronouncement, 1986.

CHAPTER TWO

1. Mark and Ellen Lukas, *Teilhard* (Collins, 1977); Teilhard de Chardin, *The Making of a Mind* (Collins, 1965); Teilhard de Chardin, *Let Me Explain* (Collins, Harper and Row, 1965); Satprem, *Sri Aurobindo, or The Adventure of Consciousness* (Aurobindo Ashram, 1968, Watkins Bookshop, London, WC2).
2. C.G. Jung, *Memories, Dreams, Reflections* (Fontana).
3. John Bliebtreu, *The Parable of the Beast* (Gollancz, 1968)

4. See, for instance, Lancelot Law Whyte, *Aspects of Form* (Indiana University Press, 1971); Arthur M. Young, *The Reflexive Universe*, (Delacorte, New York, 1975); Jean Charon, *The Unknown Spirit*, (Coventure, 1983); Paul Davies, *God and the New Physics* (Penguin, 1983); Paul Davies, *The Cosmic Blueprint* (Penguin, 1988); Ilya Prigogine, *Order out of Chaos*, (Flamingo, 1984); A.N. Whitehead, *Science and the Modern World* (The Free Press, New York, 1967); A.N. Whitehead, *Process and Reality*, (CUP, 1929); C.H. Waddington, *The Evolution of an Evolutionist* (Edinburgh University Press, 1975); Ed. Koestler and J.R. Smythies, *Beyond Reductionism*, (Hutchinson, London, 1969); Henry Margenau, 'Einstein's Conception of Reality' in P.A. Schilpp, *Albert Einstein: Philosopher-Scientist* (Harper and Row, New York, 1959).
5. See, for instance, Harold Saxton Burr, *Blueprint for Immortality*, (Neville Spearman, London, 1972); H.S. Burr, *The Fields of Life: Our Links with the Universe*, (Ballantine, New York, 1973); Shafica Karagula, *Breakthrough to Creativity*, (De Vorss, Santa Monica, Ca, 1967); Charles Tart, *Altered States of Consciousness*, (Wiley, New York, 1969); Albert Szent-Gyorgyi, *Bioelectronics, A Study in Cellular Regulation Defence and Cancer* (Academic Press, New York, 1968); S. Krippner and D. Rubin, *Galaxies of Life: The Human Aura in Acupuncture and Kirlian Photography* (Gordon and Breah, London, 1973).
6. The last group to die by fire were the 'witches', the wise women, and millions of ordinary women.

CHAPTER THREE

1. The use of these colours should be explained, especially for readers outside Britain. The colour *purple* is often associated with spiritual values. *Dark blue* reflects the beauty of the planet as a whole. *Pale blue* is the colour used by Britain's Conservative party, which emphasizes economic values above all else. *Green* reflects ecological values. *Yellow* is a colour many people associate with creativity. *Orange* is the colour of Britain's Liberal party, which emphasizes local community values. *Red* is the colour of socialist values the world over.
2. Michael Phillips and Salli Rasberry, *Honest Business: A Superior Strategy for Starting and Managing Your Own Business* (Clear Glass, San Francisco/Random, New York, 1981).
3. I do not pretend that this is an adequate treatment of the complex politics of macro-economic management. Mea culpa.

4. On Lowell, see *Business Matters* Notes No. 4, (BBC, 1988); on Massachusetts, see *The Guardian*, May 2 and 3, 1988.

5. Lancashire Enterprises Ltd, Lancashire House, Watery Lane, Preston, PR2 2XE.

6. An ancient North American Indian legend predicts that when the Earth has been ravaged and the animals killed, a tribe of people from all races, creeds and colours will arrive who will put their faith in deeds, not in words, to make the land green again. They will be called 'The Warriors of the Rainbow', the protectors of the environment. Those who work to build the rainbow economy stand alongside those who work for Greenpeace and for the environment as joint 'Warriors of the Rainbow'. The international co-operative movement uses the colours of the rainbow on its flag. Rainbows appear when the light of the sun hits the rain, after the storm, the refraction of light made each raindrop creating a prism effect, and breaking the light into separate colours.

CHAPTER FOUR

1. In 1932–33, at a time of very high unemployment and depression, the Austrian town of Wurgl created its own interest-free currency which was distributed in return for public works. The notes were date-stamped, and decreased in value by one cent each month, which encouraged rapid circulation. Taxes were paid, unemployment greatly reduced and local shopkeepers flourished. There was great interest, but the Austrian National Bank took legal action against it and closed it down. (Ekins, 1986 and Cole, 1930). In Chicago, in the 1930s, a local scrip called 'United Trade Dollars' was set up by businessmen, secured by US currency held in trust. These circulated three times as fast as US currency. As in Wurgl, each note had to be certified with a monthly one cent exchange stamp. United Trade dollars could be changed back into federal dollars at a discount, creating a high incentive to use them. The system was ended in 1943 due to war-time scarcities. (*Community Comments* magazine, USA, January 1970.) In Basle, Switzerland, a self-help 'Economic Ring' was set up in 1935 using a local exchange currency, following models developed in Scandinavia. In 1949, it was used for four million Swiss Francs worth of trade, half in cheques and half in cash. You bought the exchange currency with Swiss Francs, and each new payment of national currency gave you an additional 5% of exchange currency credit as reward for joining the Ring. A daily levy of 0.001% was charged on your daily credit balance to encourage you to circulate it. The Ring was

still operating in 1970, and may be operating today. A similar scheme was started in Stuttgart. The island of Guernsey in the English Channel has an ancient prerogative to issue its own money. Between 1815 and 1936, the island government issued £4000 in interest-free notes, using them initially to pay for public road and building repairs. Thereafter, they remained in general circulation, and could be used for interest-free loans. They have gone on issuing their own money from 1914 to the present in spite of attempts by the banks to prevent them. (Ekins, 1986.) The Wurgl experiment, and probably the Basle and Chicago experiments, were inspired by the writings of Silvio Gesell, a German businessman working in the Argentine. (Gesell, 1904, Kennedy 1987.) Further writings on the subject of local currencies can be found in Galbraith, 1975 and Hayek, 1976.

2. 'LETS' originally meant 'Local Exchange Trading Scheme'. The first six members started trading in February 1983. In 1987 the name was changed to 'Local Employment and Trading Scheme'. Special thanks to Michael Linton for his help on this chapter.

3. Don Haythorne, an Edmonton consultant in economic affairs, *Credit Union Way*, Vancouver, September 1986.

4. 1982 Revenue Canada bulletin on barter transactions.

5. VAT is the European Common Market equivalent of sales tax.

6. Christine Langlois, 'Is Bartering Back?' *Canadian Living*, Oct 31, 1987.

7. These rules have now been changed (1996).

CHAPTER FIVE

1. The Universe may never have 'started' at all. Some physicists (e.g. Stephen Hawking) argue for continuous creation.

2. Yankelovich and Immerwarh, *Putting the Work Ethic to Work* (Public Agenda Foundation, New York, 1983).

3. Charles Handy, *The Future of Work*, p.133, (Blackwell, 1984).

4. The journal TVEI *Insight* (free from Training Commission, Distribution Unit (Dept TVEI), Room E825, Moorfoot, Sheffield S1 4PQ) often runs good stories on action learning approaches.

5. The journal SCAN covers developments in community education in Scotland.

6. Taranaki . . . information from Vivian Hutchinson, Taranaki Work Trust, see Chapter Six, Ref. 14.

7. *LEDIS Sheet* A293 (Coventry Consortium), B56 (Local Exchange, Glasgow. (See Appendix)

8. *SCAN*, April 1984.

9. As reference 2, above.

10. The achievements exercise was developed by Bernard Haldane, author of *Job Power Now!* (Acropolis, Washington DC, 1976). The exercise and skills list can be found in *The New Unemployment Handbook*.

11. One of the best books on lifeplanning is *Build Your Own Rainbow*.

12. Job Change Project, Polytechnic of Central London, 35 Marylebone Rd, London NW1 5LS. Similar work is done commercially by DMA, 25 Cholmeley Lodge, Cholmeley Park, London N6 5EN, Tel: 0171-341 6027, and 27 Congress St, Salem, MA 01970, USA, Tel: (508) 741 0780.

13. *Development Forum*, March-April 1988 (*Resources*, Chapter Twelve).

14. London Work Out, 8 Strutton Ground, London SW1 2HP, Tel: 0171-222 0222.

15. *New Synthesis Think Tank Papers*, Sirius, Baker Rd, Shutesbury, MA 01072, USA, 1987. The Door, 618 Ave of the Americas, New York, NY 10011.

16. Professor Frank Reid, Economics Dept, University of Toronto, Canada.

17. The information on worksharing has been taken from *The New Unemployment Handbook*.

18. *New Ways to Work*, (London).

19. Rocky Mountain Institute (See Appendix).

CHAPTER SIX

1. Quoted in *Reckoning: The Rise and Fall of American Business Culture* (National Film Board of Canada, November 1987).

2. 'Eldonians', undated Guardian article, 1987.

3. *The Honor of All*, 1985 video the Alkali Lake Sushwap band, Box 4306 Williams Lake, BC V2D 2V4, Canada. Four Worlds Development Project, University of Lethbridge, lethbridge, Alberta T1K 3M4, Canada.

4. David Caley, *New Ideas in Ecology and Economics* (CBC transcript, 1986, $5.00 from CBC Enterprises, PO Box 6440, Station A, Montreal, Canada H3C 3L4).

5. Celine Sachs, 'Mutirao in Brazil – Initiatives for Self-Reliance' in *Development* (Rome, 1986:4).

6. *Future Workshops* – Institute for Social Inventions (Appendix).

7. Brainstorming is a technique which releases imagination and creativity in a group in a short period of time. Everyone's ideas are

encouraged without comment or criticism, however crazy. (Institute for Social Inventions [Appendix].)
8. Information on Connemara West from Kieran O'Donohue and Ian Scott Connemara West Letterfrack, Co. Galway, Eire (LEDIS Sheet A238).
9. *Community Business News*, Oct 87.
10. Greg MacLeod, *New Age Corporations – Community Corporations that Work* (see Appendix).
11. *Community Business News*, Feb 88.
12. *Building Economic Alternatives*, Summer 1987.
13. *Community Business Scotland Directory*, 1986.
14. Information from Vivian Hutchinson, Taranaki Work Trust, PO Box 274, New Plymouth, Taranaki, New Zealand.

CHAPTER SEVEN

1. For the Esperance story, thanks to the Australian magazine *Work Matters* (date unknown).
2. Stories about the initiatives can be found in *Initiatives* magazine and the *LEDIS Sheets* (see Appendix).
3. *LEDIS Overview sheet* B55; study done by the Open University Co-operative Research Unit.
4. *The Entrepreneurial Economy*, January 1986.
5. *LEDIS sheets*, see Appendix.
6. *Initiatives*, October 1987.
7. *Resurgence*, March 1987 – see Appendix.
8. Business in the Community, *Small Firms: Survival and Job Creation – the contribution of Enterprise Agencies* (see below).
9. Briarpatch, Business Network.
10, 11. Rocky Mountain Institute (see Appendix).
12. David Morris, *The New City-States*.
13. LEDIS sheet Overview B26, see Appendix.
14. As reference 12.
15. As reference 10.
16. Lester Thurow, *The Zero-Sum Solution*, p.193 (Penguin, 1987).
17. Ed. Rick Carlson, *The Frontiers of Science and Medicine* (Wildwood House, London, 1973).
18. *New Age Business*.
19. Thanks to Hazel Henderson for this lucid description of the 'whole economy'. See Appendix.
20. The possibilities of this kind of co-operation can be further grasped by considering the experiment in computer-based

economic co-ordination undertaken by Professor Stafford Beer, Fernando Flores and others in Chile in 1972–73, under President Salvador Allende's democratically-elected communist government. In 'Project Cybersin' a computerized command centre was set up linking Chile's major producers, suppliers, government offices and finance houses. Essential data was sent in electronically on a daily basis, enabling the command room to carry a real-time picture of key indicators in the Chilean economy. This allowed intelligent policy-oriented planning to proceed, avoiding the litany of stock-piles, queues and shortages that often accompanies centrally-run economies. The command centre became, in effect, the brain of the economy. On 11 September 1973 Allende was assassinated, and the government overthrown. One of the Cybersin workers rushed to the command centre and magnetised the discs to protect the identity of the people involved. The 'brain' died. On a smaller scale, local businesses could create a similar brain for themselves. Computer intelligence offers a capacity for co-ordinated information, forecasting and projection far beyond anything one person or team of people can provide, and the experience of Mondragon and Chile could potentially be applied in a community economy. For a detailed write up on Project Cybersin, see Stafford Beer, *Brain of the Firm* (John Wiley & Sons, 1981).

21. Louis Burghes, *Made in the USA: a review of Workfare* (Unemployment Unit, 9 Poland St, London W1V 3DG).

22. *I Ching*, Hexagram 59, (Arkana/Routledge, London).

23. Participative approaches to planning have been explored over recent years. The Greater London Council experimented with 'Popular Planning', enabling local people to plan the kind of future they want to see for their area. Tony Gibson has developed 'Planning for Real' in which people construct a model of their community, and try out new arrangements of streets, houses, shops, parks and playgrounds. (Town and Country Planning Association, 17 Carlton House, London SW1Y 5AS.)

CHAPTER EIGHT

1. Peters & Waterman, *In Search of Excellence: Lessons from America's Best-Run Companies* (Harper and Row, 1982).

2. The term 'Third Era' is not synonymous with Toffler's 'Third Wave', which follows the Agricultural Age and the Industrial Age. The First and Second Eras of business both arise during the Industrial Age.

3. John Naisbitt and Patricia Aburdene, *Re-inventing the*

Corporation (Warner, New York, 1985).
4. John Elkington, *The Green Capitalists* (Gollancz, London, 1987).
5. *Re-inventing the Corporation and The Pursuit of Excellence* give examples of progressive innovations.
6. Martin Stott, *Beyond Isolation – Constructing a Co-ops Sector in the UK Economy* (ICOM, Leeds, 1986).
7. Naisbitt & Aburdene (reference 3), p. 63.
8. *New Options*, Washington DC, May 1988.
9. Newsletter of the Social Investment Forum, USA, October 1987 (see Appendix).
10. Lester Thurow, *The Zero Sum Solution* (Penguin, 1985).
11. Naisbitt & Aburdene (reference 3), p.27.
12. John Love *TWA, Ambassador* magazine, August 1979.
13. Hilary Wainwright & Dave Elliott, *The Lucas Plan: A New Trade Unionism in the Making?* (Allison & Busby, London 1982).
14. Thurow (reference 10), p.187.
15. Mark Dowie & Theodore Brown, 'The Best and Worst of American Business', *Mother Jones magazine*, June 1985. Also Naisbitt and Aburdene, p.43.
16. Anita Roddick, 'The Responsibilities of Profit', *One Earth* magazine, Spring 1988 (see Appendix).
17. Linda Ackerman, 'Fear or Flow – What's the state of your organisation?', *One Earth*, Spring 1988 (see Appendix), 6121 Castle Drive, Oakland, CA 94611, USA.
18. Roger Harrison, 'Organising Love', *One Earth*, Spring 1988 (see Appendix). 2719 Woolsey Street, Berkely, CA 94705, USA.
19. Naisbitt & Aburdene (reference 3), p.257.
20. Naisbitt & Aburdene (reference 3), p.36.
21. The Guardian, 16 July 1987.
22. *No Single Model: Participation, Organisation and Democracy in Larger Co-ops* (ICOM, 1987, see Appendix).
23. *Noren News*, Noren Institute, 62 Stanton St, San Francisco, CA 94114, USA, Spring 1988.
24. *Environmental Aspects of the Activities of Transnational Corporations*, UN Centre on Transnational Corporations, New York, 1985.
25. Elkington (reference 4), pp 23 & 179.
26. Elkington, p.140.
27. Anita Roddick, *One Earth*, Spring 1988.
28. *Our Common Future* (The Brundtland Report, Oxford University Press, 1987).
29. Elkington (reference 4), p.228.

30. Business in the Community – see Appendix.

31. *Initiatives*, London, April 1987 (no longer printed).

32. Elkington (see reference 4).

33. Ed. John Button, *Green Pages – a Directory of Natural Products, Services, Resources & Ideas* (Optima, London, 1988); Ed. Elkington, *Green Pages – the Business of Saving the World* (Routledge, London, 1988).

34. Personal talk by Michael Phillips at 'The Other Economic Summit', London, 1985.

CHAPTER NINE

1. In indigenous native societies, the sense of 'this is ours' reflects the sense of a shared partnership with nature, not of ownership in the modern sense.

2. R.T. Taylor, *Hot Money – And the Politics of Debt*, (Unwin Hyman, London, 1987).

3. For further notes on current banking policies, see Susan George, *A Fate Worse Than Debt* (Penguin, 1988) and Anthony Sampson, *The Money Lenders – Bankers in a Dangerous World* (Hodder & Stoughton, 1981).

4. 1985 Scott Bader Common Ownership Lecture, 1985. (Woolaston, Wellingborough, Northants, NN9 7RC, UK). See also James Robertson, *Future World* (Temple Smith/Gower, 1985).

5. Dominique La Pierre, *The City of Joy* (Arrow, London, 1986).

6. *Scottish Community Business News*, February 1988 and personal conversations (see Appendix).

8. CBC interview in *New Ideas in Ecology and Economics*, (Toronto, 1986).

9. Another Vancouver credit union, the Community Congress for Economic Change, has followed community-oriented lending policies since its inception in 1974.

10. Information on CELT from Vivian Hutchinson, Taranski Work Trust, New Zealand.

11. *Building Economic Alternatives* Spring 1987 (Co-op America, Washington DC – see Appendix).

12. As reference 11.

13. Data from Gordon Davidson, Director of the Social Investment Forum, Boston, USA.

14. Josh Martin, 'Happy Returns for Do-Gooders', *Financial World*, March 18 1986, USA.

15. Susan Meeker-Lowry, *Building Economic Alternatives*, Spring 1987.

16, 17. As reference 11.

18. Sue Ward, *Socially Responsible Investment*. (Directory of Social Change, Radius Works, Back St, London NW3 1HL, £6.95).

19. *LEDIS sheets* B34 (Pension Funds, Investment and Jobs) and B46 (Socially Responsible Investment).

20. As reference 14.

21. Maxine Waters, *The Forum*, newsletter of the Social Investment Forum, October 1987.

22. Lester Thurow, *The Zero Sum Solution* (Penguin, 1987).

23. Personal conversations and correspondence.

24. *LEDIS sheets* A172 (Northumbria Unit Trust), A332 (Highland Opportunity Ltd), A211 (Northern Investors Co Ltd), A120 (Valleys of Enterprise Trust Fund).

25. *Enterprise Boards*, (Centre for Local Employment Strategies, Heron House, Brazennose St, Manchester M2 5HD) £2.50.

26. Mark Kidel, *Financial Times*, 8 October 1981.

27. *New York Times*, 25 December 1987.

28. Rocky Mountain Institute (see Appendix).

29. *Initiatives*, June 1987, and David Osborne, 'Bootstrap Banking', *Inc Magazine*, August 1987.

30. Quoted in 'Socially Responsible Banking' by Rob Baird, *Building Economic Alternatives*, Spring 1987.

31. *The Entrepreneurial Economy*, Washington DC, July 1987.

32. Marj Halperin, 'Women Helping Women Worldwide', *Building Economic Alternatives*, Spring 1987.

33. *The Entrepreneurial Economy*, Washington DC, July 1987.

34. Mushtaq Parker, 'Islam's Challenge to the System', *South* magazine, November 1986.

35. Ken Marshall, 'The Grameen Bank of Bangladesh', *Appropriate Technology* Vol. 13, No.3.

36. An anonymous banker who was personally involved in lending more than $50 billion to developing countries wrote in the *Herald International Tribune*, 16 October 1985: *'We rushed blindly along chasing a rainbow we thought would lead to easy profits. Our painful experience has demonstrated that private banks are incapable of making reliable judgements about the risks involved in financing economic development. The disastrous record of private financing for economic development shows this is no place for banks.'* (Quoted in Susan George, *A Fate Worse Than Debt*).

37. Information on community land trusts from the Institute for Community Economics (see below).

38. Shann Turnbull, 'Co-operative Land Banks', in *The Living Economy*, (Routledge, 1986).

CHAPTER TEN

1. Jacob von Uexkull, *Towards a Responsible World View* (unpublished Paper).
2. William Chandler, *Energy Productivity: Key to Environmental Protection and Economic Progress* (Worldwatch paper No. 63, 1985) (see Appendix).
3. Nuclear power may contribute to the greenhouse effect through thermal heating. Research by staff at the Rocky Mountain Institute has shown that an all-nuclear anti-greenhouse strategy would require the construction of a new nuclear power plant every one to three days for 40 years, cost $200 billion a year, and only reduce greenhouse warming by 20%–30% (February 1988, RMI Newsletter).
4, 5. Hunter and Amory Lovins, *Energy Unbound*, (Sierra Books, 730 Polk St, San Francisco, CA 94109, USA, 1986). Recommended as a key source.
6, 7. As reference 2.
8. Developing countries have three-quarters of the world's population, and use just 18% of its electricity. Average consumption is around 500 kilowatt hours per year, compared with 10,500 kWh in America. Since 1980, electricity consumption in poor countries has grown by 7% p.a. (compared with 2% p.a. in rich countries). On existing efficiency rates, if developing countries grow at 4.5% p.a., they will need to invest $125 per year in generating capacity, compared with $50–60 billion now. Existing capital expenditure and loans are already causing crippling problems. Efficiency and demand-management methods are therefore as important for the Third World as for the industrial north. (*Economist*, 7 May 1988).
9. A reduction to 30% of existing demand may be a feasible goal – *New Scientist*, 14 April 1988.
10. The Rocky Mountain Institute's Economic Renewal Project has prepared an easy off-the-shelf format for a community energy study – see Appendix.
11–13. *Energy Unbound* (see note 4 above).
14. *The Guardian*, 30 January, 1988.
15. As reference 4.
16. Newcastle Energy Centre.
17. *Living with Energy*, Lothian Energy Group, Edinburgh, 1983.
18. The evolution of the bridge gives a good example of this subtle mind/matter relationship. With each new advance, a bridge incorporates more mind and less matter. Consider first no bridge at all

(getting wet); the stone clapper bridge; the arched bridge; the early suspension bridge; modern suspension bridges. Advances in ceramics may take us further yet. If the mind-matter curve continues, we may see 'Scotty, Beam-Me-Over' bridges. The same evolution from matter to mind is true of computers, transport, energy-use, healing, etc.

19. Lester Brown and Pamela Shaw, *Six Steps to a Sustainable Society* (Worldwatch Paper No. 48, 1982).

20. Cynthia Pollock, *Mining Urban Wastes: The Potential for Recycling* (Worldwatch Paper No. 76, April 1987). See Appendix.

21. Data in this paragraph from Worldwatch paper No. 76.

22. De Allen Hershowitz & De Eugene Salerni, *Garbage Management in Japan: Leading the Way* (Inform, NY 10016).

23. Jo Gordon, *Waste Recycling in the Community* (NCVO, London 1987). See also Jon Vogler, *Recycling for Change* (Christian Aid, PO Box 1, London SW9 8BH, 1985, 50p).

24. *Warmer* Bulletin, March 1988.

25. Neil Seldman, 'Recycling by Any Other Name Won't Smell As Sweet', *Friends of the Earth newsletter*, USA, January 1987.

26. Worldwatch Paper No. 76.

27. For examples of partnerships, see reference 23.

28. John Seymour and Herbert Girardet, *Blueprint for a Green Planet* (Dorling Kindersley, London, 1987).

29. Farmer suicides – *The Guardian*, London, 12 March 1987. From 1980/81 to 1987, total farm debt in Britain increased from £500 million to over £6 billion (*Trade Indemnity, Guardian*, 24 February 1988).

30. *Pacific News Service/Utne Reader*, USA, November 1987.

31. *Centre for Rural Affairs Newsletter/Utne Reader*, USA, November 1987.

32. *Technology Review/Utne Reader*, July 1987, USA, November 1987.

33. John Seymour and Herbert Girardet, *Far from Paradise* (Green Print, Basingstoke, 1988). Recommended as a key source.

34–36. David Nicholson-Lord, *The Greening of the City* (Routledge, 1987). Recommended as a key source.

37. Thanks to Martin Stott, Oxford City Councillor, for this information.

38. Thanks to Vera Elliott, Sutton Centre for Environmental Information, for this information.

39. Thanks for the '5% Effect' to Liz Shephard.

40. 75%–80% – Friends of the Earth MORI-commissioned survey; 95% – *Which?* magazine survey; 60% – 500 people survey

in Reading, Newbury and Hungerford (Soil Association Review, June 1986).

CHAPTER ELEVEN

1. Alex Henney, *Inside Local Government* (Sinclair Brown, 1984).
2. The terms 'council' and 'local government' are used collectively to refer to Britain's different rural and urban situations, while recognising that city councils, county councils and borough councils have differing powers and responsibilities.
3. *Going Local: Decentralisation in Practice* (London Borough of Islington, 1986).
4. The Liberals became known as the Liberal Democrats in 1988 when they merged with the Social Democrats.
5. *Decentralisation: A Change for the Better* (Tower Hamlets Borough Council, 1988); and *Urban Development Sheet D24*, The Planning Exchange, Glasgow (see Appendix).
6. On integrated unemployment strategies, see Guy Dauncey and Jane Mountain, *The New Unemployment Handbook*, Chapter 14 (National Extension College, 18 Brooklands Avenue, Cambridge CB2 2HN 1988) £6.95.
7. For information on Oxford City Council, thanks to Martin Stott.
8. David Morris, *The New City States* (Institute for Local Self-Reliance, Washington DC, 1982).
9. Ed. Bassand *et al., Self-Reliant Development in Europe* (see Appendix).
10. *The Guardian*, 8 April 1988.
11, 12. Figures from *The Cost of Crime – The Balance Sheet*, Apex Trust, Brixton Hill Place, London SW2 1HJ, with thanks to Bill Mather.
13. Martin Stott and Phil Fryer, 'Beginning to make Oxford Healthier', *Town and Country Planning*, London, March 1988.
14. *The Economist*, 23 January, 1987.
15. These initiatives are discussed in detail in ed. Clement Bezold, *Anticipatory Democracy* (Vintage/Random, New York, 1978).
16. *The Guardian*, 26 November 1987.
17. Oxford's female leadership at the time included the Labour Leader, Deputy and Chief Whip, the Conservative Leader and Deputy, the Mayor and the Sheriff. The city's symbol is a bull.

CHAPTER TWELVE

1. *State of the World*, 1988 (see Appendix).
2. Information from Canadian National Task Force (see below).
3. In 1988, Massachusetts held a major 'Blueprint 2,000' exercise, asking where the state should go, and developing an action plan for the state based on principles of sustainability and equality. Questionnaires were sent to 351 municipalities, and regional hearings held across the state. (C/o Eleanor LeCain, Governor's Office, State House-Room 259, Boston MA, 02133.) (*New Options* #48, May 30, 1988.) Wisconsin hneld a statewide 'Globescope' conference in 1988 on sustainable development, relating global trends to practical environmental issues that Wisconsin corporations and government bodies must deal with. (*New Synthesis Think Tank Papers*, Sirius, Baker Rd, Shutesbury, MA 01072).
4. *Our Common Future* (Chapter Eight, reference 28), p.303.
5. 'Redefining National Security' (Rocky Mountain Institute, see Appendix).
6. 'To Balance the Budget, Build a Sustainable Society', *New Options* #48, May 30, 1988 (no longer being published).
7. *New Internationalist*, Oxford, February 1988 (see Appendix).
8. World Conservation Bank, contact via Michael Sweatman, International Wilderness Leadership Foundation, USA. Tel: (802) 253 8142.
9. Susan George, *A Fate Worse Than Debt* (Penguin, 1988),

CHAPTER 13

1. UNDP Development Report, 1993.
2. For general references, see O'Hara 'Working Harder Isn't Working' and 'In Context' Journal, Issue 37.
3. 'Europe weighs 4-day week to tackle jobs crisis. UK Guardian, Nov 24, 1993
4. 'Dear Europe, IOU $1.6 trillion'. European, Sept 2 1993.

CHAPTER 14

1. Daly, Herman E., and John B. Cobb, *For the Common Good*.
2. Paul Hawken, *The Ecology of Commerce*.
3. In Context #41, Paul Hawken interview, p.20.

4. Oakland/Berkeley RMDZ, City of Oakland, 1333 Broadway, Suite 900, Oakland, CA 94612, USA. Tel (510) 238-3703 Fax (510) 238-3691.
5. In Context #41, p.43.
6. State of the World 1995, 'Creating a Sustainable Materials Economy'.
7. Vermont Businesses for Social Responsibility, PO Box 462, Burlington, VT 05402 (802) 655-4300 Fax (802) 655-2700 VBSR@together.org.
8. In Business, Vol 17, 5, 'How Vermont Businesses Put Sustainability Into Law'.
9. Green Builder Program, Environmental & Conservation Services Dept, PO Box 1088, Austin, Texas 78767 (512) 499-STAR.
10. See Huey Johnson, *Green Plans*.
11. Earthword #4, 'Transportation Planning, Restoration of Cities', for excellent overall coverage.
12. The Rocky Mountain Institute produces some of the best materials showing the links between CO_2 reduction and economic gain.
13. Mondragon is the best model for the integrated management of welfare, training and business development.
14. Chinese grain – WorldWatch Magazine Vol 8, No 5.
15. In Context #42 (whole issue).
16. Huey Johnson, *Green Plans* p.127.
17. In Context #42, p.10.
18. For Hazel Henderson's ideas, see Whole Earth Review #86, pp.22–29, and 'Futures', Vol 27 No 2, 'The United Nations at 50' p.119.
19. Gulf of Mexico – Reuter report, Victoria Times Colonist Nov 3rd 1995.
20. *Rachel's Environment and Health Weekly*, #455.
21. CERES – see LEDIS Sheet E143.
22. David Korten, *When Corporations Rule the World*.
23. *Green Plans*, p.117.
24. For Co-op America, Shared Interest, see Resources.
25. 'Futures', Vol 27 No 2, 'The United Nations at 50'.
26. State of the World 1995, p.185.
27. See New Road Map Foundation and Voluntary Simplicity, see Appendix.
28. For ecovillages, see EcoVillages Report, Context Institute, PO Box 11470, Bainbridge Island, WA 98110. $15 + shipping (ci@context.org), and Global EcoVillages Network, Fjorvang,

Skyumjes 101, 7752 Snedsted, Denmark (gen@gaia.org). For intentional communities, see the 400-page thick Communities Directory 1995, $20 from Communities, Rt 4, Box 169-D, Louisa VA 23093. For cohousing, see *Cohousing: A Contemporary Approach to Housing Ourselves* by Kathryn McCamant and Charles Durrett (Cohousing Company, 1250 Addison St, #113, Berkeley CA 94702, and the Cohousing Network, PO Box 2584, Berkeley, CA 94702).

29. *The Power of One*, by Sharif Abdullah.

30. This story may be copied and passed around freely. Just credit the author, and this book.

Appendix :
Resources and Opportunities in the Rainbow Economy

COMMUNITY CURRENCIES

Cahn, Edgar, and Jonathan Rowe. *Time Dollars: The New Currency that Enables Americans to Turn their Hidden Resource - Time - into Personal Security and Community Renewal*. Rodale Press, Emmaus, PA 18098, 1992.

Dobson, Ross. *Bringing the Economy Home from the Market*. Black Rose Books, Montreal, 1994.

Galbraith, J.K. *Money - Whence It Came, Where It Went*. Pelican, Harmondsworth, UK, 1975.

Gesell, Silvio. *Die Naturlich Wirtschaftsordnung*. Rudolf Zitmann Verlag, Nuremberg, 1904; IXth edition 1949.

Glover, Paul. *Hometown Money: How to Enrich Your Community with Local Currency*. Ithaca Money, Box 6578, Ithaca, NY 14851. 1995. $25 + $3 shipping. Overseas $33.

Greco, Tom. *New Money for Healthy Communities*. Tom Greco Publications, PO Box 42663, Tucson, AZ 85733. $15.95 + $3 shipping.

Hayek, F.A. *Choice of Currency* and *Denationalisation of Currency*. Institute of Economic Affairs, London, 1976.

Kennedy, Margrit. *Interest and Inflation Free Money*. New Society Publishers, PA; PO Box 189, Gabriola Island, BC V0R 1X0, Canada, 1995.

Lang, Peter. LETS Work – *Rebuilding the Local Economy*. Grover Books, c/o Ecologic, 19 Maple Grove, Bath BA2 3AF, £8.99 + £1.80 postage in UK, overseas £2.25

Organisations & Resources

LETSLink, Liz Shephard, 61 Woodcock Rd, Warminster, Wilts BA12 9DH, UK (01985) 217871. Introductory literature (£1.20).

347

LETS Info Pack (£6.95+75p postage). Let'sLink (local currency magazine) £10pa.
Michael Linton, 1600 Embledon Cresc, Courtenay V9N 6N8, B.C., Canada (604) 338-0213. Send $50 fee for all LETS materials, discs, postage and packing, and prepayment for service calls. lcs@mars.ark.com. Also http://www.u-net.com/gmlets/home.html
Green$Quarterly, PO Box 21140, Christchurch, New Zealand (03) 661-992. Basic resource for New Zealand groups.
OZLETS, PO Box 183, Kurrajong, NSW 2758, Australia. National magazine for Australian LETS groups, A$12pa, A$50pa overseas.
Ithaca Money - Home Town Money Starter Kit. $25 ($35 overseas), Box 6578, Ithaca, NY 14851. (607) 273-8025. Ithacahour@aol.com
Time Dollar Network, PO Box 42160, Washington, DC 20015. (202) 686-5200.
Amy Bellanger, PO Box 7132, Milton, FL 32570. Send $1 for listing of community currency projects in USA.

COMMUNITY ECONOMIC DEVELOPMENT

Douglas, David. *Community Economic Development in Canada*, Vols 1 & 2. 1994/95. Libra, 366 Adelaide St E., #443, Toronto, Ontario M5A 3X9.
Jungk, Robert and Norbert Muller, *Future Workshops – How to Create Desirable Futures*. Institute for Social Inventions, 1988, see below.
MacLeod, Greg. *New Age Business: Community Corporations that Work*. Canadian Council on Social Development, PO Box 3505, Station C, Ottawa, K1Y 4G1 1986.
MacLeod, Greg. *Ideas with Legs: From Mondragon to America*. CCE Publications, Vernon, Canada, 1995.
M'Gonigle, Michael and Ben Parfitt. *Forestopia: A Practical Guide to The New Forest Economy*. Harbour Publishing, PO Box 219, Madeira Park, BC V0N 2H0 Canada, 1994.
Morrison, Roy. *We Build the Road as We Travel, Mondragon: A Co-operative Solution*. New Society Publishers, PA; PO Box 189, Gabriola Island, BC V0R 1X0, Canada, 1991.
Quartier, Jack. *Canada's Social Economy*. CCE Publications, Vernon, Canada, 1994.
Pearce, John. *At the Heart of the Community Economy: Community Enterprise in a Changing World*. Calouste Gulbenkian Foundation, London 1993.
Perry, Stewart, and Mike Lewis. *Reinventing the Local Economy: What 10 Canadian Initiatives Can Teach Us About Building*

Creative, Inclusive and Sustainable Communities. CCE Publications, Vernon, Canada, 1994.

Roberts, Wayne, John Bacher & Brian Nelson. *Get A Life: A Green Cure for Canada's Economic Blues.* Ontario CED Publications, #402-130 Spadina Ave, Toronto M5V 2L4, 1993.

Organisations & Resources:

Center for Economic Conversion, 222 View St, Mountain View, CA 94041-1344. Publish *Alternatives*.

Business and Community Development. 8-part video series on Mondragon, co-ops in Canada & UK, CDCs in the USA. University College of Cape Breton Press, PO Box 5300, Sydney, Nova Scotia, Canada.

Community Supported Agriculture, PO Box 550, Kimberton PA 19442. (215) 935-7797.

Commonwealth Association for Local Action and Economic Development, c/o DACE, University of Durham, 32 Old Elvet, Durham DH1 3HN, UK.

Connemara West Centre, Kieran O'Donohue, Letterfrack, Co. Galway, Eire. (095) 41047.

Co-op America, 1612 K St. NW, #600, Washington DC 20006. (202) 872-5307. *Co-op America Quarterly* ($20US pa) and *National Green Pages* (annual).

Dean Clough Industrial Park, Halifax HX3 5AX, UK (01422) 344555.

E.F. Schumacher Society, Box 76, RD3 Great Barrington, MA 01230. (413) 528-1737. Focus on community land trusts, community currencies, affordable housing.

GEO - Grassroots Economic Organising Newsletter, PO Box 5065, New Haven, CT 06525. $15pa.

Industrial Common Ownership Movement (ICOM), Vassalli House, 20 Central Rd, Leeds LS1 6DE, UK. (0113) 246-1738.

Institute for Community Economics, 57 School St, Springfield MA. 01105 (413) 774-7956. *Community Economics,* $15pa. Community land trusts, community development loan funds, co-op housing.

Institute for Local Self-Reliance, 1313 5th St SE, #306, Minneapolis, MN 55414-1546. (612) 379-3815 ilsr@igc.apc.org

LEDIS Sheets. Monthly mailing on community economic development initiatives from The Planning Exchange, Tontine House, 8 Gordon St, Glasgow G1 3PL, UK. (0141) 248-8541.

Making Waves: Canada's Community Economic Development Quarterly. CCE, 2905 - 31st St, #5, Vernon, BC V1T 5H6,

Canada. (604) 542-7057. $30pa

Mondragon Study Tours, Intercommunity Justice & Peace Centre, 215 E.14th St, Cincinatti, OH 45210. (513) 579-8547.

Mondragon (Information and study tours), Palacio Otalora, Barrio Aozaraza #2, 20550 Aretxabaleta (Guipuzcoa), Spain. Tel (43) 79 79 99.

The Mondragon Experiment (video). BBC Enterprises Ltd, 80 Wood Lane, London W12 0TT, UK.

National Center for Employee Ownership, 1201 Martin Luther King Jr. Way, Oakland, CA 94612. (510) 272-9461.

National Congress for Community Economic Development, 1875 Connecticut Ave. NW, Washington DC 20009.

National Network of Community Business, Society Place, West Calder, West Lothian, Scotland EH55 8EA. (01506) 871370. *New Sector Magazine.*

The Neighbourhood Works: Building Alternatives for the City. 2125 W. North Ave, Chicago IL 60647(312) 278-4800 $30pa.

Ontario CED Alliance, 130 Spadina Ave, #402, Toronto M5V 2L4, Canada. (416) 594-9255. *Community Economics*, $16pa, and a range of books and papers. commecon@web.apc.org

Prosperity Press, Paul Wildman, PO Box 244, Ashgrove, Qld 4012, Australia. Books and materials on community economic development, sustainability and self-sufficiency. pwildman@scu.edu.an

Social Planning and Research Council, #106-2182 West 12th Ave, Vancouver, BC V6K 2N4, Canada. (604) 736-8118.

Trusteeship Institute, 15 Edwards Sq, MA 01060. (413) 584-8191 (re Mondragon).

Youth Business Kit. Project North-East, 60 Grainger St, Newcastle upon Tyne, NE1 1BR, UK.

ENVIRONMENT

Brown, Lester, et al *State of the World (Annual): A Worldwatch Institute Report on Progress Toward A Sustainable Society.* Norton, New York.

Brown, Lester, *et. al., Vital Signs: The Trends that are Shaping Our Future.* Norton, New York, 1994.

Callenbach, Ernest *Ecotopia* Bantam, New York, 1978.

Callenbach, Ernest *Ecotopia Emerging* Bantam, New York, London 1982.

Engwicht, David. *Toward an Eco-City: Calming the Traffic.* New Society Publishers, PA; PO Box 189, Gabriola Island, BC V0R 1X0, Canada. Envirobook, Sidney, Australia 1993.

Gore, Al. *Earth in the Balance: Ecology and the Human Spirit* Plume/Penguin, 1993.

Meadows, Donella, Dennis Meadows & Jörgen Randers. *Beyond the Limits: Confronting Global Collapse, Envisioning a Sustainable Future.* Chelsea

Green, Vermont; McLelland & Stewart, Toronto, 1992.

Merchant, Carolyn. *The Death of Nature: Ecology and the Scientific Revolution.* Harper & Row, San Francisco, 1980.

Roseland, Mark. *Toward Sustainable Communities: A Resource Book for Municipal and Local Governments.* National Round Table, 1 Nicholas St #520, Ottawa, Ontario K1N 7B7, Canada.

Walter, Bob, Lois Arkin & Richard Crenshaw. *Sustainable Cities: Concepts & Strategies for Eco-City Development.* EcoHome Media, 4344 Russell Ave, LA 90027, 1992. $20US + $3.50 shipping. Superb overall coverage, and resource listing.

Organisations and Resources:

Amicus Journal, Natural Resources Defense Council, 40 West 20th St, New York NY 10011. (212) 727-2700.

E: The Environmental Magazine, PO Box 699, Mt Morris, IL 61054-7589. (203) 854-5559. $20US.

Earth Island Journal, 300 Broadway, #28, San Francisco, CA 94133-3312 $25US, $32 overseas.

Friends of the Earth, 26 Underwood St, London N1 7JQ, UK (0171) 490-1555. *Earth Matters* magazine, and numerous reports.

Friends of the Earth, 1025 Vermont Ave NW, Washington DC 20005. (202) 783-7400. foedc@igc.apc.org

Friends of the Earth, #701-251 Laurier Ave West, Ottawa, ON K1P 5J6

Permaculture Magazine, Hyden House, Little Hyden Lane, Clanfield, Hants PO8 0RU, UK (01705) 596500

Permaculture: Bill Mollison, PO Box 1, Tyalgum, NSW Australia. 2484 (066) 79-3442.

NorthWest Environment Watch, 1402 Third Ave #1127, Seattle, WA 98101-2118. (206) 447-1880.

Rachel's Environment and Health Weekly, PO Box 5036, Annapolis, MD 21403-7036 Weekly, $25 pa. erf@igc.apc.org.

Rocky Mountain Institute, 1739 Snowmass Creek Rd, Snowmass CO 81654, USA (303) 927-3851 Quarterly Newsletter. orders@rmi.org

Sutton Centre for Environmental Information, 24 Rosebery Rd, Sutton, Surrey SM1 2BW, UK. (0181) 642-3030.

Urban Ecologist. 405, 14th St, #701, Oakland, CA 94612 (510)

251-6330. US $30; Canada/Mexico $35; Overseas $40pa urbane-cology@igc.apc.org

Women's Environment and Development Organisation, 845 Third Ave, 15th flr, New York, NY 10022 (212) 759-7982.

Women's Environment Network, Aberdeen Studios, 22 Highbury Grove, London N5 2EA. (0171) 354-8823.

GLOBAL SUSTAINABILITY

Brown, Lester, et al. *State of the World* (annually). WW Norton, New York, 1995. wwpub@igc.apc.org

Durning, Alan. *How Much Is Enough? The Consumer Society and the Future of the Earth*. WW Norton, New York, 1992.

Ekins, Paul. *A New World Order: Grassroots movement for global change*. Routledge, London, 1994.

Futures: *The UN at 50: Policy and Financing Alternatives*. Global Commission to Fund the United Nations, 1511 K St NW, Suite 1120, Washington DC 20005. $12.95US

George, Susan. *A Fate Worse Than Debt*. Penguin, London; Food First Books, 145 Ninth St, San Francisco 94103, 1988.

George, Susan. *The Debt Boomerang*. Pluto Press, London, 1991.

Johnson, Huey D. *Green Plans: Greenprint for Sustainability*. Univ. Nebraska Press, Lincoln, NE 68588-0484. 1995.

Korten, David. *When Corporations Rule the World*. Kumarian Press, USA. 1995. KPBooks@aol.com

New Consumer Magazine. The Global Consumer. Gollancz 1991.

Myers, Norman. *The Gaia Atlas of Planet Management*. Pan, London, 1985.

Pye-Smith, Charlie, and Grazia Borrini-Feyerabend. *The Wealth of Communities: Stories of Success in Local Environmental Management*. Kumarian Press, USA, 1994. KPBooks@aol.com

Shiva, Vandana. *Staying Alive: Women, Ecology and Development*. Zed Books, London, 1989.

Organisations and Resources

The Bulletin: Quarterly Review of Progress Towards Sustainable Development. and *The Network*. Centre for Our Common Future, 33 route de Valavran, 1293 Bellevue, Switzerland. (22-774-4530) commonfuture@gn.apc.org. Tracks global progress towards sustainability.

Bootstrap/Apex Press, c/o Council on International and Public Affairs, 777 UN Plaza #3C, NY 10017 (212)953-6920. Books on sustainable community economics, western and third world.

Debt Crisis Network, c/o Christian Aid, PO Box 100, London SE1 7RT (0171) 620-4444.

Earthword, Journal of Environmental and Social Responsibility, EOS Institute, 580 Broadway, #200, Laguna Beach, CA 92651 $20US

In Context, PO Box 11470, Bainbridge Island WA 98110 USA. Perhaps the best overall journal on sustainability issues. (206) 842-0216. $24pa. Now called YES magazine.

Greenpeace USA, 1436 U St, NW, Washington, DC 20009. (202) 462-1177.

Greenpeace Canada, 185 Spadina Ave, 6th flr, Toronto, Ontario M5T 2C6. (800) 320-7183.

Greenpeace UK, Canonbury Villas, London N1 2PN.

National Round Table on the Environment and the Economy, 1 Nicholas St, #1500, Ottawa, Ontario K1N 7B7, Canada. (613) 992-7189

New Road Map Foundation, PO Box 15981, Seattle, WA 98115. Resource centre for voluntary simplicity.

New Internationalist, Freepost SG559, PO Box 79, Hertford SG14, 1YB, UK.

Resurgence Magazine, Salem Cottage, Trelill, Bodmin, Cornwall, UK PL30 3HZ. £16 or US$45 pa.

Schumacher College: International Centre for Ecological Study, The Old Postern, Dartington, Devon TQ9 6EA, UK.

SPUR, Newspaper of the World Development Movement, 25 Beehive Place, London SW9 7QR. (0171) 737-6215. The WDM leads a hard-hitting movement on behalf of the world's poorest.

Tranet, PO Box 567, Rangeley, ME 04970. (207) 864-2252. Old-as-the-hills bimonthly newsletter covering social and ecological transformation all over the world.

World Resources Institute, 1709 New York Ave NW, Washington DC 20006. (202) 638-6300.

Worldwatch Institute, 1776 Massachusetts Ave, N.W., Washington DC 20036 (202) 452 1999. wwpub@igc.apc.org. *World Watch Magazine* and the annual *State of the World* report.

NEW ECONOMICS

Brandt, Barbara. *Whole Life Economics: Revaluing Daily Life*. New Society Publishers, Philadelphia; Gabriola Island, B.C. VOR1X0, 1995.

Daly, Herman E., and John B.Cobb. *For the Common Good:*

Redirecting the Economy Toward Community, the Environment, and a Sustainable Future. Beacon Press, Boston, 1989.

Robertson, James. *Future Wealth: a New Economics for the 21st Century*. Cassell, London, 1990. Also direct from Old Bakehouse, Cholsey, Oxon, UK.

Ekins, Paul. *The Living Economy: A New Economy in the Making*. London, Routledge, 1986.

Ekins, Paul, Mayer Hillman and Robert Hutchinson. *Wealth Beyond Measure: An Atlas of New Economics*. Gaia Books, UK; Doubleday, New York 1992.

Henderson, Hazel. *The Politics of the Solar Age: Alternatives to Economics*. (1981) Knowledge Systems, Indianapolis, 1988.

Henderson, Hazel. *Paradigms in Progress: Life Beyond Economics*. Berrett-Koehler, San Fransisco. 1995.

Henderson, Hazel: *Building a Win-Win World*. Berret-Koehler, San Francisco, 1996.

Korten, David. *When Corporations Rule the World*. Berrett-Koehler, San Fransisco. 1995

McQuaig, Linda. *Shooting the Hippo*. Viking, 1995. A hard-hitting critique of the financial policies that led to Canada's massive debt-problem.

Meeker-Lowry, Susan. *Economics As If The Earth Really Mattered*. New Society Publishers, Philadelphia, 1988.

Meeker-Lowry, Susan. *Invested in the Common Good*. *New Society Publishers*, Philadelphia, 1995.

Plant, Chris and Judith Plant (ed). *Green Business: Hope or Hoax ? Toward and Authentic Strategy for Restoring the Earth*. New Society Publishers, Philadelphia, PA, and Gabriola Island, B.C. VOR 1X0.

Organisations and Resources

Human Economy Newsletter, PO Box 28, W.Swanzey, NH 03469-0028. (603) 355-1250.

International Society for Ecological Economics, PO Box 1589, Solomons, MD 20688. (410) 326-0794.

Internet – support@igc.apc.org. New economics discussions via EcoNet.

New Economics, New Economics Foundation, Vine Court, 1st flr, 112-116 Whitechapel Rd, London E1 1JE. (0171) 377-5720. £18pa. Indispensable! neweconomics@gn.apc.org

Whole Life Economics Network, Barbara Brandt, PO Box 44-1615, West Somerville, MA. 02144-0013.

Turning Point 2000. Twice-yearly digest of people, events, publications. James Robertson, The Old Bakehouse, Cholsey, Oxon OX10 9NU, UK. (01491) 652346 £5pa (£6 overseas)

SOCIALLY RESPONSIBLE BUSINESS

Chappell, Tom. *The Soul of a Business: Managing for Profit and the Common Good.* Bantam, New York, 1993.

Elkington, John. *The Green Capitalists: Industry's Search for Environmental Excellence.* Gollancz, London 1987.

Elkington, John, Julia Hailes and Peter Knight. *The Green Business Guide. How to Take up – and Profit from – The Environmental Challenge.* Gollancz, London, 1992.

Hawken, Paul. *The Ecology of Commerce: A Declaration of Sustainability.* Harper Business, New York, 1993.

Makower, Joel. *The E-Factor: The Bottom-Line Approach to Environmentally Responsible Business* Plume/Penguin, New York 1994.

Naisbitt, John and Patrician Aburdene. *Re-inventing the Corporation.*Warner, New York 1986.

Reder, Alan. *75 Best Business Practices for Socially Responsible Companies.* Examples from the Social Venture Network. 1995. Libra, 366 Adelaide St E., #443, Toronto, Ontario M5A 3X9.

Thurow, Lester. *The Zero-Sum Solution* Penguin, 1987.

Semler, Ricardo. *Maverick!* Century, London, 1992. Astonishing tale of a Brazilian industrial transformation.

50 Simple Things Your Business Can Do To Save the Earth. Earthworks Group, Berkeley, USA 1991.

Organisations & Resources

Business Ethics, 52 S. 10th St, #110, Minneapolis, MN 55403-2001. $25US pa.

Business in the Community, 8 Stratton St, London W1X 5FD, UK. (0171) 629-1600

Business in the Environment, 5 Cleveland Place, London SW1Y 6JJ, UK.

Businesses for Social Responsibility, 1850 M St., #110, NW, Washington, DC 20036. (202) 467-5566

CERES - Coalition for Environmentally Responsible Economies, 711 Atlantic Ave, 5th flr, Boston MA 02111 (617) 451-0927. + 29 Lincoln's Inn Fields, London WC2A 3EE, UK.

Council on Economic Priorities, 30 Irving Place, New York NY 10003 (212) 420-1133. *Rating America's Corporate Conscience* and *Shopping for a Better World*. Sierra Club Books, 1994.

Green Business Letter. Monthly from Joel Makower, Tilden Press, 1519 Connecticut Ave, NW, Washington DC 20036. 800-955-GREEN.

In Business: the Magazine of Environmental Entrepreneuring, 419 State Ave, Emmaus, PA 18049. (215) 967-4135. $23US; $31 outside USA.

SustainAbility, The People's House, 91-97 Freston Rd, London W11 4BD. (0171) 243-1277 (John Elkington & Julia Hailes).

Tomorrow Magazine. Kungsgatan 27, 11156 Stockholm, Sweden (8) 243-480.

Businesses for Social Responsibility, 1030 15th St.NW, Suite 1010, Washington DC 20005. (202) 842-5400

SOCIALLY RESPONSIBLE FINANCE

Brill, Jack and Alan Reder, *Investing from the Heart*. Crown Publishers, New York, 1992.

Kinder, Peter, et al. *Investing for Good: Making Money while being Socially Responsible*. 1994. Libra, 366 Adelaide St E., #443, Toronto, Ontario M5A 3X9.

Lowry, Ritchie, *Good Money: Profitable Investing in the '90s*. WW Norton, New York, 1991.

Sparkes, Russell, *The Ethical Investor*. Harper Collins, London, 1995.

Organisations & Resources

ACCION International, 1385 Cambridge St, Cambridge MA 02139. (617) 492-4930.

Association of British Credit Unions, #305, 339 Kennington Lane, London SE11 5QY.

Aston Reinvestment Trust, Swan House, Hospital St & Summer Lane, Birmingham B19 3PY. (0121) 236-4808.

Calvert Social Investment Fund, 4550 Montgomery Ave, Suite 1000N, Bethesda, Maryland 20814. 800-368-2748.

Community Capital Bank, 111 Livingston St, Brooklyn, NY 11201. 800-827-6699.

Ecology Building Society, 18 Station Rd, Cross Hills, Nr Keighley, W.Yorks BD20 7EH, UK. (01535) 635933.

Ethical Investment Research and Information Service (EIRIS), 401 Bondway Business Centre, 71 Bondway, London SW8 1SQ. (0171) 735-1351.

Franklin Research and Development Corporation, 711 Atlantic Ave, Boston, MA 02111. (617) 423-6655.

Good Money Publications, PO Box 363, Worcester VT 05682. Publishes *Good Money* bimonthly ($75pa) (800) 535-3551.

Grameen Bank Newsletter, Head Office, Mirpur Two, Dhaka 1216, Bangladesh (23) 830-8185.

Greenmoney Journal, $25US for 6 issues. West 608 Glass Ave, Spokane, WA 99205.

Industrial Common Ownership Fund, 12 - 14 Gold St, Northampton NN1 1BR, UK.

Mercury Provident, Orlingbury House, Lewes Rd, Forest Row, Sussex RH18 5AA, UK.

National Association of Community Development Loan Funds, 924 Cherry St, 3rd flr, Philadelphia, PA 19107-5085. (215) 923-4754.

National Federation of Community Development Credit Unions, 59 John St, 8th flr, New York, NY 10038. (212) 513-7191.

Progressive Asset Management, 1814 Franklin St, #710, Oakland, CA 94612. (510) 834-3722

Prometheus Foundation, PO Box 969, Napier, New Zealand. Socially responsible investment fund.

Shared Interest, 31 Mosley St, Newcastle upon Tyne, NE1 1HX, UK. 0191-261-5943.

South Shore Bank, 7054 South Jeffery Blvd, Chicago, IL 60649-2096. (800) NOW-SSBK.

Social Investment Forum, PO Box 2234, Boston, MA 02107. (617) 451-3369.

Social Investment Organisation, 336 Adelaide St. E, #447, Toronto, Ontario M5A 3X9, Canada. (416) 360-6047. sio@web.apc.org

UK Social Investment Forum, 318 Summer Lane, Birmingham B19 3RL, UK. (0121) 359-3562. uksif@gn.apc.org

Vermont National Bank, Socially Responsible Banking Fund, PO Box 804, Brattleboro, VT 05302-9987. (802) 257-7151.

Women's World Banking, 8 West 40th St, New York, NY 10018. (212) 768-8513

Working Assets, 111 Pine St, #1415, San Fransisco CA 94111. 800-223-7010. Leading SRI fund in US.

SPIRITUAL/EVOLUTION/FUTURE

Abdullah, Sharif. *The Power of One: Authentic Leadership in Turbulent Times*. New Society Publishers, 1995.

Berry, Thomas. *The Dream of the Earth*. Sierra Club Books, San Francisco, 1988.

Capra, Fritjof. *The Turning Point: Science, Society and the Rising Culture*. Fontana, London; Simon & Schuster, New York, 1983.

de Chardin, Teilhard. *The Phenomenon of Man*. Collins, London, 1955.

Ferguson, Marilyn. *The Aquarian Conspiracy: Personal and Social Transformation in the 1980s*. Granada, London; Tarcher, Los Angeles, 1980.

McLaughlin, Corinne and Gordon Davidson. *Spiritual Politics: Changing the World from the Inside Out*. Ballantine Books, NY; Findhorn Press, Forres IV36 OTZ, Scotland. $14.95 from Sirius Educational Resources, 56F Crescent Rd, Greenbelt MD 20770.

Russell, Peter. *The Global Brain – The Awakening Earth: Our Next Evolutionary Leap*. Tarcher, LA and Routledge, London, 1982.

Swimme, Brian, and Thomas Berry. *The Universe Story: A Celebration of the Unfolding of the Cosmos*. Harper, San Francisco, 1992.

Planetary Connections: Positive News from Around the World, Six Bells, Church St, Bishops Castle, Shropshire SY9 5AA £15 pa.

One Earth, Findhorn Press, Nr. Forres, Scotland IV36 0TZ.

WORKSHARING, FUTURE OF WORK,

Dauncey, Guy, and Jane Mountain. *The New Unemployment Handbook*. National Extension College, Cambridge, UK, 1987.

O'Hara, Bruce. *Working Harder Isn't Working*. New Star Books, 2504 York St, Vancouver, B.C. V6K 1E3, Canada, 1993, $19.00.

Rifkin, Jeremy. *The End of Work: The Decline of the Global Labor-Force in the Post-Market Era*. Putnam, New York, 1995.

Robertson, James. *Future Work: Jobs, Self-Employment and Leisure after the Industrial Age*. Temple Smith/Gower, Aldershot, UK, 1985.

Schor, Juliet. *The Overworked American: The Unexpected Decline of Leisure*. Basic Books, New York 1991.

Organisations

New Road Map Foundation, PO Box 15981 Seattle, WA 98115. (206) 527-0437.

New Ways to Work, 309 Upper St, London N1 2TY, UK. 0171-226-4026.

New Ways to Work, 485 Market Street, #950, San Francisco, CA

9410. (415) 995-9860. *Work Times, Creating A Flexible Workplace.*
Society for the Reduction of Human Labor, c/o B.K.Hunnicutt, 1610 E.College St, Iowa City, IA 52245. National clearinghouse; quarterly newsletter $25pa.
Voluntary Simplicity Association, c/o Phinney Neighbourhood Ass'n, 6532 Phinney Ave, N., Seattle WA 98103 (206) 783-2244. Send stamped addressed envelope for information on how to organise a voluntary simplicity study circle and support group.
Work Well Network, c/o Bruce O'Hara, Box 3483, Courtenay, B.C. V9N 6Z8, Canada. Publish Share Times, quarterly, $10pa.

IN A CATEGORY ALL OF ITS OWN

Institute for Social Inventions, Nic Albery, 20 Heber Rd, London NW2 6AA, UK. (0181) 208-2853. rhino@bbcnc.org.uk. *The Book of Visions: An Encyclopedia of Social Innovations*, 1993, £18.49. £20.65 overseas, and *Re-Inventing Society : A Bumper Book of Best Ideas, Schemes and Speculations*, 1994, £14.85. Published 'Future Workshops' and many other useful materials.

Index